SWT
A Developer's Notebook™

Tim Hatton

Beijing · Cambridge · Farnham · Köln · Paris · Sebastopol · Taipei · Tokyo

SWT: A Developer's Notebook™
by Tim Hatton

Published by O'Reilly Media, Inc., 1005 Gravenstein Highway North, Sebastopol, CA 95472.

O'Reilly books may be purchased for educational, business, or sales promotional use. Online editions are also available for most titles (*safari.oreilly.com*). For more information, contact our corporate/institutional sales department: (800) 998-9938 or *corporate@oreilly.com*.

Editor:	Brett D. McLaughlin
Production Editor:	Jamie Peppard
Cover Designer:	Edie Freedman
Interior Designer:	David Futato

Printing History:

October 2004:	First Edition.

 This book uses RepKover™, a durable and flexible lay-flat binding.

ISBN: 0-596-00838-4

[M]

Contents

The Developer's Notebook
Series

So, you've managed to pick this book up. Cool. Really, I'm excited about that! Of course, you may be wondering why these books have the odd-looking, college notebook sort of cover. I mean, this is O'Reilly, right? Where are the animals? And, really, do you *need* another series? Couldn't this just be a cookbook? How about a nutshell, or one of those cool hacks books that seems to be everywhere? The short answer is that a developer's notebook is none of those things—in fact, it's such an important idea that we came up with an entirely new look and feel, complete with cover, fonts, and even some notes in the margin. This is all a result of trying to get something into your hands you can actually use.

It's my strong belief that while the nineties were characterized by everyone wanting to learn everything (Why not? We all had six-figure incomes from dot-com companies), the new millennium is about information pain. People don't have time (or the income) to read through 600-page books, often learning 200 things, of which only about 4 apply to their current job. It would be much nicer to just sit near one of the uber-coders and look over his shoulder, wouldn't it? To ask the guys that are neck-deep in this stuff why they chose a particular method, how they performed this one tricky task, or how they avoided that threading issue when working with piped streams? The thinking has always been that books can't serve that particular need—they can inform, and let you decide, but ultimately a coder's mind was something that couldn't really be captured on a piece of paper.

This series says that assumption is patently wrong—and we aim to prove it.

A Developer's Notebook is just what it claims to be: the often-frantic scribbling and notes that a true-blue alpha geek mentally makes when working with a new language, API, or project. It's the no-nonsense code that solves problems, stripped of page-filling commentary that often serves more as a paperweight than an epiphany. It's hackery, focused not on what is nifty or might be fun to do when you've got some free time (when's the last time that happened?), but on what you need to simply "make it work." This isn't a lecture, folks—it's a lab. If you want a lot of concept, architecture, and UML diagrams, I'll happily and proudly point you to our animal and nutshell books. If you want every answer to every problem under the sun, our omnibus cookbooks are killer. And if you are into arcane and often quirky uses of technology, hacks books simply rock. But if you're a coder, down to your core, and you just want to get on with it, then you want a Developer's Notebook. Coffee stains and all, this is from the mind of a developer to yours, barely even cleaned up enough for print. I hope you enjoy it...we sure had a good time writing them.

Notebooks Are...

Example-driven guides

As you'll see in the "Organization" section, developer's notebooks are built entirely around example code. You'll see code on nearly every page, and it's code that *does something*—not trivial "Hello World!" programs that aren't worth more than the paper they're printed on.

Aimed at developers

Ever read a book that seems to be aimed at pointy-haired bosses, filled with buzzwords, and feels more like a marketing manifesto than a programming text? We have too—and these books are the antithesis of that. In fact, a good notebook is incomprehensible to someone who can't program (don't say we didn't warn you!), and that's just the way it's supposed to be. But for developers...it's as good as it gets.

Actually enjoyable to work through

Do you really have time to sit around reading something that isn't any fun? If you do, then maybe you're into thousand-page language references—but if you're like the rest of us, notebooks are a much better fit. Practical code samples, terse dialogue centered around practical examples, and even some humor here and there—these are the ingredients of a good developer's notebook.

About doing, not talking about doing

If you want to read a book late at night without a computer nearby, these books might not be that useful. The intent is that you're coding as you go along, knee deep in bytecode. For that reason, notebooks talk code, code, code. Fire up your editor before digging in.

Notebooks Aren't...

Lectures

We don't let just anyone write a developer's notebook—you've got to be a bona fide programmer, and preferably one who stays up a little too late coding. While full-time writers, academics, and theorists are great in some areas, these books are about programming in the trenches, and are filled with instruction, not lecture.

Filled with conceptual drawings and class hierarchies

This isn't a nutshell (there, we said it). You won't find 100-page indices with every method listed, and you won't see full-page UML diagrams with methods, inheritance trees, and flow charts. What you will find is page after page of source code. Are you starting to sense a recurring theme?

Long on explanation, light on application

It seems that many programming books these days have three, four, or more chapters before you even see any working code. I'm not sure who has authors convinced that it's good to keep a reader waiting this long, but it's not anybody working on *this* series. We believe that if you're not coding within ten pages, something's wrong. These books are also chock-full of practical application, taking you from an example in a book to putting things to work on your job, as quickly as possible.

Organization

Developer's Notebooks try to communicate different information than most books, and as a result, are organized differently. They do indeed have chapters, but that's about as far as the similarity between a notebook and a traditional programming book goes. First, you'll find that all the headings in each chapter are organized around a specific task. You'll note that we said *task*, not *concept*. That's one of the important things to get about these books—they are first and foremost about doing something. Each of these headings represents a single *lab*. A lab is just what it sounds like—steps to accomplish a specific goal. In fact, that's the first heading you'll see under each lab: "How do I do that?" This is the central question of each lab, and you'll find lots of down-and-dirty code and detail in these sections. Many labs offer alternatives and address common questions about different approaches to similar problems. These are the "What about…" sections, which will help give each task some context within the programming big picture.

And one last thing—on many pages, you'll find notes scrawled in the margins of the page. These aren't for decoration; they contain tips, tricks, insights from the developers of a product, and sometimes even a little humor, just to keep you going. These notes represent part of the overall communication flow—getting you as close to reading the mind of the developer-author as we can. Hopefully they'll get you that much closer to feeling like you are indeed learning from a master.

And most of all, remember—these books are…

All Lab, No Lecture

—Brett McLaughlin, Series Creator

Preface

In this book, you'll find information about the Standard Widget Toolkit, part of the Eclipse project. Eclipse is an open source Integrated Development Environment (IDE) project supported by IBM and others. The purpose of the Eclipse project is to provide a standardized development environment across platforms.

The Standard Widget Toolkit (SWT) provides a set of Java class files and native code libraries that permit the developer to deliver graphical user interfaces that completely mirror the look and feel of the target platform. If your code is executing on the MS Windows operating system, the interface elements will have the identical look and feel of applications that are compiled natively to Windows. If your code executes on the Mac OS, it will have the identical look and feel of all applications compiled natively to that platform.

What's Inside

This book covers many widgets from the SWT, including the following components:

```
Shell              Menu
MenuItem           Toolbar
ToolItem           Text
Button             Combo
List               Composite
Group              Trees
Tabbed Folders     Layouts
Listeners          CoolBar
CoolItem           MessageBox
ColorDialog        PrintDialog
FileDialog
```

These widgets are covered in detail in the following chapters. Here's what's in each chapter.

Chapter 1, *Getting Started*
> This chapter introduces the SWT and how to download and configure Eclipse to perform SWT development.

Chapter 2, *SWT Shells*
> In the SWT the Shell class is used to create the basic window. In this chapter you learn how to create windows and manipulate their attributes to achieve the desired appearance.

Chapter 3, *SWT Menus*
> Menus are an essential element of most GUI designs. In this chapter you learn how to create SWT menus and how to respond to the events fired when the user interacts with the menu items.

Chapter 4, *SWT Toolbars*
> Toolbars are a companion widget for adding functionality to menus. They provide buttons that are used to initiate a specific menu action without the user navigating the menu structure. In this chapter you learn how to create and manipulate toolbars.

Chapter 5, *SWT Text Fields*
> Text fields are used in a GUI to present information to the user or to enable the user to input information into the application. In the SWT, text fields are created using a single Text widget class. In this chapter you learn how to create and manipulate text fields.

Chapter 6, *SWT Buttons*
> In the SWT a single Button class is used to create Push, Check, and Radio buttons. In this chapter you learn how to add buttons to your user interface and how to create each button style, as well as how to cause the button to perform the indicated task when the user interacts with it.

Chapter 7, *SWT Lists*
> Lists (or listboxes as they are sometimes called) are used to present the user with a set of items from which to choose. In this chapter you learn how to create lists, add and delete items from the list, and determine what item or items the user has selected.

Chapter 8, *The SWT Combo*
> The Combo (also known as the drop-down list) acts like a list, except that it takes up much less room in the GUI. This chapter looks at how to create Combo objects and interact with them as you do lists.

Chapter 9, *SWT Layouts*

Layouts make the task of positioning and sizing your widgets much easier than using the x and y coordinate method. SWT has four basic layout types—FillLayout, RowLayout, GridLayout and FormLayout. In this chapter you learn how to use each of these layout types.

Chapter 10, *SWT Composites and Groups*

To achieve complex layouts, you need to be able to do more than just add widgets directly to a window. The Composite and Group classes permit you to create "containers within containers," which is the subject of this chapter.

Chapter 11, *SWT Tabbed Folders*

The tabbed folder is a very common user interface element, and the SWT makes coding them a snap. You learn how in this chapter.

Chapter 12, *SWT Tables*

Tables are used to display information in a grid. The SWT contains an easy-to-use Table class to assist in creating tables and populating them with data. This chapter shows you how.

Chapter 13, *SWT Trees*

The tree interface is a useful construct for presenting hierarchical information. This chapter shows you how to create a tree, add items and icons, and determine how the user is interacting with the tree.

Chapter 14, *Other SWT Listeners*

In earlier chapters you learned how to add listeners to specific widgets. In this chapter you learn how to use other common listener types not associated with a single widget type.

Chapter 15, *SWT CoolBars*

CoolBars are super toolbars that permit the user to move buttons from place to place. They also enable you to use widgets other than buttons to initiate actions directly from the CoolBar. In this chapter you learn how to create CoolBars, add widgets (and even other toolbars) to the CoolBar, and react to user interaction with the CoolBar widgets.

Chapter 16, *SWT Slider and ProgressBar*

Sliders enable the users to choose from a range of values by sliding a single widget. Progress bars are similar, except that they position the slider within a range of values depending upon program conditions. This chapter explores how to use both sliders and progress bars.

Chapter 17, *SWT Standard Dialogs*

As a time-saving device, the SWT provides a set of standard dialogs that automate functions such as opening a file or choosing a printer. This chapter looks at the SWT standard dialog classes.

Chapter 18, *A Complete SWT Application*

Throughout this book, examples are built using only a single widget type at a time. In this chapter you learn how to build a complete GUI, in the form of a text editor, demonstrating how to utilize in a production application many of the techniques shown in earlier chapters.

As with all technology, the Eclipse IDE and the SWT are subject to changes—and often rapid ones, at that. For example, just before this book was finalized, Eclipse IDE version 3 was released and all code for the book had to be retested on that platform. If you find that a more recent version of a component has been released, you should download that more recent version and check the O'Reilly web site for updates related to this book.

Conventions Used in This Book

I'll use a number of conventions you should know about in this book. For example, menu items are separated with an → like this: File → New → Project. To make them stand out, new lines of code will be highlighted when they're first added. Example code is often presented out of context; instead of developing an entire class, only the relevant block of code is presented. Most examples will include the necessary import statements for Commons-relevant classes, and other import statements will be implied. When code is omitted or implied, it is represented by ellipses:

```
import org.apache.commons.digester.Digester;
...
Digester digester = new Digester( );
digester.doSomething( );
```

The following typographical conventions are also used in this book:

Plain text

Indicates menu titles, menu options, menu buttons, and keyboard accelerators.

Italic

Indicates new terms, URLs, email addresses, filenames, file extensions, pathnames, directories, and Unix utilities.

Constant width

Indicates commands, options, switches, variables, types, classes, namespaces, methods, modules, properties, parameters, values, objects, events, event handlers, and XML tags.

Constant width italic

Indicates text that should be replaced with user-supplied values.

TIP

This icon designates a note that is an important aside to the nearby text.

WARNING

This icon designates a warning relating to the nearby text.

What You'll Need

To experiment with the various libraries introduced in this book, you need the J2SE 1.4 SDK that can be obtained at *http://www.javasoft.com*. The examples in this book were developed using Eclipse, which can be downloaded from the Eclipse project site at *http://www.eclipse.org*. Chapter 1 contains full instructions on how to download and configure Eclipse and the SWT classes and libraries.

Using Code Examples

The code developed in this book is available for download for free from *http://www.oreilly.com/catalog/swtadn/*. Before installing, take a look at *readme.txt* in the download.

This book is here to help you get your job done. In general, you may use the code in this book in your programs and documentation. You do not need to contact us for permission unless you're reproducing a significant portion of the code. For example, writing a program that uses several chunks of code from this book does not require permission. Selling or distributing a CD-ROM of examples from O'Reilly books *does* require permission. Answering a question by citing this book and quoting example code does not require permission. Incorporating a significant amount of example code from this book into your product's documentation *does* require permission.

We appreciate, but do not require, attribution. An attribution usually includes the title, author, publisher, and ISBN. For example: "*SWT: A Developer's Notebook* by Tim Hatton. Copyright 2005 O'Reilly Media, Inc., 0-596-00838-4."

If you feel your use of code examples falls outside fair use or the permission given here, feel free to contact us at *permissions@oreilly.com*.

We'd Like to Hear from You

Please address comments and questions concerning this book to the publisher:

> O'Reilly Media, Inc.
> 1005 Gravenstein Highway North
> Sebastopol, CA 95472
> (800) 998-9938 (in the United States or Canada)
> (707) 829-0515 (international or local)
> (707) 829-0104 (fax)

We have a web page for this book, where we list errata, examples, and any additional information. You can access this page at:

> *http://www.oreilly.com/catalog/swtadn/*

To comment or ask technical questions about this book, send email to:

> *bookquestions@oreilly.com*

For more information about our books, conferences, Resource Centers, and the O'Reilly Network, see our web site at:

> *http://www.oreilly.com*

Acknowledgments

As with any large project, this book was written with the support of a large number of colleagues, friends, and family.

Thanks to Brett McLaughlin, my editor, who had a great impact on the quality, structure, and content of the book. His feedback and insistence that I make my writing style conform to the guidelines for the Developer's Notebook series made this a much better book than it otherwise would have been. With each editing cycle the book became more concise and readable, and imparted more information.

Of course, the book would never have been written if it were not for the many developers who write code for and manage the Eclipse project. They deserve the support of the development community (as do other open source pioneers).

Many thanks go out to Jed Levine for his constant email chats, which kept me from getting too wrapped up in the project, and for all his assistance when I sometimes got stuck to the point where I couldn't string words into coherent sentences.

The folks over at LexisNexis in Dayton deserve credit for giving me the chance to write a full, production, SWT system. I might not have looked at the SWT if they hadn't given me the leeway to choose the tool I wanted to use for a small GUI project.

There are many friends and family members who deserve acknowledgment. Kermit Lowery and Drew Miller are great golfing companions (after all, you can't think about tech matters all the time). Lizard Breath and The Sequel were always ready to make cookies when I didn't feel like writing anymore. And Mother, who sometimes doesn't get the appreciation she's due, gave me a place to hide and work while getting this one done.

This book represents perhaps my last large technology-related project. From here, I am returning to the practice of law, where I hope to use what I've learned over the past 14 years to make my practice more efficient, profitable, and exciting. Thanks are due to the good folks at Thompson & DeVeny in Dayton, for giving me a chance to ease back into the legal sector while at the same time keeping my tech muscles active.

CHAPTER 1

Getting Started

One of the most exciting trends in software development is the move toward the use of open source tools and components to assist developers in quickly and easily completing assigned programming tasks. One of the most successful of the open source platforms is Eclipse, an open source Integrated Development Environment (IDE) which is designed to enable developers to write code in any language, for any platform, using a standardized IDE. Eclipse has been downloaded by more than 18 million developers worldwide and forms the basis for IBM's WebSphere Application Developer, perhaps the most popular Java development environment in the corporate world.

One aspect of Eclipse is the Standard Widget Toolkit (SWT), a set of components that enable the developer to easily build GUIs. Although Java itself has built-in capability to develop graphical applications using the Abstract Windowing Toolkit (AWT) and the Java Foundation Classes (Swing) components, these toolkits have been tarred with the brush of sluggish performance and an inability to deliver user interfaces that appear to seamlessly integrate with the operating system platform for which the GUI was developed. Such is the price we pay for the promise of Java—*write once, run anywhere*.

The SWT provides the ability to *write once, run natively*. SWT delivers this capability by delivering the code necessary to create the on-screen widgets in an operating-system-specific library, and allowing access to that library from a thin layer of Java classes that make calls to that native code using the Java Native Interfaces (JNI). This affords developers the best of both worlds. Graphical interfaces run in fast native code, while applications can be developed entirely in Java, preserving the ability to write a single code base across multiple platforms. By shifting the on-screen presentation to native code, Java applications have the same look

In this chapter:
- *Downloading the SWT Library*
- *Configuring Eclipse for SWT Development*
- *Supplying the SWT Package to the Java Compiler*
- *Specifying the Location of the Native Library*
- *Using swt.jar in Multiple Projects*

and feel as applications developed entirely in native code on a particular platform. SWT developers also gain from the performance boost of having the code that does the heavy lifting of drawing graphics being performed in compiled code executing outside the Java Virtual Machine (JVM). The only downside is the requirement that you deploy a separate, and different, runtime library for each platform upon which you want to execute your finished product.

Although nothing in the SWT requires it, this book uses the Eclipse IDE to look at the nuts and bolts of SWT development. The command-line tools of the Java SDK could be used just as easily.

I begin the discussion with how to set up the Eclipse IDE for SWT development. I then proceed with a look at how each of the most commonly used widgets works, developing real working code along the way. I also provide you with some useful hints and tips for developing GUIs—what widget to use under which circumstances.

Downloading the SWT Library

The basic Eclipse download doesn't contain the classes and libraries needed to do SWT development. These must be downloaded separately from the Eclipse web site.

How do I do that?

The Eclipse web site has a list of mirror sites for downloading in case the Eclipse site happens to be overloaded.

Visit *http://www.eclipse.org/downloads/index.php* online for the SWT download (the web page is shown in Figure 1-1).

From here, click Main Eclipse Download Site, which will take you to the window shown in Figure 1-2.

From this window, choose the build of Eclipse that you wish to use. This book uses the 3.0M8 version. Clicking that version in Figure 1-1 takes you to Figure 1-3.

Here you will find 11 (as of this writing) different versions of the SWT, one for each supported platform. Download the file that matches your development environment and extract the files to a location on your development machine.

For my system, I downloaded the version for Windows 98/ME/2000/XP. This downloaded a file called *swt-3.0M8-win32.zip*, which I then expanded into a directory on my local machine, *C:\swt*.

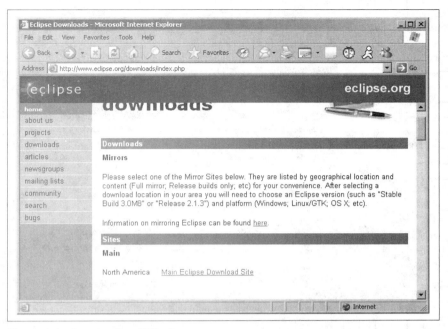

Figure 1-1. Downloading SWT releases

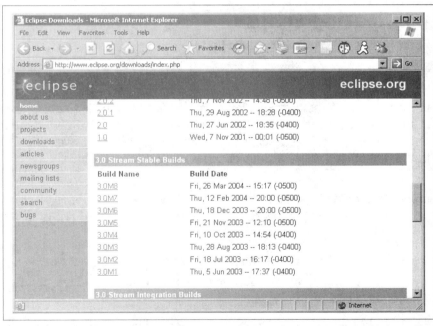

The contents of these pages change frequently, as new builds are released.

Figure 1-2. The current Eclipse builds

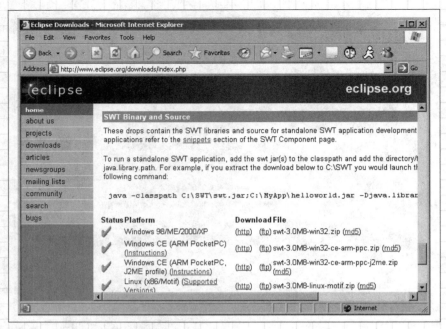

Figure 1-3. The SWT download area

Configuring Eclipse for SWT Development

To gain access to the promise of the SWT, you must first configure your development environment to allow access to the packages and libraries that contain both the thin Java layer as well as the compiled native layer. In this book, all examples are developed using Eclipse 3.0M8, but there is nothing to stop you from writing the code using any other available IDE, including Notepad or vi, with no changes necessary to the code.

How do I do that?

No matter what development tool you use, you must do two things before you can develop using the SWT:

- Add the SWT JAR to the compiler classpath.
- Add the native library for your platform to your Java Runtime Engine's (JRE's) library path.

If you are using Notepad or vi, do this by specifying command-line parameters at compile and execution time, as shown in Figures 1-4 and 1-5.

Figure 1-4. Specifying the classpath from the command line

Figure 1-5. Specifying the location of the SWT classes and native library for the JRE

The same requirements apply even if you are using an environment such as Eclipse. The difference is that, in Eclipse, you can specify these settings using graphical tools on a per-project basis and have them applied every time you compile or run your code, just as if you were using an Ant script or a batch file from the command line. Since these are two distinct steps, each is covered in a separate lab in the following sections.

Supplying the SWT Package to the Java Compiler

First, you've got to let `javac` know where to find the SWT libraries so that it can compile your applications.

How do I do that?

You first need to create a Java project, and then specify the Java Build Path for that project.

The Java Build Path in Eclipse may be specified either at the time the project is created, or later by selecting Project → Properties from the Eclipse menu. Either way, you will invoke a dialog similar to that shown in Figure 1-6, the Project Properties dialog. Select Java Build Path from the list on the left side of the dialog, which will reveal the set of tabs shown in the figure. Click the Libraries tab to specify the SWT packages required for your project.

On the Libraries tab, click the Add External JARs button and use the dialog shown in Figure 1-7 to locate the JAR file that contains the SWT

The Java Build Path in Eclipse is the equivalent of specifying the -classpath option for the javac compiler on the command line.

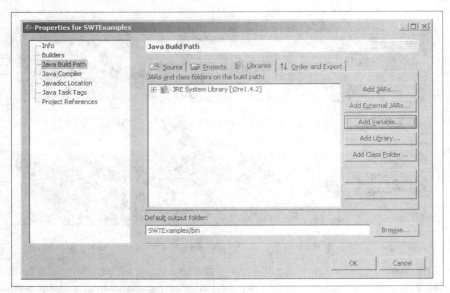

Figure 1-6. Specifying the Java Build Path

Make sure you include swt.jar in your final distribution so that your code can locate the SWT classes at runtime.

classes (you should have these from "Downloading the SWT Library." This file is normally called *swt.jar* and will be located in the directory where you extracted the SWT development files.

Navigate to the JAR file and click Open; this adds *swt.jar* into the Java Build Path for the project and returns you to the Project Properties dialog, as shown in Figure 1-8. You should see a reference to *swt.jar* listed under JARs and class folders on the build path.

If you need them, you can proceed to add other custom libraries to your project. For our purposes, the SWT classes are all that are needed. Make certain that your properties appear as shown in Figure 1-8 before clicking OK to save these settings in your project.

To test your configuration, simply create a Java class and enter the following lines of code:

```
import org.eclipse.swt.*;
import org.eclipse.swt.custom.*;
import org.eclipse.swt.graphics.*;
import org.eclipse.swt.widgets.*;
import org.eclipse.swt.layout.*;
```

If these lines appear in the Eclipse editor with red lines underneath the package identifiers, the project still can't locate the SWT classes and you should repeat the preceding steps. If the problem persists, try downloading the SWT classes again, as the original download may have been corrupt.

Figure 1-7. Locating the *swt.jar* file

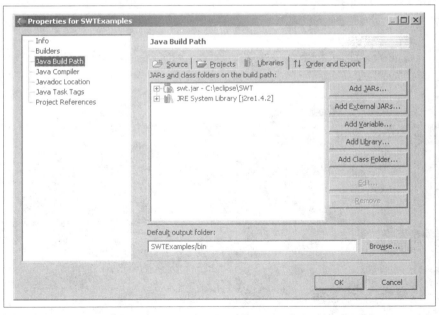

If you don't see swt.jar listed, repeat these steps, making sure to highlight swt.jar in the File dialog after clicking Add External JARs.

Figure 1-8. The Java Build Path specifying the location of *swt.jar*

What about...

if your import statements have yellow lines underneath them? That's okay—those mean only that you haven't yet referred to any of those classes in your code, which is normal at this stage of the process.

Specifying the Location of the Native Library

The second step in configuring Eclipse for SWT development is to specify the location of the SWT native library that will be passed to the JRE when you run your code within Eclipse for testing purposes. This allows the JRE to load up the native code that handles the tasks of creating and drawing the on-screen widgets. If the JRE is not able to locate this file, a runtime exception will occur.

How do I do that?

Since this is a runtime setting, it must be specified as a Run Configuration for your Eclipse project. To specify a Run Configuration, select Run → Run from the Eclipse menu. This will invoke the properties dialog shown in Figure 1-9.

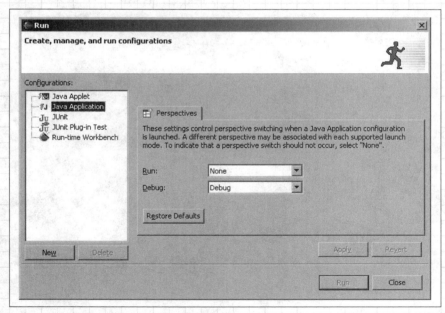

Figure 1-9. The Run Configurations dialog

In the Run Configurations dialog, select the type of application (Java Application), then click the New button. This loads the Run Properties dialog, shown in Figure 1-10, where you specify settings that govern how your project is loaded into the JRE. The setting you need to set is located on the Arguments tab.

Since this argument is to be passed to the JVM, it must be entered into the VM arguments text box. The same rules for constructing the argument to pass apply here as when running from the command line.

The argument to pass to `java` is `-Djava.library.path=`*`pathtolibrary`*, substituting the actual path to the location where you extracted the SWT library files.

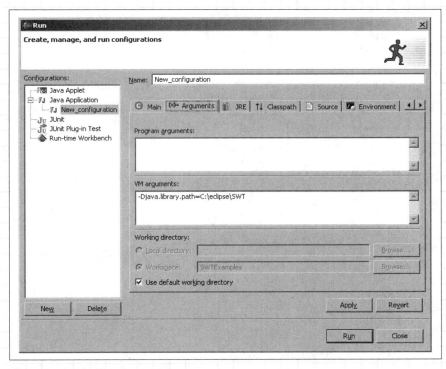

Figure 1-10. Setting the runtime arguments

Now Eclipse is configured to allow SWT development and to run your SWT programs from within the Eclipse IDE for testing.

What just happened?

You learned how to specify a runtime property to be passed into the JVM when executing your program. You can learn more about the other arguments that can be passed into the JVM by consulting the Java SDK documentation, or by opening a command prompt and entering java.

This causes help text to appear in the Console window:

```
C:\Documents and Settings\Administrator>java
Usage: java [-options] class [args...]
           (to execute a class)
   or  java [-options] -jar jarfile [args...]
           (to execute a jar file)

where options include:
    -client       to select the "client" VM
    -server       to select the "server" VM
    -hotspot      is a synonym for the "client" VM  [deprecated]
                  The default VM is client.

    -cp <class search path of directories and zip/jar files>
    -classpath <class search path of directories and zip/jar files>
                  A ; separated list of directories, JAR archives,
                  and ZIP archives to search for class files.
    -D<name>=<value>
                  set a system property
    -verbose[:class|gc|jni]
                  enable verbose output
    -version      print product version and exit
    -version:<value>
                  require the specified version to run
    -showversion  print product version and continue
    -jre-restrict-search | -jre-no-restrict-search
                  include/exclude user private JREs in the version search
    -? -help      print this help message
    -X            print help on non-standard options
    -ea[:<packagename>...|:<classname>]
    -enableassertions[:<packagename>...|:<classname>]
                  enable assertions
    -da[:<packagename>...|:<classname>]
    -disableassertions[:<packagename>...|:<classname>]
                  disable assertions
    -esa | -enablesystemassertions
                  enable system assertions
    -dsa | -disablesystemassertions
                  disable system assertions
```

The setting detailed in this lab is the same as passing the −D option to the java program from the command line, as shown in Figure 1-5. You must remember this when distributing your application for running in standalone mode outside Eclipse. The proper command to invoke your SWT application from the command line would be:

```
java -classpath C:\SWT\swt.jar;C:\MyApp\my.jar
    -Djava.library.path=C:\SWT  MyApp
```

TIP

In this and other code samples, I've added some formatting to
allow this to appear on the printed page. This should all be on one
line in reality.

Of course, you'll need to substitute the proper values for JAR file locations, the native library location, and the application class name.

What about...

this odd error message you keep getting:

```
java.lang.UnsatisfiedLinkError: no swt-win32-3038 in java.library.path
    at java.lang.ClassLoader.loadLibrary(Unknown Source)
    at java.lang.Runtime.loadLibrary0(Unknown Source)
    at java.lang.System.loadLibrary(Unknown Source)
    at org.eclipse.swt.internal.Library.loadLibrary(Library.java:100)
    at org.eclipse.swt.internal.win32.OS.<clinit>(OS.java:46)
    at org.eclipse.swt.widgets.Display.internal_new_GC(Display.java:1548)
    at org.eclipse.swt.graphics.Device.init(Device.java:541)
    at org.eclipse.swt.widgets.Display.init(Display.java:1573)
    at org.eclipse.swt.graphics.Device.<init>(Device.java:96)
    at org.eclipse.swt.widgets.Display.<init>(Display.java:331)
    at org.eclipse.swt.widgets.Display.<init>(Display.java:327)
    at ToolbarShellExample.<init>(SWTExample.java:24)
    at Runner.main(Runner.java:20)
Exception in thread "main"
```

Running within Eclipse without specifying the location of the SWT library
file, or specifying an incorrect location, causes this exception to appear in
the Console (class names and line numbers will vary). An identical error
would appear in the Java Console if running from the command prompt
using java. If you get this error, check your configuration settings and
run again.

Using swt.jar in Multiple Projects

The Build path set here does not persist across projects. If you have multiple SWT projects, you will need to repeat this process for each. If you
are planning on developing many SWT projects, you should consider creating a classpath variable pointing to the location of *swt.jar*, then using
this variable in each project.

How do I do that?

To create a classpath variable that can be used in multiple projects, select Windows → Preferences from the Eclipse menu; this invokes the dialog shown in Figure 1-11.

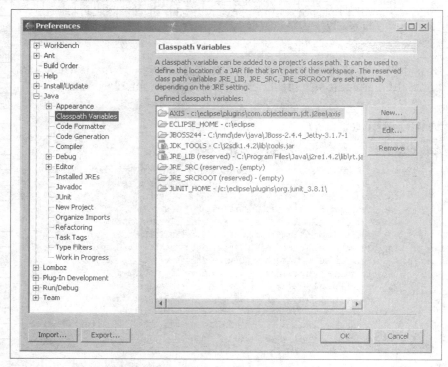

Figure 1-11. Specifying classpath variables

In the tree on the lefthand side of the window, expand the Java branch and select Classpath Variables, then click the New button to display Figure 1-12.

In this window, provide a name for the variable (SWT) and the path to the location of the *swt.jar* file. Click OK to return to the dialog shown in Figure 1-11, with your new entry displayed.

To use your variable in a project, use the Project Properties page, as you did earlier (Figure 1-8). Instead of locating the *swt.jar* file manually by clicking Add External JARs, click Add Variable to invoke Figure 1-13.

In Figure 1-13, you see all the variables that are declared in Eclipse. Select SWT and click OK. This returns you to the Project Properties dialog showing your selection as part of the project, as shown in Figure 1-14.

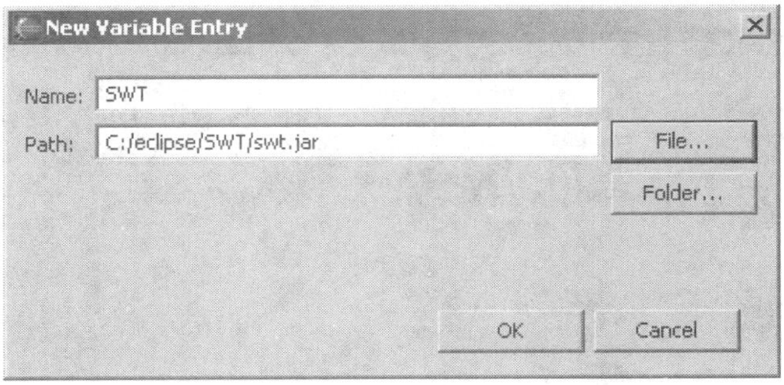

Figure 1-12. Creating a variable entry

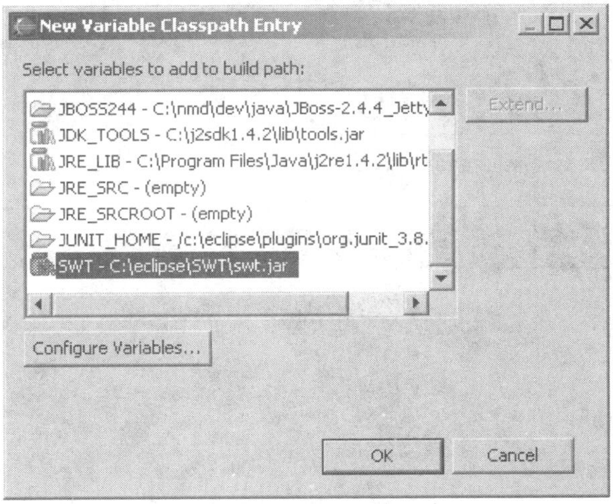

Figure 1-13. Selecting a classpath variable

What about...

persistence across projects? Unfortunately, in today's Eclipse there doesn't seem to be a way to have a classpath variable become a part of every new project. If you look at the Preferences dialog's New Project section (see Figure 1-15), there seems to be a logical location to allow this to be specified. Perhaps this feature will be added in a later version.

But I haven't seen it on anyone's list.

Eclipse is now configured to develop and execute SWT applications.

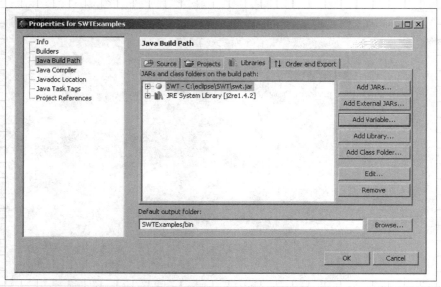

Figure 1-14. A classpath variable as a project property

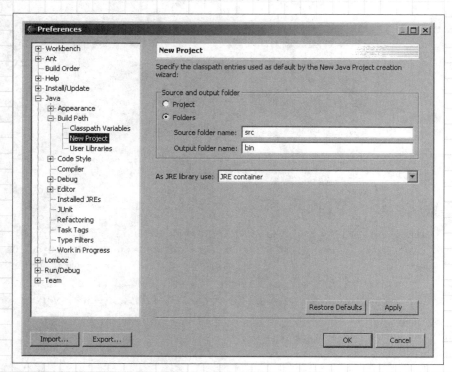

Figure 1-15. Specifying persistent classpath variables

CHAPTER 2

SWT Shells

The foundation from which you build every GUI is the window, so it's appropriate to begin discussion of the SWT by examining the classes that provide you with the ability to rapidly develop windows of all types.

If you look at all the different operating systems available, you soon realize that GUI windows come in all manner of types. These windows look and behave differently on the MS Windows platform than they do on Motif running under Unix, or KDE running under Linux. Even on a single platform, GUI windows may look and behave differently across versions—compare, for example, applications running under Windows 95, 98, NT, 2000, or XP. Fortunately for us developers, the code necessary to manage these differences is contained in the SWT library for a particular platform and is nicely abstracted for us in the SWT Java classes that we use to access that library. You write your code once, and allow the SWT native library to handle the differences between platforms.

We use two SWT classes to create windows: Display and Shell. Display is the class responsible for managing the interaction between all SWT widgets and the underlying operating system. It is in Display that you find methods that enable you to directly query the operating system for information about things such as which control currently has the focus and what windows are currently open and attached to the display. You will not need to interact directly with the display very often.

The second class, Shell, is much more important to the programmer. Instances of Shell represent windows which are currently being managed by the desktop (on MS Windows) or the windows manager (on Unix or Linux systems). Shells can be created either directly on the display, or within the confines of a parent shell. In this chapter, you will learn to develop code that creates both types of shells.

Creating a Simple Shell

The first type of shell you need to learn to create is the simple, high-level window that is opened directly on the display.

How do I do that?

Two coding steps are always needed to create a window:

1. Create an instance of the Display class.
2. Pass the instance of Display to the Shell constructor to create an instance of the Shell class.

Example 2-1 is the code that creates a basic shell, managed directly by the display.

Example 2-1. A very simple shell

```
import org.eclipse.swt.widgets.*;

public class SimpleShell {

    SimpleShell()     {
        Display d = new Display();
        Shell s = new Shell(d);
        s.setSize(500,500);
        s.open();
        while(!s.isDisposed()){
            if(!d.readAndDispatch())
                d.sleep();
        }
        d.dispose();
    }
}
```

Running on a Windows XP system, this code creates the dialog shown in Figure 2-1 when executed.

Executing the Example

To execute the examples in this book, you will need to do one of two things—either create a runner class or include a main() method in each example.

How do I do that?

The first approach is to create a simple class called Runner, shown in Example 2-2.

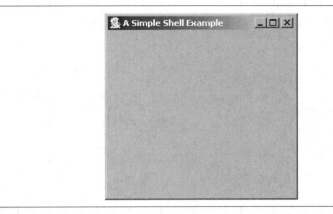

Figure 2-1. SimpleShell executing on Windows XP

Example 2-2. A Runner class to execute examples

```
public class Runner {

    public static void main(String[] args){
        SimpleShell ss = new SimpleShell();
    }
}
```

Each time you change the class name of the example you wish to run, you must change the name of the class that's being instantiated in your Runner class (which is a bit of a pain, admittedly).

The second approach is to embed a main() method in each example class you create, like this:

```
import org.eclipse.swt.widgets.*;

public class SimpleShell {

    // Class body from previous lab
    public static void main(String [] args)
    {
        SimpleShell ss = new SimpleShell();
    }
}
```

In this book, I will use the Runner class method so that I can keep the example code clean of code not directly related to the technique being demonstrated.

In Eclipse, to execute a class that contains a main() method you must create a Run Configuration. To do this, select Run → Run from the Eclipse menu. This invokes the dialog shown in Figure 2-2.

If you embed a main() method in each class, you have to go through the process of creating a Run Configuration for each one. What a mess that is.

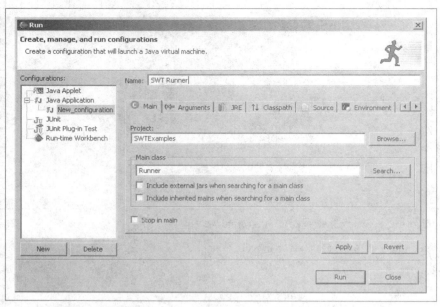

Figure 2-2. The Eclipse Run settings dialog

If you're more comfortable using Run Configurations than creating a Runner class, go for it.

You saw this dialog in Chapter 1, but there you dealt with settings on the Arguments tab. Here, specify the name of your Runner class on the Main tab, then check the Arguments tab to make certain you passed the location of the SWT native library to the JRE, as you learned to do in Chapter 1.

Once you have configured the Run Configuration, clicking Run from the Eclipse menu executes the code.

What just happened?

As you see, the SimpleShell code is straightforward. There are three key sections. The first contains the lines that create the required instances of the Shell and Display classes:

```
Display d = new Display();
Shell s = new Shell(d);
```

The next lines simply set the initial size of the shell to 500x500 pixels and invoke the open method to cause the shell to appear on the screen:

```
s.setSize(500,500);
s.open();
```

The final code segment constitutes the shell's event loop:

```
while(!s.isDisposed()){
    if(!d.readAndDispatch())
      d.sleep();
    }
```

Shells respond to events, some fired by the operating system, others by user actions. Examples of events are things such as the user clicking the maximize button or closing the window created by the shell. The event loop continuously listens for these events and dispatches them to the appropriate handler (this is the purpose of the readAndDispatch() method of the Display class). This means that every shell you create must have this event loop. Failure to provide the event loop results in the shell being created, then immediately disposed of. The event loop continues to execute until the isDisposed() method of the Shell class returns true, indicating that the window has been closed by the user.

The last line releases the memory resources captured when you created the display:

```
d.dispose();
```

It is important in SWT programming to remember to dispose of any widget you explicitly create. This prevents memory leaks.

Working with Shell Styles

Windows come in all types, shapes, and sizes. Some have titlebars, some don't. Some have minimize, maximize, and close buttons, and some don't. You need some way to control the appearance of windows, and with the SWT Shell class, you do that by using a second constructor that enables you to pass a style—an integer value the class uses to determine what attributes to show or hide.

How do I do that?

To specify a style for a shell, the SWT provides us with a set of enumerated values encapsulated in another class called SWT. The SWT class is located in the org.eclipse.swt package. For shells, the enumerated values are BORDER, CLOSE, MIN, MAX, NO_TRIM, RESIZE, and TITLE. Also, two convenience values—SHELL_TRIM and DIALOG_TRIM—combine several of the style attributes to create two common looks for windows.

The Shell class has multiple constructors. You utilized one of those earlier when you created an instance of your first shell:

```
Shell s = new Shell(d);
```

This constructor accepted only an instance of the Display class as an argument. To open an instance of Shell that accepts a style value, you must use a different constructor:

```
Shell(Display display, int style)
```

As you can see from this constructor's prototype, you are permitted to pass in only a single int value to control all the attributes. This means that you must have some way to combine the enumerated values in any combination you require. In Java programming, you can combine these values using the | operator, as follows:

```
Shell s = new Shell(d, SWT.CLOSE | SWT.RESIZE);
```

You can use any combination of the enumerated values to achieve the effect you desire, or you can use one of the two convenience values, SHELL_TRIM or DIALOG_TRIM, to specify the two most common combinations.

What about...

if you specify a style combination that isn't supported by the platform? That is certainly possible, since not all platforms have the same window attributes (suppose a window manager doesn't allow titles, for example).

SWT styles act merely as hints to the window manager or desktop, giving a suggestion as to how the window should be displayed. No error will be produced if an unusable combination is specified—it will simply be ignored.

Creating a Shell Styles Example

To demonstrate how different style combinations affect the appearance and functionality of a shell, create a modification to your earlier SimpleShell example and pass the Shell constructor a different combination of styles.

How do I do that?

Example 2-3 is similar to the earlier SimpleShell class, modified to specify a window that has a close button, has no min or max button, and is resizable.

Example 2-3. Setting the shell styles

```
import org.eclipse.swt.*;
import org.eclipse.swt.widgets.*;

public class ShellStylesExample {
    ShellStyles()   {
        Display d = new Display();
        Shell s = new Shell(d, SWT.CLOSE | SWT.RESIZE);
        s.setSize(300,300);
        s.open();
```

Example 2-3. *Setting the shell styles (continued)*

```
        while(!s.isDisposed()){
            if(!d.readAndDispatch())
                d.sleep();
        }
        d.dispose();
    }
}
```

The only difference between this class and the SimpleShell example is that the second constructor form is used and the style parameter is used to specify the desired window attributes.

Next, modify the Runner program to load up an instance of ShellStylesExample, as demonstrated in Example 2-4.

Example 2-4. *Revised Runner class*

```
public class Runner {

    public static void main(String[] args){
        ShellStylesExample sse = new ShellStylesExample ();
    }
}
```

Or you can create a Run Configuration for the new class.

TIP

This is the last time I will show you how to modify the Runner class. You should have the idea down pat by now.

The result of ShellStylesExample is as shown in Figure 2-3. You see only a close button displayed on the titlebar and the window is resizable.

Creating Child Shells

It is often necessary to open windows that appear not on the desktop or window manager, but within another window. One example of this is the ever-popular Multiple Document Interface (MDI) found in earlier versions of applications such as Microsoft Excel. Another example would be a prompt to the user for information or a display of some type of message.

TIP

MessageBox and other common forms of dialogs are created from another set of SWT classes and are discussed in Chapter 17.

Figure 2-3. Result of ShellStylesExample

How do I do that?

To open a window within a window, use a third constructor of the Shell class:

```
Shell(Shell parent)
```

You can also use a similar constructor that enables you to specify a style:

```
Shell(Shell parent, int style)
```

These constructors behave exactly the same as in the earlier examples, except that they cause the shell being opened to be displayed within the shell that is the parent, instead of displaying directly upon the desktop or the window manager.

Example 2-5 creates an instance of Shell that is suitable for opening within the confines of a parent shell.

Example 2-5. A child shell

```
import org.eclipse.swt.widgets.*;
public class ChildShell {

    ChildShell(Shell parent){
        Shell child = new Shell(parent);
        child.setSize(200,200);
        child.open( );
    }
}
```

The ChildShell constructor enables you to pass in a reference to the shell that will serve as the parent:

```
ChildShell(Shell parent)
```

That reference is then passed to a Shell constructor that accepts a reference to another instance of Shell as a parent rather than as a Display reference:

```
Shell child = new Shell(parent);
```

This causes child to be created within the confines of the parent shell.

No event loop is required for the ChildShell. Why? Because the event loop for the parent shell handles the dispatching of events for all objects opened within the parent. The child remains open until it is closed by the user or until the parent is closed.

To execute ChildShell, you must create a class that creates an instance of Shell to serve as the parent, and then creates an instance of ChildShell. This is demonstrated in Example 2-6.

Example 2-6. Opening ChildShell within a parent shell

```
import org.eclipse.swt.widgets.*;

public class ChildShellExample {
    Display d = new Display();


    ChildShellExample()    {
        Shell s = new Shell(d);
        s.setSize(500,500);
        s.open();
        ChildShell cs = new ChildShell(s);
        while(!s.isDisposed()){
            if(!d.readAndDispatch())
                d.sleep();
        }
        d.dispose();
    }
}
```

When you create an instance of ChildShellExample you see the result shown in Figure 2-4.

What about...

the ChildShell? You will notice that the child shell doesn't create a true MDI interface, since the child shell can be moved outside the confines of the parent. Many developers are creating MDI-like applications by forcing the parent shell to remain maximized whenever it is open. This can be done in a single line of code:

```
s.setMaximized(true);
```

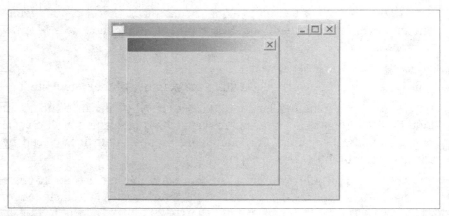

Figure 2-4. Window within a window

If you also set the parent shell's style attribute so that the minimize and maximize buttons are not displayed, the user will be unable to change the parent shell's size or position. The normal behavior for shells created in this manner is to pass on events from parent to child so that minimizing the parent will cause all child shells to also minimize. Admittedly, it's a bit contrived, but it comes as close as possible to creating MDI applications using the SWT—until the developers provide true MDI functionality.

It's on the official bug list, so it will get done.

Creating Multiple Child Windows

Often you will need to create more than just a single child window within your main window. You can create many instances of ChildShell, using ChildShellExample as the parent, simply by creating new instances of ChildShell.

How do I do that?

The code required to create multiple child windows is shown in Example 2-7. All you do is create a new instance of ChildShell for each window desired.

Example 2-7. Creating multiple instances of ChildShell

```
import org.eclipse.swt.widgets.*;

public class ChildShellExample {
    Display d = new Display();

    ChildShellExample()    {
        Shell s = new Shell(d);
```

Example 2-7. Creating multiple instances of ChildShell (continued)

```
        s.setSize(500,500);
        s.open( );
        ChildShell cs1 = new ChildShell(s);
        ChildShell cs2 = new ChildShell(s);
        ChildShell cs3 = new ChildShell(s);
        while(!s.isDisposed( )){
            if(!d.readAndDispatch( ))
                d.sleep( );
        }
        d.dispose( );

    }
}
```

Running Example 2-7 creates three child windows, as shown in Figure 2-5.

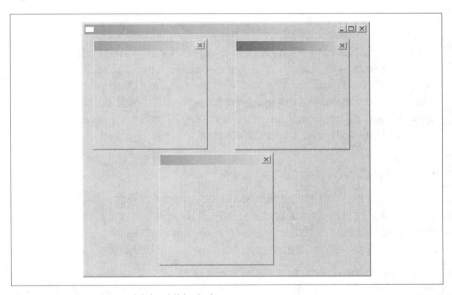

Figure 2-5. Opening multiple child windows

Opening True Dialogs

ChildShellExample demonstrated how to open a child window within the confines of a parent window, but this is not the same as opening a true dialog. A dialog window is one that halts processing of code in the parent window until the user takes some action in the dialog. In ChildShellExample, the parent window code continued to execute even while the child window was opened. You can see the effect if you execute Example 2-8.

Example 2-8. Demonstrating the effect of opening a child on the parent

```
import org.eclipse.swt.widgets.*;

public class ChildShellExample {
    Display d = new Display();

    ChildShellExample()    {
        Shell s = new Shell(d);
        s.setSize(500,500);
        s.open();
        ChildShell cs1 = new ChildShell(s);
        System.out.println("Execution Continues");
        while(!s.isDisposed()){
            if(!d.readAndDispatch())
                d.sleep();
        }
        d.dispose();

    }
}
```

If you execute this version of `ChildShellExample`, you see that the message is printed to the Console immediately after the child window is opened. What if you need to wait for the user to take some action in the child window before knowing how to proceed? For this, you must use a special form of window known as a *dialog*. The SWT provides the capability to work with dialogs in the form of the `Dialog` class.

How do I do that?

The `Dialog` class enables you to create custom dialogs—those on which you can place any widget you desire. A dialog is simply another type of `shell`, except that it extends the `Dialog` class, which encapsulates some additional methods and accepts additional style attributes.

Using SYSTEM_MODAL is generally a bad idea since it prevents the user from switching from your application to another application running in the operating system.

The `Dialog` class has two style attributes: `SWT.APPLICATION_MODAL` and `SWT.SYSTEM_MODAL`. `APPLICATION_MODAL`, as the name implies, will cause the dialog to halt all processing in the application until the dialog is dismissed. `SYSTEM_MODAL` will prevent the user from performing other tasks in any application running in the operating system while the dialog is open (although background tasks will still run on most platforms).

As with `Shell`, you specify the dialog type at construction time by passing the style attributes desired to the `Dialog` constructor. Example 2-9 creates an application modal dialog.

Example 2-9. An application modal dialog

```
import org.eclipse.swt.SWT;
import org.eclipse.swt.widgets.*;

public class DialogExample extends Dialog {
    DialogExample(Shell parent)
    {
        super(parent);
    }
    public String open()
    {
        Shell parent = getParent();
        Shell dialog = new Shell(parent,
            SWT.DIALOG_TRIM | SWT.APPLICATION_MODAL);
        dialog.setSize(100,100);
        dialog.setText("A Dialog");
        dialog.open();
        Display display = parent.getDisplay();
        while (!dialog.isDisposed())
        { if (!display.readAndDispatch()) display.sleep();
        }
        return "After Dialog";
    }
}
```

Next, you need a parent shell in which to open this dialog. To create that, just modify one of the earlier examples, as shown in Example 2-10.

Example 2-10. Opening a dialog

```
import org.eclipse.swt.widgets.*;

public class ShellDialogExample {
    ShellDialogExample()
    {
        Display d = new Display();
        Shell s = new Shell(d);
        s.setSize(300,300);
        s.open();
        DialogExample de = new DialogExample(s);
        String result = de.open();
        System.out.println(result);
        while(!s.isDisposed()){
            if(!d.readAndDispatch())
                d.sleep();
        }
        d.dispose();

    }
}
```

Creating an instance of ShellDialogExample causes Figure 2-6 to display.

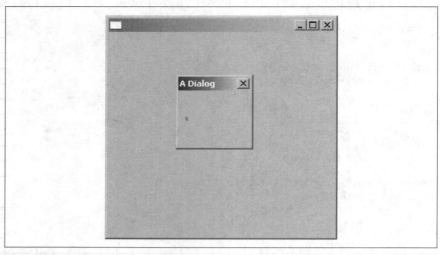

Figure 2-6. A shell with a dialog

What just happened?

If you examine the running application, you see that while the dialog is open it is not possible to take any action within the parent shell (such as closing, minimizing, or maximizing). Closing the dialog returns control to the parent. If you follow the execution of the `ShellDialogExample` code in a debugger or by watching the Console output, you see that program execution halts on the line:

```
String result = de.open();
```

Execution does not resume until the dialog is closed. Upon closing the dialog, you see the contents of the variable `result` printed to the Console.

The fact that execution is halted while the dialog is open is what permits you to use the dialog to gather information from the user that is required for further program execution. Dialogs should be used sparingly and only when you must have input from the user to determine how to proceed.

Setting the Shell Title Text

To create professional-looking windows—those that meet the user's expectations for what a window should look like on a particular platform—it's not enough to just rely upon the SWT to manage the look and feel of the window. Sure, it will have the same look and feel as other windows running on the platform, but it will still be missing certain elements that users expect to see. One of these elements is the title text, used to tell the user the subject matter of the window contents.

How do I do that?

Every window that opens in an application should have text in the title-bar area. Setting the text is simply a matter of calling the setText() method on the Shell class:

```
s.setText("A Shell Example");
```

Setting the Shell Icon

Another window element is the window icon. If you examine the parent shell in the ShellDialogExample, you notice that there is a generic "window" icon on the right side of the titlebar. Although this icon does not appear on all platforms, when it does appear the user will almost certainly expect that it reflect the type of application and not be the generic "window" icon.

How do I do that?

Use the setImage() method of the Shell class to specify the image you wish to display, as shown in Example 2-11.

Example 2-11. Setting the shell icon

```
import org.eclipse.swt.graphics.Image;
import org.eclipse.swt.widgets.*;

public class ProfessionalShell {

    ProfessionalShell()    {
        Display d = new Display();
        Shell s = new Shell(d);
        s.setSize(500,500);
        s.setImage(new Image(d, "c:\\icons\\JavaCup.ico"));
        s.setText("A Shell Example");
        s.open();
        while(!s.isDisposed()){
            if(!d.readAndDispatch())
                d.sleep();
        }
        d.dispose();
    }
}
```

Creating an instance of ProfessionalShell generates Figure 2-7, showing a distinct improvement over the generic "window" icon from previous examples.

Figure 2-7. A professional shell

Adding an icon, displaying the appropriate title text, and specifying the correct style for a particular window type will go a long way toward making your windows look the way users expect them to look.

Creating the basic window using the Shell class is only the first step toward generating a professional GUI that users will enjoy using. Most GUIs contain many other elements that users will expect to see in your applications. These include menus, which are discussed in the next chapter, and toolbars, which are examined in Chapter 4.

The window, including menus and toolbars, will be the foundation for everything you will add as you build your user interfaces. A thorough understanding of window design will give you the coding skills upon which you can build throughout this book.

CHAPTER 3

SWT Menus

In this chapter you continue your examination of the SWT by looking at another component for designing professional-looking windows—menus. In SWT, the classes provided to help you create menus are Menu and MenuItem, both located in the org.eclipse.swt.widgets package.

Menus are the primary application navigation tool you provide for your users, and it is a rare application that doesn't make use of them. The published standards for designing GUIs specify the types of windows that should display a menu, the functionality the menu should provide, and the names of specific menu items. You can get the same guidance by examining the menu structure of almost any application running on your target platform.

TIP

The menu guidelines vary somewhat by platform as far as specific names to be given to menu items and the actual menu structure (what appears under File or Edit, for example). This presents somewhat of a problem for "write once, run anywhere" programming, because SWT won't help when it comes to names, labels, or locations of menu items. As time goes by, the standards for graphical design are merging and this issue will someday vanish into these (theoretical) merged standards. For now, following the Microsoft guidelines should suffice for most platforms.

Most applications will have a minimum of File, Edit, Window, and Help as high-level menu choices, with submenu items varying depending upon the application's functionality. Edit, for example, will almost certainly have Cut, Copy, and Paste items for programs with text capability, but might have directory or folder movement capability for programs that work extensively with lists of items. Other high-level menu items will be application-specific, such as a Report menu if the application generates reports.

The SWT provides two classes to assist in menu creation. These are the Menu and MenuItem classes. Menu is a container class that holds other menus and menu items. Menu represents the highest level of any menu system, the menu bar that appears just below the title of the window. Instances of Menu are also used to create the individual drop-down menus that appear on the menu bar—File, Edit, and so on.

To create any menu system, you first create an instance of the Menu class to represent the menu bar, and then attach instances of the MenuItem class that represent each of the high level choices you wish to present to the user (File, Edit, Window, and Help in a typical menu system are all instances of the MenuItem class). You then add instances of the MenuItem class to each of these menus, representing the individual choices presented to the user.

And if you don't take the time to plan, your menu will look like it grew like a weed instead of being cultivated like a garden.

Menus require a great deal of thought and planning in their design phase, if you want to achieve the best possible design for a particular application. If you take the time to plan, the actual development of the menu in code is a much easier process

Creating the Menu Bar

The first step in creating a menu system is to create an instance of Menu to serve as the menu bar and attach it to an instance of the Shell class.

How do I do that?

Example 3-1 demonstrates how to create a menu bar attached to a simple window..

Example 3-1. Creating the menu bar

```
import org.eclipse.swt.SWT;
import org.eclipse.swt.graphics.Image;
import org.eclipse.swt.widgets.*;

public class MenuShell {
    Display d;
    Shell s;
    MenuShell()
    {
        d = new Display();
        s = new Shell(d);
```

Example 3-1. Creating the menu bar (continued)

```
        s.setSize(500,500);
        s.setImage(new Image(d, "c:\\icons\\JavaCup.ico"));
        s.setText("A Shell Menu Example");

        Menu m = new Menu(s,SWT.BAR );
        s.setMenuBar(m);

        s.open( );
        while(!s.isDisposed( )){
            if(!d.readAndDispatch( ))
                d.sleep( );
        }
        d.dispose( );
    }
}
```

What just happened?

The important code in the example comprises only two lines:

```
Menu m = new Menu(s,SWT.BAR );
s.setMenuBar(m);
```

With these two lines you have created an instance of Menu, passing it a reference to its containing Shell, and specifying the SWT.BAR style. The menu is then attached to the window by calling the setMenuBar( ) method of the Shell class.

How does the Menu class know whether it serves as a menu bar or a high-level menu item such as File? You specify the type of menu created by passing a style attribute to the Menu constructor. As with Shell, the style attributes are specified in the SWT class as enumerated values. For Menu, there are three values to choose from—SWT.BAR, SWT.DROP_DOWN, and SWT.POP_UP.

Adding Drop-Down Menus

Executing MenuShell won't display a menu system because no high-level menus have been created and added to the menu bar. To do that, you need to create instances of the MenuItem class using the SWT.CASCADE style.

How do I do that?

Create an instance of the MenuItem class for each desired drop down and set the text attribute of each such instance to represent the clickable text the user will see. These instances of MenuItem are what the user will see running across the menu bar (e.g., File). Instances of MenuItem are attached directly to the menu bar by passing a reference to the menu bar in the MenuItem constructor. These MenuItem objects must be given the SWT.CASCADE style. The setText() method is called to specify the text you wish to appear on the menu:

```
MenuItem file = new MenuItem(m, SWT.CASCADE);
file.setText("File");
```

Next, create a Menu instance to attach to the cascading menu item. This instance of Menu is the container for the individual menu items that appear when the user clicks the cascading menu (i.e., when the menu drops down). This time you pass the Menu constructor the SWT.DROP_DOWN style in addition to a reference to the containing Shell:

```
Menu filemenu = new Menu(s, SWT.DROP_DOWN);
file.setMenu(filemenu);
```

Finally, create instances of MenuItem to add to the DROP_DOWN style menu, passing them a reference to the containing Menu instance and specifying the SWT.PUSH style (one of the other available MenuItem styles):

```
MenuItem openItem = new MenuItem(filemenu, SWT.PUSH);
openItem.setText("Open");
MenuItem separator = new MenuItem(filemenu, SWT.SEPARATOR);
MenuItem exitItem = new MenuItem(filemenu, SWT.PUSH);
exitItem.setText("Exit");
```

TIP

Menu items attached to the drop-down menu can have one of five styles—SWT.CHECK, SWT.CASCADE, SWT.PUSH, SWT.RADIO, or SWT.SEPARATOR. The most often used style is SWT.PUSH, which creates a menu item the user can click to perform some action.

When you pull all these techniques together, as shown in Example 3-2, you create a menu bar with one menu (File) that, when clicked by the user, cascades to reveal two choices (Open and Exit).

Example 3-2. A File menu system

```
import org.eclipse.swt.SWT;
import org.eclipse.swt.graphics.Image;
import org.eclipse.swt.widgets.*;

public class MenuShell {
    Display d;
    Shell s;
    MenuShell()
    {
```

Example 3-2. *A File menu system (continued)*

```
        d = new Display();
        s = new Shell(d);
        s.setSize(500,500);
        s.setImage(new Image(d, "c:\\icons\\JavaCup.ico"));
        s.setText("A Shell Menu Example");

        Menu m = new Menu(s,SWT.BAR );

        MenuItem file = new MenuItem(m, SWT.CASCADE);
        file.setText("File");
        Menu filemenu = new Menu(s, SWT.DROP_DOWN);
        file.setMenu(filemenu);
        MenuItem openItem = new MenuItem(filemenu, SWT.PUSH);
        openItem.setText("Open");
        MenuItem exitItem = new MenuItem(filemenu, SWT.PUSH);
        exitItem.setText("Exit");

        s.setMenuBar(m);

        s.open();
        while(!s.isDisposed()){
            if(!d.readAndDispatch())
                d.sleep();
        }
        d.dispose();
    }
}
```

Adding Separator Bars

If you examine the menu system for an application running on your chosen platform, you may see that individual menu items are often separated by a line, enabling you to divide the items in a cascading menu into functional groups.

A menu without separators may function okay, but it just won't look good.

How do I do that?

A separator is simply an instance of MenuItem that has been given the SWT.SEPARATOR style:

```
    MenuItem separator = new MenuItem(filemenu, SWT.SEPARATOR);
```

A separator menu item will take no action and cannot be clicked.

Creating a Complete Menu System

Creating a complete menu system is a matter of duplicating the code seen in Example 3-2 for each high-level menu item that appears on the menu bar.

How do I do that?

Example 3-3 creates a menu bar with File, Edit, Window, and Help cascading menus. Each cascading menu drops down to display menu items appropriate to the top-level menu.

Example 3-3. A complete menu system

```java
import org.eclipse.swt.SWT;
import org.eclipse.swt.graphics.Image;
import org.eclipse.swt.widgets.*;

public class MenuShell {
    Display d;
    Shell s;
     MenuShell()    {
         d = new Display();
         s = new Shell(d);
        s.setSize(300,300);
        s.setImage(new Image(d, "c:\\icons\\JavaCup.ico"));
        s.setText("A Shell Menu Example");

        Menu m = new Menu(s,SWT.BAR );

        // create a File menu and add an Exit item
        final MenuItem file = new MenuItem(m, SWT.CASCADE);
        file.setText("File");
        final Menu filemenu = new Menu(s, SWT.DROP_DOWN);
        file.setMenu(filemenu);
        final MenuItem openItem = new MenuItem(filemenu, SWT.PUSH);
        openItem.setText("Open");
        final MenuItem separator = new MenuItem(filemenu, SWT.SEPARATOR);
        final MenuItem exitItem = new MenuItem(filemenu, SWT.PUSH);
        exitItem.setText("Exit");

        // create an Edit menu and add Cut, Copy, and Paste items
        final MenuItem edit = new MenuItem(m, SWT.CASCADE);
        edit.setText("Edit");
        final Menu editmenu = new Menu(s, SWT.DROP_DOWN);
        edit.setMenu(editmenu);
        final MenuItem cutItem = new MenuItem(editmenu, SWT.PUSH);
        cutItem.setText("Cut");
        final MenuItem copyItem = new MenuItem(editmenu, SWT.PUSH);
        copyItem.setText("Copy");
        final MenuItem pasteItem = new MenuItem(editmenu, SWT.PUSH);
```

Example 3-3. A complete menu system (continued)

```
        pasteItem.setText("Paste");

        //create a Window menu and add Child items
        final MenuItem window = new MenuItem(m, SWT.CASCADE);
        window.setText("Window");
        final Menu windowmenu = new Menu(s, SWT.DROP_DOWN);
        window.setMenu(windowmenu);
        final MenuItem maxItem = new MenuItem(windowmenu, SWT.PUSH);
        maxItem.setText("Maximize");
        final MenuItem minItem = new MenuItem(windowmenu, SWT.PUSH);
        minItem.setText("Minimize");

        // create a Help menu and add an About item
        final MenuItem help = new MenuItem(m, SWT.CASCADE);
        help.setText("Help");
        final Menu helpmenu = new Menu(s, SWT.DROP_DOWN);
        help.setMenu(helpmenu);
        final MenuItem aboutItem = new MenuItem(helpmenu, SWT.PUSH);
        aboutItem.setText("About");

        s.setMenuBar(m);

        s.open();
        while(!s.isDisposed()){
            if(!d.readAndDispatch())
                d.sleep();
        }
        d.dispose();
    }
}
```

TIP

Why are the menu variables final? There are many reasons for making these variables final. One is that they must be declared as final if you are going to refer to them in an inner class, as you will see in Example 3-5. Another reason is that the Java compiler can perform certain optimizations upon variables declared final or static (or both).

Creating an instance of MenuShell displays Figure 3-1; dropping down the Edit menu yields Figure 3-2.

What about...

creating menus in a class of their own? Most SWT developers code menus as shown here—in the same class that creates the shell. One reason to use this approach is that the SWT classes are generally not

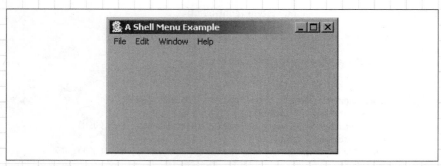

Figure 3-1. Executing MenuShell on Windows XP

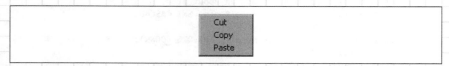

Figure 3-2. Dropping down the Edit menu

extendable, so it is not possible to create a class that extends Menu, populate it with menu items, and then attach that class to another class that extends Shell.

It is possible, however, to place the code that creates the menu system in a separate class, and then create an instance of that class, passing it a reference to the shell to which the menu will attach.

Either approach works as well as the other and you are free to choose which best fits your coding style.

Adding Cascading Submenus

Some menu items that appear in a drop-down menu won't have an action directly associated with them, but will cause another menu to cascade out to the side when the user points to that item (without clicking).

How do I do that?

A good demonstration of the ability to cascade submenus is extending the code in Example 3-3 so that the File → Open selection permits the user to choose whether to open the ChildExample or DialogExample (from Chapter 2). Such a menu system is shown in Figure 3-3.

On some platforms, the user must actually click the Open item to cause the submenu to appear.

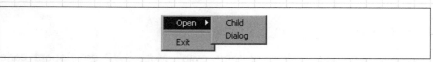

Figure 3-3. The cascading Open menu

To convert the Open menu item into a cascading menu to allow for a submenu, first change its style from SWT.PUSH to SWT.CASCADE, and then create menu items to attach to it. The following code creates menu items, with the SWT.PUSH style, with the text Child and Dialog:

```
final MenuItem openItem = new MenuItem(filemenu, SWT.CASCADE);
openItem.setText("Open");
final Menu submenu = new Menu(s, SWT.DROP_DOWN);
openItem.setMenu(submenu);
final MenuItem childItem = new MenuItem(submenu, SWT.PUSH);
childItem.setText("Child");
final MenuItem dialogItem = new MenuItem(submenu, SWT.PUSH);
dialogItem.setText("Dialog");
```

To see the effect, alter MenuShell by replacing the code that created the Open menu item with the preceding code, as shown in Example 3-4.

Example 3-4. Creating cascading submenus

```
import org.eclipse.swt.SWT;
import org.eclipse.swt.graphics.Image;
import org.eclipse.swt.widgets.*;

public class MenuShell {
    Display d;
    Shell s;
     MenuShell( )     {
         d = new Display( );
         s = new Shell(d);
        s.setSize(300,300);
        s.setImage(new Image(d, "c:\\icons\\JavaCup.ico"));
        s.setText("A Shell Menu Example");

        Menu m = new Menu(s,SWT.BAR );

         // create a File menu and add an Exit item
         final MenuItem file = new MenuItem(m, SWT.CASCADE);
         file.setText("File");
         final Menu filemenu = new Menu(s, SWT.DROP_DOWN);
         file.setMenu(filemenu);

         final MenuItem openItem = new MenuItem(filemenu, SWT.CASCADE);
         openItem.setText("Open");
         final Menu submenu = new Menu(s, SWT.DROP_DOWN);
         openItem.setMenu(submenu);
         final MenuItem childItem = new MenuItem(submenu, SWT.PUSH);
         childItem.setText("Child");
         final MenuItem dialogItem = new MenuItem(submenu, SWT.PUSH);
         dialogItem.setText("Dialog");

         final MenuItem separator = new MenuItem(filemenu, SWT.SEPARATOR);
         final MenuItem exitItem = new MenuItem(filemenu, SWT.PUSH);
         exitItem.setText("Exit");
```

Example 3-4. Creating cascading submenus (continued)

```
        // create an Edit menu and add Cut, Copy, and Paste items
        final MenuItem edit = new MenuItem(m, SWT.CASCADE);
        edit.setText("Edit");
        final Menu editmenu = new Menu(s, SWT.DROP_DOWN);
        edit.setMenu(editmenu);
        final MenuItem cutItem = new MenuItem(editmenu, SWT.PUSH);
        cutItem.setText("Cut");
        final MenuItem copyItem = new MenuItem(editmenu, SWT.PUSH);
        copyItem.setText("Copy");
        final MenuItem pasteItem = new MenuItem(editmenu, SWT.PUSH);
        pasteItem.setText("Paste");

        //create a Window menu and add Child items
        final MenuItem window = new MenuItem(m, SWT.CASCADE);
        window.setText("Window");
        final Menu windowmenu = new Menu(s, SWT.DROP_DOWN);
        window.setMenu(windowmenu);
        final MenuItem maxItem = new MenuItem(windowmenu, SWT.PUSH);
        maxItem.setText("Maximize");
        final MenuItem minItem = new MenuItem(windowmenu, SWT.PUSH);
        minItem.setText("Minimize");

        // create a Help menu and add an About item
        final MenuItem help = new MenuItem(m, SWT.CASCADE);
        help.setText("Help");
        final Menu helpmenu = new Menu(s, SWT.DROP_DOWN);
        help.setMenu(helpmenu);
        final MenuItem aboutItem = new MenuItem(helpmenu, SWT.PUSH);
        aboutItem.setText("About");

        s.setMenuBar(m);

        s.open();
        while(!s.isDisposed()){
            if(!d.readAndDispatch())
                d.sleep();
        }
        d.dispose();
    }
}
```

Creating an instance of this version of MenuShell displays the menu shown in Figure 3-3 when the user clicks File, then positions the mouse over the Open item.

Making Menus Perform the Intended Action

Of course, if you click any of the menu items in the MenuShell example, nothing happens. You must complete one more task to make your menu items perform their intended function—you must attach a Listener to your menu items. As the name implies, a Listener listens for a particular event to occur and then takes some action upon the occurrence.

A Listener is a class that extends one of the Listener interfaces. When an event occurs, the event loop for the main shell of the application dispatches that event to be handled by the Listener attached to the widget that is causing the event to occur. The result is that one of the methods of the Listener will be called. It is in those methods that you develop the code that executes when the event occurs.

The SWT provides you with several Listener interfaces, all a part of the org.eclipse.swt.events or org.eclipse.swt.widgets packages. To use a Listener, first identify the type of event that you are listening for, then call a method to attach that Listener to the widget. Finally, add code to the listener's methods to perform the desired task.

How do I do that?

To add a SelectionListener to the MenuItem childItem in MenuExample, use the following code:

```
childItem.addSelectionListener(new SelectionListener() {
    public void widgetSelected(SelectionEvent e) {
        Shell parent = (Shell)maxItem.getParent().getParent();
        ChildShell cs = new ChildShell(parent);
    }
    public void widgetDefaultSelected(SelectionEvent e) {
    }
});
```

Every widget in the SWT, including MenuItem, has one or more add methods that attach a Listener to the widget. To listen for mouse click events, add a SelectionListener to be called by addSelectionListener(). You pass addSelectionListener() a reference to a class that implements the SelectionListener interface. Usually, this is accomplished by using an anonymous inner class.

What happens next depends on the code you write in the widgetSelected() method. The preceding code simply opens one of the ChildShell examples from Chapter 2.

You must add a SelectionListener to every menu item you create,
except those you create using the SWT.CASCADE or SWT.SEPARATOR styles.
The complete menu system code, with SelectionListener added where
appropriate, is shown in Example 3-5.

Example 3-5. Menu items with listeners

```
import org.eclipse.swt.SWT;
import org.eclipse.swt.graphics.Image;
import org.eclipse.swt.widgets.*;

public class MenuShell {
    Display d;
    Shell s;
     MenuShell( )     {
         d = new Display( );
         s = new Shell(d);
         s.setSize(500,500);
         s.setImage(new Image(d, "c:\\icons\\JavaCup.ico"));
         s.setText("A Shell Menu Example");
         Menu m = new Menu(s,SWT.BAR );

         // create a File menu and add an Exit item
         final MenuItem file = new MenuItem(m, SWT.CASCADE);
         file.setText("File");
         final Menu filemenu = new Menu(s, SWT.DROP_DOWN);
         file.setMenu(filemenu);
        // create an Open menu and two submenu items
        final MenuItem openItem = new MenuItem(filemenu, SWT.CASCADE);
        openItem.setText("Open");
        final Menu submenu = new Menu(s, SWT.DROP_DOWN);
        openItem.setMenu(submenu);
        final MenuItem childItem = new MenuItem(submenu, SWT.PUSH);
        childItem.setText("Child");
        final MenuItem dialogItem = new MenuItem(submenu, SWT.PUSH);
        dialogItem.setText("Dialog");
        //add a separator
         final MenuItem separator = new MenuItem(filemenu, SWT.SEPARATOR);
        // create an Exit menu item
         final MenuItem exitItem = new MenuItem(filemenu, SWT.PUSH);
         exitItem.setText("Exit");

         // create an Edit menu and add Cut, Copy, and Paste items
```

Example 3-5. Menu items with listeners (continued)

```
        final MenuItem edit = new MenuItem(m, SWT.CASCADE);
        edit.setText("Edit");
        final Menu editmenu = new Menu(s, SWT.DROP_DOWN);
        edit.setMenu(editmenu);
        final MenuItem cutItem = new MenuItem(editmenu, SWT.PUSH);
        cutItem.setText("Cut");
        final MenuItem copyItem = new MenuItem(editmenu, SWT.PUSH);
        copyItem.setText("Copy");
        final MenuItem pasteItem = new MenuItem(editmenu, SWT.PUSH);
        pasteItem.setText("Paste");

        //create a Window menu and add Child items
        final MenuItem window = new MenuItem(m, SWT.CASCADE);
        window.setText("Window");
        final Menu windowmenu = new Menu(s, SWT.DROP_DOWN);
        window.setMenu(windowmenu);
        final MenuItem maxItem = new MenuItem(windowmenu, SWT.PUSH);
        maxItem.setText("Maximize");
        final MenuItem minItem = new MenuItem(windowmenu, SWT.PUSH);
        minItem.setText("Minimize");

        // create a Help menu and add an About item
        final MenuItem help = new MenuItem(m, SWT.CASCADE);
        help.setText("Help");
        final Menu helpmenu = new Menu(s, SWT.DROP_DOWN);
        help.setMenu(helpmenu);
        final MenuItem aboutItem = new MenuItem(helpmenu, SWT.PUSH);
        aboutItem.setText("About");

    childItem.addSelectionListener(new SelectionListener() {
        public void widgetSelected(SelectionEvent e) {
            Shell parent = (Shell)maxItem.getParent().getParent();
            ChildShell cs = new ChildShell(parent);
        }
        public void widgetDefaultSelected(SelectionEvent e) {

        }
    });


    dialogItem.addSelectionListener(new SelectionListener() {
        public void widgetSelected(SelectionEvent e) {
            Shell parent = (Shell)maxItem.getParent().getParent();
            DialogExample de = new DialogExample(parent);
            de.open();
        }
        public void widgetDefaultSelected(SelectionEvent e) {

        }
    });

    exitItem.addSelectionListener(new SelectionListener() {
```

Example 3-5. Menu items with listeners (continued)

```
            public void widgetSelected(SelectionEvent e) {
                System.exit(0);
            }
            public void widgetDefaultSelected(SelectionEvent e) {

            }
        });

        cutItem.addSelectionListener(new SelectionListener() {
            public void widgetSelected(SelectionEvent e) {
                System.out.println("Cut");
            }
            public void widgetDefaultSelected(SelectionEvent e) {

            }
        });

        copyItem.addSelectionListener(new SelectionListener() {
            public void widgetSelected(SelectionEvent e) {
                System.out.println("Copy");
            }
            public void widgetDefaultSelected(SelectionEvent e) {

            }
        });

        pasteItem.addSelectionListener(new SelectionListener() {
            public void widgetSelected(SelectionEvent e) {
                System.out.println("Paste");
            }
            public void widgetDefaultSelected(SelectionEvent e) {

            }
        });

        maxItem.addSelectionListener(new SelectionListener() {
            public void widgetSelected(SelectionEvent e) {
                Shell parent = (Shell)maxItem.getParent().getParent();
                parent.setMaximized(true);
            }
            public void widgetDefaultSelected(SelectionEvent e) {
            }
        });

        minItem.addSelectionListener(new SelectionListener() {
            public void widgetSelected(SelectionEvent e) {
                Shell parent = (Shell)minItem.getParent().getParent();
                parent.setMaximized(false);
            }
            public void widgetDefaultSelected(SelectionEvent e) {
            }
        });
```

Example 3-5. Menu items with listeners (continued)

```
aboutItem.addSelectionListener(new SelectionListener() {
    public void widgetSelected(SelectionEvent e) {
        Shell parent = (Shell)minItem.getParent().getParent();
        parent.setMaximized(false);
    }
    public void widgetDefaultSelected(SelectionEvent e) {
    }
});

s.setMenuBar(m);
s.open();
while(!s.isDisposed()){
    if(!d.readAndDispatch())
        d.sleep();
}
d.dispose();
    }
}
```

Menus sure require a lot of code to create. Also, a lot of objects are being created. Menus are very expensive constructs.

TIP

Some of these menu items currently do nothing except print to the console when they are clicked. In Chapter 18, you examine the code to make Cut, Copy, and Paste actually work.

What about...

code organization for the SelectionListener inner classes? After all, an inner class can be created anywhere inside the outer class.

To keep code grouped according to functionality, I suggest that you keep the anonymous inner classes in the same location as your menu creation code—usually placing it immediately after the code that creates the menu items. That way you don't have to bounce all over what may be a very large class file looking for the code that makes your menus perform.

Working with Other Menu Item Styles

In addition to SWT.SEPARATOR, SWT.PUSH, and SWT.CASCADE, which you have exercised earlier, menu items can have one of two other styles: SWT.RADIO and SWT.CHECK.

There's no right or wrong way to do these things. Just find the approach that works for you and your project. What works for one project may not be the best for another.

The RADIO style assigns multiple menu items to a group of items and allows only one of those items to be selected at any given time. It is analogous to the RADIO style for buttons that you will examine in Chapter 5.

The CHECK style simply places a check icon next to a menu item when the user has selected that option and removes it when the user deselects that option (by clicking the menu while it is in its checked state).

Both of these styles are useful when you want to enable the user to set a system option from the menu and to retain a visual indication of what options have been previously selected.

How do I do that?

The following code creates an Options menu with three menu items (plus a separator):

```
final MenuItem options = new MenuItem(m, SWT.CASCADE);
options.setText("Options");
final Menu optionsmenu = new Menu(s, SWT.DROP_DOWN);
options.setMenu(optionsmenu);
final MenuItem checkItem = new MenuItem(optionsmenu, SWT.CHECK);
checkItem.setText("Checked Option");
final MenuItem optionsseparator = new MenuItem(optionsmenu, SWT.SEPARATOR);
final MenuItem radioItem1 = new MenuItem(optionsmenu, SWT.RADIO);
radioItem1.setText("Radio One");
final MenuItem radioItem2 = new MenuItem(optionsmenu, SWT.RADIO);
radioItem2.setText("Radio Two");
```

Adding this code to the ShellMenu example class results in the menu shown in Figure 3-4. You can experiment with the menu to see the effects of clicking the various options (see Figure 3-5 and Figure 3-6).

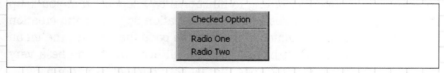

Figure 3-4. The Options menu

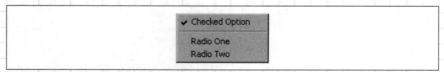

Figure 3-5. Clicking Checked Option

Figure 3-6. Clicking the Radio One option—clicking Radio Two deselects Radio One

Determining the State of CHECK and RADIO Menu Items

When you add a Listener to a menu item with the SWT.CHECK or SWT.RADIO style, you need to take extra steps to determine the state of the item. After all, it is the state of the item that controls what action you take in your code.

How do I do that?

You add a Listener to a CHECK or RADIO menu item in exactly the same manner as you do for a regular menu item. The difference comes in what code you write in the widgetSelected( ) method for your Listener. Specifically, the action you take will depend upon the state of the menu item (whether checked or unchecked). SWT provides a method to use to determine the menu's state. A typical Listener looks like this:

```
checkItem.addSelectionListener(new SelectionListener( ) {
    public void widgetSelected(SelectionEvent e) {
        if(checkItem.getSelection( ))
        {
            System.out.println("Check Menu was Checked");
        }
        else
        {
            System.out.println("Check Menu was Un-Checked");
        }
    }
    public void widgetDefaultSelected(SelectionEvent e)
    {
    }
});

radioItem1.addSelectionListener(new SelectionListener( ) {
    public void widgetSelected(SelectionEvent e) {
        if(radioItem1.getSelection( ))
        {
            System.out.println("Radio One was Checked");
        }
    }
    public void widgetDefaultSelected(SelectionEvent e)
    {
```

```
            }
        });

        radioItem2.addSelectionListener(new SelectionListener( ) {
            public void widgetSelected(SelectionEvent e) {
                if(radioItem2.getSelection( ))
                {
                    System.out.println("Radio Two was Checked");
                }
            }
            public void widgetDefaultSelected(SelectionEvent e)
            {
            }
        });
```

What about...

times when you want the menu to open for the first time with an item already checked? Neither CHECK nor RADIO style menu items have a default—meaning that unless you take action, the menu will open with no item initially selected.

A single line of code causes a CHECK or RADIO menu item to be selected:

```
        radioItem2.setSelection(true);
```

setSelection( ) works with CHECK style menu items, too.

Addition of this code causes the menu to cascade with the second RADIO menu item selected. Of course, selecting radioItem1 will deselect radioItem2 according to the normal rules.

Adding Keyboard Shortcuts

You've already seen how adding a separator bar to a menu can make a drop-down more visually pleasing, but users expect another professional touch from a menu system—the ability to access the menu items via keyboard keystroke combinations.

How do I do that?

SWT provides two approaches to assigning keyboard combinations to menu items. The approach you use depends upon which of the two keyboard shortcut types you wish to provide.

The first shortcut type is a single-key mnemonic that activates the menu if—and only if—that menu item is visible (i.e., it is one of the high-level menu items that appear on the menu bar or one of the menu items that appear when a menu is in its dropped-down state). It's easy to set this type of shortcut; just add an ampersand before the menu item text when calling the setText( ) method:

```
file.setText("&File");
```

You should consult guidelines for your target platform to determine the generally accepted keyboard shortcuts for particular functionality and design your menu to conform to those standards.

TIP

This type of keyboard shortcut depends upon the operating system to function. The results you get may vary from system to system. For example, on some versions of Windows you will see the *F* in File underlined at all times. On other versions, the *F* will be underlined only when the ALT key is pressed. On Windows XP, it could be either, depending on user settings. You must remember to execute your code on all target platforms to test for proper behavior.

The second keyboard shortcut is called an accelerator. An accelerator is a two-key combination (the first key normally being the Control key), that causes the menu item's action event to fire whether or not the menu item is currently visible. To set an accelerator, use the setAccelerator( ) method on MenuItem:

```
childItem.setAccelerator(SWT.CTRL+'C');
dialogItem.setAccelerator(SWT.CTRL+'D');
```

Making all the changes discussed earlier to the ShellMenu example yields the class shown in Example 3-6.

Example 3-6. Menu system with keyboard shortcuts

```
import org.eclipse.swt.SWT;
import org.eclipse.swt.events.HelpEvent;
import org.eclipse.swt.events.HelpListener;
import org.eclipse.swt.graphics.Image;
import org.eclipse.swt.widgets.*;

public class MenuShell {
    Display d;
    Shell s;
    MenuShell( )     {
        d = new Display( );
        s = new Shell(d);
        s.setSize(500,500);
        s.setImage(new Image(d, "c:\\icons\\JavaCup.ico"));
        s.setText("A Shell Menu Example");
        final Menu m = new Menu(s,SWT.BAR );

        // create a File menu and add an Exit item
        final MenuItem file = new MenuItem(m, SWT.CASCADE);
        file.setText("&File");
        final Menu filemenu = new Menu(s, SWT.DROP_DOWN);
```

Example 3-6. Menu system with keyboard shortcuts (continued)

```
                file.setMenu(filemenu);
                final MenuItem openItem = new MenuItem(filemenu, SWT.CASCADE);
                openItem.setText("&Open");
                final Menu submenu = new Menu(s, SWT.DROP_DOWN);
                openItem.setMenu(submenu);
                final MenuItem childItem = new MenuItem(submenu, SWT.PUSH);
                childItem.setText("&Child\tCTRL+C");
                childItem.setAccelerator(SWT.CTRL+'C');
                final MenuItem dialogItem = new MenuItem(submenu, SWT.PUSH);
                dialogItem.setText("&Dialog\tCTRL+D");
                dialogItem.setAccelerator(SWT.CTRL+'D');
                final MenuItem separator = new MenuItem(filemenu, SWT.SEPARATOR);
                final MenuItem exitItem = new MenuItem(filemenu, SWT.PUSH);
                exitItem.setText("E&xit");

                // create an Edit menu and add Cut, Copy, and Paste items
                final MenuItem edit = new MenuItem(m, SWT.CASCADE);
                edit.setText("&Edit");
                final Menu editmenu = new Menu(s, SWT.DROP_DOWN);
                edit.setMenu(editmenu);
                final MenuItem cutItem = new MenuItem(editmenu, SWT.PUSH);
                cutItem.setText("&Cut");
                final MenuItem copyItem = new MenuItem(editmenu, SWT.PUSH);
                copyItem.setText("Co&py");
                final MenuItem pasteItem = new MenuItem(editmenu, SWT.PUSH);
                pasteItem.setText("&Paste");

                //create an Options menu and add Menu items
                final MenuItem options = new MenuItem(m, SWT.CASCADE);
                options.setText("&Options");
                final Menu optionsmenu = new Menu(s, SWT.DROP_DOWN);
                options.setMenu(optionsmenu);
                final MenuItem checkItem = new MenuItem(optionsmenu, SWT.CHECK);
                checkItem.setText("&Checked Option");
                final MenuItem optionsseparator = new MenuItem(optionsmenu,
                    SWT.SEPARATOR);
                final MenuItem radioItem1 = new MenuItem(optionsmenu, SWT.RADIO);
                radioItem1.setText("Radio &One");
                final MenuItem radioItem2 = new MenuItem(optionsmenu, SWT.RADIO);
                radioItem2.setText("Radio &Two");

                //create a Window menu and add Child items
                final MenuItem window = new MenuItem(m, SWT.CASCADE);
                window.setText("&Window");
                final Menu windowmenu = new Menu(s, SWT.DROP_DOWN);
                window.setMenu(windowmenu);
                final MenuItem maxItem = new MenuItem(windowmenu, SWT.PUSH);
                maxItem.setText("Ma&ximize");
                final MenuItem minItem = new MenuItem(windowmenu, SWT.PUSH);
                minItem.setText("Mi&nimize");

                // create a Help menu and add an About item
```

Example 3-6. Menu system with keyboard shortcuts (continued)

```
        final MenuItem help = new MenuItem(m, SWT.CASCADE);
        help.setText("&Help");
        final Menu helpmenu = new Menu(s, SWT.DROP_DOWN);
        help.setMenu(helpmenu);
        final MenuItem aboutItem = new MenuItem(helpmenu, SWT.PUSH);
        aboutItem.setText("&About");

        // add action listeners for the menu items
        // this code is the same as seen previously, so it is
        // omitted here


        s.setMenBar(m);
        s.open();
        while(!s.isDisposed()){
            if(!d.readAndDispatch())
                d.sleep();
        }
        d.dispose();
    }
}
```

Creating an instance of this version of MenuShell results in a menu that responds to keyboard shortcuts. You should experiment with the running program and various key combinations to ensure the desired effect.

Creating Pop-Up Menus

The last type of menu to examine is called the *pop-up menu*. A pop-up menu is one that appears at the current mouse cursor position whenever the user right-clicks (on Windows and most Unix systems) or Ctrl-clicks (on a Mac). Pop-up menus are often used to create context-sensitive menu choices when the user right-clicks a particular widget in a window. For example, if the cursor is located within the confines of a text widget, a right-click could pop up a menu giving instant access to Cut, Copy, and Paste functionality.

Users love pop-up menus.

How do I do that?

Pop-up menus are easy to create and the steps are similar to those used to create a menu bar. In the case of a pop-up menu, the difference is that the highest-level menu has the style SWT.POP_UP rather than SWT.BAR. To create a pop-up of an Edit menu with Cut, Copy, and Paste menu items, you would use the following:

```
private Menu createEditPopup(){
        final Menu p = new Menu(s,SWT.POP_UP);
        final MenuItem cutItem = new MenuItem(p, SWT.PUSH);
```

```
cutItem.setText("&Cut");
final MenuItem copyItem = new MenuItem(p, SWT.PUSH);
copyItem.setText("Co&py");
final MenuItem pasteItem = new MenuItem(p, SWT.PUSH);
pasteItem.setText("&Paste");

cutItem.addSelectionListener(new SelectionListener() {
    public void widgetSelected(SelectionEvent e) {
        System.out.println("Cut");
    }
    public void widgetDefaultSelected(SelectionEvent e) {

    }
});

copyItem.addSelectionListener(new SelectionListener() {
    public void widgetSelected(SelectionEvent e) {
        System.out.println("Copy");
    }
    public void widgetDefaultSelected(SelectionEvent e) {

    }
});

pasteItem.addSelectionListener(new SelectionListener() {
    public void widgetSelected(SelectionEvent e) {
        System.out.println("Paste");
    }
    public void widgetDefaultSelected(SelectionEvent e) {

    }
});

    return p;

}
```

TIP

You see that I've taken a slightly different approach with the pop-up menu than I did with the main menu by placing the code to create the menu in a separate method. Why? By placing the code in a separate method, I keep the code that creates the pop-up in one easily accessible location so I can attach it to any widget on the shell, simply by calling the method as needed.

To attach a pop-up menu to a Shell or other widget you call the setMenu() method. Since the preceding pop-up menu is created in a separate method in the MenuExample class, attach it to the Shell with this code:

```
s.setMenu(createEditPopup());
```

Adding this code to MenuShell results in the pop-up menu shown in Figure 3-7, appearing at the cursor location when the user right-clicks anywhere inside the Shell.

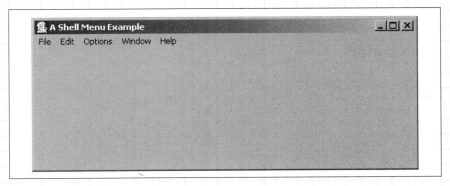

Figure 3-7. The Edit menu pop-up

Menus are an essential element of GUI design and, as you have seen, SWT provides everything you need for their creation. Almost every application you design should make extensive use of menus. You should strive to create menus with an efficient design that follows the generally accepted guidelines for your platform.

CHAPTER 4

SWT Toolbars

To complete the examination of building windows using the SWT you must look at the final element that end users expect to see in a well-designed window—the toolbar. A *toolbar* is a row of buttons that appears below the menu and above the working area of the window to allow one-click access to the most commonly used functionality of your application. If your application supports the use of a menu—and almost every application will—it can benefit from the use of a toolbar.

Toolbar buttons can have a text label, an image, or both; the use of images that provide a hint about the functionality of the button is a nice touch. If you examine other applications running on your chosen platform, you will likely find that the use of images, rather than text, is the norm. Toolbar buttons also often make use of pop-up Help text that appears whenever the mouse hovers over the button.

SWT provides two classes that you use in toolbar creation—the ToolBar and ToolItem classes. These classes are part of the org.eclipse.swt.widgets package. The Image class, located in the org.eclipse.swt.graphics package, is also used to load and specify an icon or bitmap for use as a toolbar button's image, just as it specified a window icon for your shell back in Chapter 2.

Creating the Toolbar

Creating toolbars is much like creating menus. Simply create an instance of the ToolBar class to serve as the container for the individual buttons, which are represented by instances of the ToolItem class.

In this chapter:
- Creating the Toolbar
- Creating Toolbar Buttons
- Creating a Complete Toolbar Example
- Making the Buttons Work— Adding Listeners
- Adding Separators to Your Toolbar
- Adding Check and Radio ToolItems
- Determining Whether a Check or Radio Button Is Selected
- Using ToolTips

Toolbars should be thoughtfully designed prior to development. There is only a small amount of space at the top of the window, so putting some thought into these decisions ahead of time (and/or talking it over with the intended user base) can save hours of programming time down the road.

Once you are armed with a list of buttons that you wish to appear on the toolbar, and you have acquired or developed images for those buttons, you are ready to begin development of your toolbar.

How do I do that?

First, create the toolbar itself—an instance of the ToolBar class:

```
final ToolBar bar = new ToolBar(s, SWT.HORIZONTAL);
```

This single line of code creates an instance of ToolBar and attaches it to a shell, referenced by the variable s.

Next, set the size and location of the toolbar:

```
bar.setSize(300, 65);
bar.setLocation(0,0);
```

What just happened?

The first line sets the toolbar's width and height. Generally, you should specify a width equal to the window's width and a height that is of sufficient size to accommodate the buttons that will be placed on the toolbar. This, of course, will depend on the size of images you plan to use for those buttons, so once again planning before coding is required.

The second line sets the X and Y coordinates of the toolbar's upper left-hand corner relative to the working area of the window. Generally, if you want the toolbar to be positioned directly below the menu, set the toolbar's location to 0, 0. If you're using a vertical toolbar, set the parameters to values that would make the toolbar position itself along either the left or right of the window. The right side position can be calculated by subtracting the width of the toolbar from the width of the window

---

TIP

Be careful when assigning a height (the second parameter). Although assigning more height than is necessary for the toolbar buttons won't affect the toolbar's appearance, it will decrease the amount of working area in the window for placing other components

---

What about...

using other styles for your toolbar? You can use five styles with the ToolBar class.

SWT.FLAT

Creates a non-3D toolbar.

SWT.HORIZONTAL

Positions the toolbar at the top of the window, below the menu bar.

SWT.WRAP

Causes the toolbar item text to wrap across multiple lines.

SWT.RIGHT

Causes the text on toolbar items to be right-justified (appearing to the right of any image) .

SWT.VERTICAL

Positions the toolbar vertically along either side of the window, depending upon the parameters passed to the setLocation( ) method.

Some styles—for example, the RIGHT and WRAP styles—can be combined to achive a desire effect.

Most toolbar buttons make use of assigned images rather than text labels.

Creating Toolbar Buttons

The next step in creating a toolbar is to add the buttons. You need one button for each function you wish to enable the user to access from the toolbar. Buttons can have assigned to them either images or labels, or both, to aid the user in understanding exactly what function the button triggers.

Either way, you create toolbar buttons by creating instances of the ToolItem class—one for each button.

TIP

There are some standards that govern what images to use for specific functions. A scissors image is used for cut, for example, while a disk image is used for save. A great way to determine what images to use is to study other applications running on your target platforms.

How do I do that?

The ToolItem class constructor accepts as arguments a reference to the containing ToolBar, and the style of the button you wish to create. There are five styles you can use when creating ToolItem buttons:

SWT.PUSH

Creates a clickable toolbar button.

SWT.CHECK

Creates a toolbar button that toggles between selected and deselected.

SWT.RADIO

Creates a toolbar button that is part of a group of buttons in which only one button can be selected.

SWT.SEPARATOR

Adds spacing between toolbar buttons.

SWT.DROP_DOWN

Creates a toolbar button to which a drop-down menu can be attached.

The code needed to create a text-only button is simple:

```
final ToolItem textItem = new ToolItem(bar, SWT.PUSH);
textItem.setText("Open Child");
```

Adding an image to a ToolItem is very similar to adding text, except that you use the setImage( ) method rather than the setText( ) method. First, you must create an instance of the Image class to load up the picture; then you associate that image with the ToolItem:

```
Image icon = new Image(d, "c:\\icons\\JavaCup.ico");
final ToolItem imageItem = new ToolItem(bar, SWT.PUSH);
imageItem.setImage(icon);
```

Creating ToolItem buttons that use both images and text is simply a matter of calling both the setImage( ) and setText( ) methods:

```
Image icon = new Image(d, "c:\\icons\\JavaCup.ico");
final ToolItem textImageItem = new ToolItem(bar, SWT.PUSH);
textImageItem.setImage(icon);
textImageItem.setText("Java Icon");
```

Creating a Complete Toolbar Example

Toolbars and menus go hand in hand, and often there is a correspondence between MenuItem and ToolItem objects that you create. To create a functional toolbar, begin by examining your menu code to determine which functions to expose as toolbar buttons. If you look at the MenuShell example from Chapter 3, you find that several common toolbar functions are included. The best candidates for a toolbar from the example are Open and Save (from the File menu), and Cut, Copy, and Paste (from the Edit menu).

Once you have planned your toolbar, you are ready to develop the code necessary to create it.

How do I do that?

Example 4-1 demonstrates how to create a window, complete with both toolbar and menu.

Example 4-1. Creating a Toolbar example

```
import org.eclipse.swt.SWT;
import org.eclipse.swt.events.*;
import org.eclipse.swt.graphics.Image;
import org.eclipse.swt.widgets.*;

public class ToolbarShellExample {
        Display d;
        Shell s;
        ToolbarShellExample( )     {
            d = new Display( );
            s = new Shell(d);
            s.setSize(300,300);
            s.setImage(new Image(d, "c:\\icons\\JavaCup.ico"));
            s.setText("A Shell Toolbar Example");

            final ToolBar bar = new ToolBar(s,SWT.HORIZONTAL);
            bar.setSize(300,70);
            bar.setLocation(0,0);

            // create images for toolbar buttons
            final Image saveIcon = new Image(d, "c:\\icons\\save.jpg");
            final Image openIcon = new Image(d, "c:\\icons\\open.jpg");
            final Image cutIcon = new Image(d, "c:\\icons\\cut.jpg");
            final Image copyIcon = new Image(d, "c:\\icons\\copy.jpg");
            final Image pasteIcon = new Image(d, "c:\\icons\\paste.jpg");

            // create and add the button for performing an open operation
            final ToolItem openToolItem = new ToolItem(bar, SWT.PUSH);
            openToolItem.setImage(openIcon);
            openToolItem.setText("Open");
            openToolItem.setToolTipText("Open File");

            //create and add the button for performing a save operation
            final ToolItem saveToolItem = new ToolItem(bar, SWT.PUSH);
            saveToolItem.setImage(saveIcon);
            saveToolItem.setText("Save");
            saveToolItem.setToolTipText("Save File");

           //create and add the button for performing a cut operation
            final ToolItem cutToolItem = new ToolItem(bar, SWT.PUSH);
            cutToolItem.setImage(cutIcon);
            cutToolItem.setText("Cut");
            cutToolItem.setToolTipText("Cut");

            // create and add the button for performing a copy operation
            final ToolItem copyToolItem = new ToolItem(bar, SWT.PUSH);
            copyToolItem.setImage(copyIcon);
```

Example 4-1. Creating a Toolbar example (continued)

```
        copyToolItem.setText("Copy");
        copyToolItem.setToolTipText("Copy");

        // create and add the button for performing a paste operation
        final ToolItem pasteToolItem = new ToolItem(bar, SWT.PUSH);
        pasteToolItem.setImage(pasteIcon);
        pasteToolItem.setText("Paste");
        pasteToolItem.setToolTipText("Paste");

        // create the menu
        Menu m = new Menu(s,SWT.BAR);

        // create a File menu and add an Exit item
        final MenuItem file = new MenuItem(m, SWT.CASCADE);
        file.setText("&File");
        final Menu filemenu = new Menu(s, SWT.DROP_DOWN);
        file.setMenu(filemenu);
        final MenuItem openMenuItem = new MenuItem(filemenu, SWT.PUSH);
        openMenuItem.setText("&Open\tCTRL+O");
        openMenuItem.setAccelerator(SWT.CTRL+'O');
        final MenuItem saveMenuItem = new MenuItem(filemenu, SWT.PUSH);
        saveMenuItem.setText("&Save\tCTRL+S");
        saveMenuItem.setAccelerator(SWT.CTRL+'S');
        final MenuItem separator = new MenuItem(filemenu, SWT.SEPARATOR);
        final MenuItem exitMenuItem = new MenuItem(filemenu, SWT.PUSH);
        exitMenuItem.setText("E&xit");

        // create an Edit menu and add Cut, Copy, and Paste items
        final MenuItem edit = new MenuItem(m, SWT.CASCADE);
        edit.setText("&Edit");
        final Menu editmenu = new Menu(s, SWT.DROP_DOWN);
        edit.setMenu(editmenu);
        final MenuItem cutMenuItem = new MenuItem(editmenu, SWT.PUSH);
        cutMenuItem.setText("&Cut");
        final MenuItem copyMenuItem = new MenuItem(editmenu, SWT.PUSH);
        copyMenuItem.setText("Co&py");
        final MenuItem pasteMenuItem = new MenuItem(editmenu, SWT.PUSH);
        pasteMenuItem.setText("&Paste");

        //create a Window menu and add Child items
        final MenuItem window = new MenuItem(m, SWT.CASCADE);
        window.setText("&Window");
        final Menu windowmenu = new Menu(s, SWT.DROP_DOWN);
        window.setMenu(windowmenu);
        final MenuItem maxMenuItem = new MenuItem(windowmenu, SWT.PUSH);
        maxMenuItem.setText("Ma&ximize");
        final MenuItem minMenuItem = new MenuItem(windowmenu, SWT.PUSH);
        minMenuItem.setText("Mi&nimize");

        // create a Help menu and add an About item
        final MenuItem help = new MenuItem(m, SWT.CASCADE);
        help.setText("&Help");
        final Menu helpmenu = new Menu(s, SWT.DROP_DOWN);
```

Example 4-1. Creating a Toolbar example (continued)

```
help.setMenu(helpmenu);
final MenuItem abouMenutItem = new MenuItem(helpmenu, SWT.PUSH);
aboutMenuItem.setText("&About");

// add action listeners for the menu items

openMenuItem.addSelectionListener(new SelectionListener( ) {
    public void widgetSelected(SelectionEvent e) {
        System.out.println("Open");
    }
    public void widgetDefaultSelected(SelectionEvent e) {
    }
});


saveMenuItem.addSelectionListener(new SelectionListener( ) {
    public void widgetSelected(SelectionEvent e) {
        System.out.println("Save");
    }
    public void widgetDefaultSelected(SelectionEvent e) {
    }
});

exitMenuItem.addSelectionListener(new SelectionListener( ) {
    public void widgetSelected(SelectionEvent e) {
        System.exit(0);
    }
    public void widgetDefaultSelected(SelectionEvent e) {
    }
});

cutMenuItem.addSelectionListener(new SelectionListener( ) {
    public void widgetSelected(SelectionEvent e) {
        System.out.println("Cut");
    }
    public void widgetDefaultSelected(SelectionEvent e) {
    }
});

copyMenuItem.addSelectionListener(new SelectionListener( ) {
    public void widgetSelected(SelectionEvent e) {
        System.out.println("Copy");
    }
    public void widgetDefaultSelected(SelectionEvent e) {
    }
});

pasteMenuItem.addSelectionListener(new SelectionListener( ) {
    public void widgetSelected(SelectionEvent e) {
        System.out.println("Paste");
    }
    public void widgetDefaultSelected(SelectionEvent e) {
```

Example 4-1. Creating a Toolbar example (continued)

```
        }
    });

    maxMenuItem.addSelectionListener(new SelectionListener() {
        public void widgetSelected(SelectionEvent e) {
            Shell parent = (Shell)maxItem.getParent().getParent();
            parent.setMaximized(true);
        }
        public void widgetDefaultSelected(SelectionEvent e) {
        }
    });

    minMenuItem.addSelectionListener(new SelectionListener() {
        public void widgetSelected(SelectionEvent e) {
            Shell parent = (Shell)minItem.getParent().getParent();
            parent.setMaximized(false);
        }
        public void widgetDefaultSelected(SelectionEvent e) {
        }
    });

    aboutMenuItem.addSelectionListener(new SelectionListener() {
        public void widgetSelected(SelectionEvent e) {
            System.out.println("Help Invoked");
        }
        public void widgetDefaultSelected(SelectionEvent e) {
        }
    });

    s.setMenuBar(m);

    s.open();
    while(!s.isDisposed()){
        if(!d.readAndDispatch())
            d.sleep();
    }
    d.dispose();
    }
}
```

As with menus, creating toolbars takes a lot of code, though fewer objects. Toolbars are expensive, but much less so than menus.

Creating an instance of ToolbarShellExample displays Figure 4-1.

Making the Buttons Work— Adding Listeners

As with menus (and, in fact, all widgets), you must now add a *listener* for each button and code the widgetSelected() method for each SelectionListener to take the appropriate action.

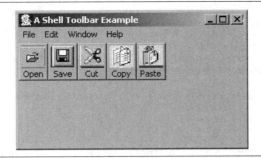

Figure 4-1. Window with toolbar

How do I do that?

The `Listener` code for the four toolbar buttons created by Example 4-1 is shown here:

```
openToolItem.addSelectionListener(new SelectionListener() {
    public void widgetSelected(SelectionEvent event) {
        System.out.println("Open");
    }
    public void widgetDefaultSelected(SelectionEvent event)
    {
    }
});

saveToolItem.addSelectionListener(new SelectionListener() {
    public void widgetSelected(SelectionEvent event) {
        System.out.println("Save");
    }
    public void widgetDefaultSelected(SelectionEvent event)
    {
    }
});

cutToolItem.addSelectionListener(new SelectionListener() {
    public void widgetSelected(SelectionEvent event) {
        System.out.println("Cut");
    }
    public void widgetDefaultSelected(SelectionEvent event)
    {
    }
});

copyToolItem.addSelectionListener(new SelectionListener() {
    public void widgetSelected(SelectionEvent event) {
        System.out.println("Copy");
    }
    public void widgetDefaultSelected(SelectionEvent event)
    {
```

```
        }
    });

    pasteToolItem.addSelectionListener(new SelectionListener() {
        public void widgetSelected(SelectionEvent event) {
            System.out.println("Paste");
        }
        public void widgetDefaultSelected(SelectionEvent event)
        {
        }
    });
```

Adding the preceding code to the constructor for `ToolbarShellExample`
results in the toolbar buttons becoming functional—at least to the point of
printing a message to the Console when they are pressed, as shown in
Figure 4-2.

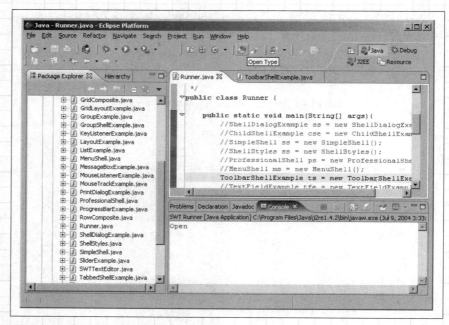

Figure 4-2. The Eclipse Console

What about...

all that duplicate code in the `SelectionListener` classes? One of the goals
of object-oriented programming is to reduce the amount of code that is
duplicated in an application, yet as you see, the `widgetSelected()` code
added to the `ToolItem` objects is identical to that added to the `MenuItem`
objects created in Example 4-1.

This can be corrected by creating named inner classes that implement the SelectionListener interface, as shown in Example 4-2.

Example 4-2. Using named inner classes for SelectionListeners

```
import org.eclipse.swt.SWT;
import org.eclipse.swt.events.SelectionEvent;
import org.eclipse.swt.events.SelectionListener;
import org.eclipse.swt.graphics.Image;
import org.eclipse.swt.widgets.*;

public class ToolbarShellExample {
        Display d;
        Shell s;
        ToolbarShellExample( )    {
            d = new Display( );
            s = new Shell(d);
            s.setSize(300,300);
            s.setImage(new Image(d, "c:\\icons\\JavaCup.ico"));
            s.setText("A Shell Toolbar Example");

            final ToolBar bar = new ToolBar(s,SWT.HORIZONTAL);
            bar.setSize(500,70);
            bar.setLocation(0,0);
            // create images for toolbar buttons
            final Image saveIcon = new Image(d, "c:\\icons\\save.jpg");
            final Image openIcon = new Image(d, "c:\\icons\\open.jpg");
            final Image childIcon = new Image(d, "c:\\icons\\userH.ico");
            final Image cutIcon = new Image(d, "c:\\icons\\cut.jpg");
            final Image copyIcon = new Image(d, "c:\\icons\\copy.jpg");
            final Image pasteIcon = new Image(d, "c:\\icons\\paste.jpg");
            // create and add the button for performing an open operation
            final ToolItem openToolItem = new ToolItem(bar, SWT.PUSH);
            openToolItem.setImage(openIcon);
            openToolItem.setText("Open");
            openToolItem.setToolTipText("Open File");

            //create and add the button for performing a save operation
            final ToolItem saveToolItem = new ToolItem(bar, SWT.PUSH);
            saveToolItem.setImage(saveIcon);
            saveToolItem.setText("Save");
            saveToolItem.setToolTipText("Save File");

            final ToolItem sep1 = new ToolItem(bar, SWT.SEPARATOR);

            //create and add the button for performing a cut operation
            final ToolItem cutToolItem = new ToolItem(bar, SWT.PUSH);
            cutToolItem.setImage(cutIcon);
            cutToolItem.setText("Cut");
            cutToolItem.setToolTipText("Cut");

            // create and add the button for performing a copy operation
            final ToolItem copyToolItem = new ToolItem(bar, SWT.PUSH);
```

```
copyToolItem.setImage(copyIcon);
copyToolItem.setText("Copy");
copyToolItem.setToolTipText("Copy");

// create and add the button for performing a paste operation
final ToolItem pasteToolItem = new ToolItem(bar, SWT.PUSH);
pasteToolItem.setImage(pasteIcon);
pasteToolItem.setText("Paste");
pasteToolItem.setToolTipText("Paste");

// create inner classes for SelectionListeners
class Open implements SelectionListener
{
    public void widgetSelected(SelectionEvent event) {
        System.out.println("Open");
    }
    public void widgetDefaultSelected(SelectionEvent event)
    {
    }
}

class Save implements SelectionListener
{
    public void widgetSelected(SelectionEvent event) {
        System.out.println("Save");
    }
    public void widgetDefaultSelected(SelectionEvent event)
    {
    }
}

class Cut implements SelectionListener
{
    public void widgetSelected(SelectionEvent event) {
        System.out.println("Cut");
    }
    public void widgetDefaultSelected(SelectionEvent event)
    {
    }
}

class Copy implements SelectionListener
{
    public void widgetSelected(SelectionEvent event) {
        System.out.println("Copy");
    }
    public void widgetDefaultSelected(SelectionEvent event)
    {
    }
}

class Paste implements SelectionListener
```

Example 4-2. Using named inner classes for SelectionListeners (continued)

```java
    {
        public void widgetSelected(SelectionEvent event) {
            System.out.println("Paste");
        }
        public void widgetDefaultSelected(SelectionEvent event)
        {
        }
    }

    openToolItem.addSelectionListener(new Open());
    saveToolItem.addSelectionListener(new Save());
    cutToolItem.addSelectionListener(new Cut());
    copyToolItem.addSelectionListener(new Copy());
    pasteToolItem.addSelectionListener(new Paste());

    // create the menu system
    Menu m = new Menu(s,SWT.BAR);
    // create a File menu and add an Exit item
    final MenuItem file = new MenuItem(m, SWT.CASCADE);
    file.setText("&File");
    final Menu filemenu = new Menu(s, SWT.DROP_DOWN);
    file.setMenu(filemenu);
    final MenuItem openMenuItem = new MenuItem(filemenu, SWT.PUSH);
    openMenuItem.setText("&Open\tCTRL+O");
    openMenuItem.setAccelerator(SWT.CTRL+'O');
    final MenuItem saveMenuItem = new MenuItem(filemenu, SWT.PUSH);
    saveMenuItem.setText("&Save\tCTRL+S");
    saveMenuItem.setAccelerator(SWT.CTRL+'S');
    final MenuItem separator = new MenuItem(filemenu, SWT.SEPARATOR);
    final MenuItem exitMenuItem = new MenuItem(filemenu, SWT.PUSH);
    exitMenuItem.setText("E&xit");

    // create an Edit menu and add Cut, Copy, and Paste items
    final MenuItem edit = new MenuItem(m, SWT.CASCADE);
    edit.setText("&Edit");
    final Menu editmenu = new Menu(s, SWT.DROP_DOWN);
    edit.setMenu(editmenu);
    final MenuItem cutMenuItem = new MenuItem(editmenu, SWT.PUSH);
    cutMenuItem.setText("&Cut");
    final MenuItem copyMenuItem = new MenuItem(editmenu, SWT.PUSH);
    copyMenuItem.setText("Co&py");
    final MenuItem pasteMenuItem = new MenuItem(editmenu, SWT.PUSH);
    pasteMenuItem.setText("&Paste");

    //create a Window menu and add Child items
    final MenuItem window = new MenuItem(m, SWT.CASCADE);
    window.setText("&Window");
    final Menu windowmenu = new Menu(s, SWT.DROP_DOWN);
    window.setMenu(windowmenu);
    final MenuItem maxMenuItem = new MenuItem(windowmenu, SWT.PUSH);
    maxMenuItem.setText("Ma&ximize");
    final MenuItem minMenuItem = new MenuItem(windowmenu, SWT.PUSH);
```

```
                minMenuItem.setText("Mi&nimize");

                // create a Help menu and add an About item
                final MenuItem help = new MenuItem(m, SWT.CASCADE);
                help.setText("&Help");
                final Menu helpmenu = new Menu(s, SWT.DROP_DOWN);
                help.setMenu(helpmenu);
                final MenuItem aboutMenuItem = new MenuItem(helpmenu, SWT.PUSH);
                aboutMenuItem.setText("&About");

                // add action listeners for the menu items

                openMenuItem.addSelectionListener(new Open());
                saveMenuItem.addSelectionListener(new Save());
                exitMenuItem.addSelectionListener(new SelectionListener() {
                    public void widgetSelected(SelectionEvent e) {
                        System.exit(0);
                    }
                    public void widgetDefaultSelected(SelectionEvent e)
                    {
                    }
                });
                cutMenuItem.addSelectionListener(new Cut());
                copyMenuItem.addSelectionListener(new Copy());
                pasteMenuItem.addSelectionListener(new Paste());
                maxMenuItem.addSelectionListener(new SelectionListener() {
                    public void widgetSelected(SelectionEvent e) {
                        Shell parent = (Shell)maxMenuItem.getParent().getParent();
                        parent.setMaximized(true);
                    }
                    public void widgetDefaultSelected(SelectionEvent e)
                    {
                    }
                });

                minMenuItem.addSelectionListener(new SelectionListener() {
                    public void widgetSelected(SelectionEvent e) {
                        Shell parent = (Shell)minMenuItem.getParent().getParent();
                        parent.setMaximized(false);
                    }
                    public void widgetDefaultSelected(SelectionEvent e)
                    {
                    }
                });

                aboutMenuItem.addSelectionListener(new SelectionListener() {
                    public void widgetSelected(SelectionEvent e) {
                        System.out.println("Help Invoked");
                    }
                    public void widgetDefaultSelected(SelectionEvent e)
                    {
                    }
```

```
        });

        s.setMenuBar(m);
        s.open();
        while(!s.isDisposed()){
            if(!d.readAndDispatch())
                d.sleep();
        }
        d.dispose();
    }
}
```

What just happened?

As you can see from Example 4-2, the number of duplicated lines is decreased. This is accomplished by adding a named inner class for each SelectionListener that was shared between a menu item and a toolbar button. For example, the inner class for the Open functionality is now written as follows:

```
class Open implements SelectionListener
{
    public void widgetSelected(SelectionEvent event) {
        System.out.println("Open");
    }
    public void widgetDefaultSelected(SelectionEvent event)
    {
    }
}
```

This saves a little code—how much depends on the contents of the inner classes. Remember, he who writes the fewest lines wins.

The inner class is then used for both the menu item and the toolbar button by calling the addSelectionListener( ) method for each:

```
openToolItem.addSelectionListener(new Open());
openMenuItem.addSelectionListener(new Open());
```

Either approach is valid: choose whichever best matches your coding philosophy.

Adding Separators to Your Toolbar

Separators enable you to group toolbar buttons into functional areas. If you look at the toolbar you created and executed in Figure 4-1, you will see that there are a couple of functional areas. The first is the Open and Save functionality. The second is the Cut, Copy, and Paste functionality. As it now appears, nothing distinguishes the two functional areas from each other as the user gazes at the toolbar. To provide that visual distinction, you must add a separator.

How do I do that?

Separators are easy to create:

```
final ToolItem separator = new ToolItem(bar, SWT.SEPARATOR);
```

If you insert this line of code in the location where you wish the separator to appear (between the code that creates the Save button and the code that creates the Cut button), the toolbar appears as in Figure 4-3— a distinct improvement.

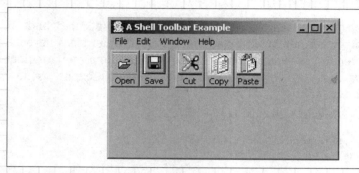

Figure 4-3. Toolbar with separator

Adding Check and Radio ToolItems

It is often helpful to supply the user with visual feedback as to what toolbar buttons have been previously selected. This is generally true when you need the user to select from a set of options. You learned in Chapter 3 how to provide visual cues in menu systems. Use checked menu items to display checkmarks next to items that have been selected. Use radio menu items to enable the user to select one, and only one, option from a group. Both types of item provide a visual indicator of selected options.

You can provide the same type of functionality on your toolbars if you use the SWT.CHECK or SWT.RADIO style when you create a ToolItem instance.

How do I do that?

As with all widgets, you can change the appearance and functionality of ToolItem objects simply by changing the style. Consider the following code:

```
final ToolItem sep2 = new ToolItem(bar, SWT.SEPARATOR);

final ToolItem checkItem = new ToolItem(bar, SWT.CHECK);
  checkItem.setText("Check");
final ToolItem sep3 = new ToolItem(bar, SWT.SEPARATOR);

final ToolItem radioItem1 = new ToolItem(bar, SWT.RADIO);
  radioItem1.setText("Radio 1");
final ToolItem radioItem2 = new ToolItem(bar, SWT.RADIO);
  radioItem2.setText("Radio 2");
final ToolItem sep4 = new ToolItem(bar, SWT.SEPARATOR);
final ToolItem radioItem3 = new ToolItem(bar, SWT.RADIO);
  radioItem3.setText("Radio 3");
final ToolItem radioItem4 = new ToolItem(bar, SWT.RADIO);
  radioItem4.setText("Radio 4");
```

Adding this code to the version of ToolbarShellExample created by Example 4-1 results in the window shown in Figure 4-4.

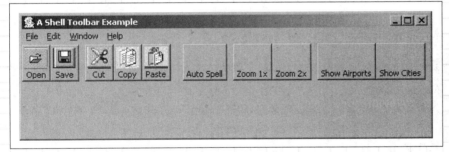

This kind of toolbar button is extremely popular: try to find an application today that doesn't make some use of it.

Figure 4-4. Toolbar with check- and radio-style buttons

What just happened?

When this window opens, all the toolbar buttons will be in their unselected state, as shown in Figure 4-4. Clicking a Check button will result in the button remaining depressed, as shown in Figure 4-5.

This provides a visual indication to the user that the option represented by the button has been selected. Clicking the button a second time returns it to its unselected state.

The behavior for radio buttons is different from that of check buttons. With radio buttons, only one member of the group can be selected at any

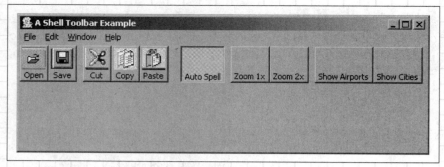

Figure 4-5. A check button in its checked state

given time. Buttons that are immediately adjacent to each other are considered to be part of a group. If another ToolItem is created between two radio buttons—even a separator—they will reside in two different groups.

In Figure 4-4, there are two radio groups. The buttons labeled in the code Radio 1 and Radio 2 are in one group, while those labeled Radio 3 and Radio 4 are in a second group. You may select either Radio One or Radio Two, and either Radio Three or Radio Four, but you may *not* select Radio One *and* Radio Two, or Radio Three *and* Radio Four.

Determining Whether a Check or Radio Button Is Selected

If you use CHECK- or RADIO-style toolbar items, at some point you must perform a check in your code to determine the current state of the button

CHECK- and RADIO-style menu items work the same way, so the code required to determine status is similar.

How do I do that?

In a SelectionListener—or any other block of code—you can determine whether a check or radio item is selected by calling the ToolItem getSelection( ) method.:

```
checkItem.addSelectionListener(new SelectionListener() {
    public void widgetSelected(SelectionEvent event) {
        if(checkItem.getSelection())
        {
            System.out.println("Check");
        }
        else
        {
            System.out.println("Uncheck");
        }
    }
    public void widgetDefaultSelected(SelectionEvent event)
```

```
        {
        }
    });
```

The code you develop for the `widgetSelected()` method depends upon the application. In place of the call to `System.out.println()`, you could set a `boolean` instance variable that could be used to govern other program logical flow. Or you could define all tool items at the class level and call `getSelection()` whenever needed.

Using Tool Tips

Tool tip text provides a hint to the user about the function triggered by clicking a toolbar button. The tip appears in a pop-up text field at the mouse cursor location whenever the user pauses the mouse over a button. This is a feature that users expect to see in any toolbar.

How do I do that?

SWT makes it very easy to create tool tips. All you must do is assign the desired text to a `ToolItem` by calling the `setToolTipText()` method, and pass the method the `String` value you wish to appear as the tool tip. Adding this line to your `ToolbarShellExample` results in Figure 4-6 when the mouse cursor is moved over the Open button:

```
openItem.setToolTipText("Open File");
```

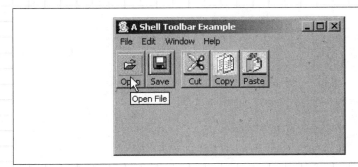

Figure 4-6. Toolbar button with tool-tip text

The SWT provides you with everything you need to create sophisticated toolbars, something your users will expect in almost every application you deliver. As you have seen in the last three chapters, the SWT makes it easy to build the windows that serve as the foundation of your applications.

CHAPTER 5

SWT Text Fields

In the next several chapters, you will expand your knowledge of the SWT by examining the four widgets that are most often a part of GUIs—text fields, buttons, lists, and combos. We begin that examination with a look at the SWT Text class, which is located in the `org.eclipse.swt.widgets` package.

Text fields are a standard part of any GUI—used either to present information to the user, or to enable the user to edit or create information. Text fields can appear as single-line edit fields, in which the user may enter or view a set amount of information (specified by the width of the field in characters), or multiline edit fields, in which the user can enter or view free-form text that wraps across lines. Text fields can also have a variety of borders, to assist in developing the look and feel that you desire for your user interface (i.e., 3D or flat boxes).

All of the necessary methods for working with text fields are encapsulated in a single class in SWT—the Text class. This is in contrast to other graphical toolkits, such as the AWT, that have separate classes for text fields of differing styles.

Adding Text Fields to a Shell

As with all of the SWT widgets, text fields must be added to a container object—an instance of Shell, Composite, or Group.

How do I do that?

Two coding steps are required to create a text field and add it to a window. First, create an instance of the Text class, passing the Text constructor a reference to the Shell and the desired style attribute(s).

Second, specify the location of the text field within the container and set its width and height. Example 5-1 demonstrates how to add a text field to a window.

Example 5-1. Adding a text field to a window

```
import org.eclipse.swt.SWT;
import org.eclipse.swt.widgets.*;

public class TextFieldExample {

    Display d;
    Shell s;
    TextFieldExample()    {
        d = new Display();
        s = new Shell(d);
        s.setSize(250,250);
        s.setImage(new Image(d, "c:\\icons\\JavaCup.ico"));
        final Text text1 = new Text(s, SWT.SINGLE);
        text1.setBounds(10,10,100,20);
        s.open();
        while(!s.isDisposed()){
            if(!d.readAndDispatch())
                d.sleep();
        }
        d.dispose();
    }
}
```

Creating an instance of TextFieldExample results in the display shown in Figure 5-1.

Figure 5-1. Results of running TextFieldExample

What just happened?

The code to add a text field to a shell is quite simple, consisting of only two lines:

```
Text text1 = new Text(s, SWT.SINGLE);
text1.setBounds(10,10,100,20);
```

In the preceding code, s represents the instance of Shell to which you are adding the text field. The SWT.SINGLE style is passed to the Text constructor, indicating creation of a single-line edit style of text field.

Although the text field is created and added to the shell using only the first line of code, it won't be visible without the second. Setting the bounds, the x and y position, and the width and height of the text field is a requirement for widget visibility.

Adding a Border to a Text Field

As you can see from Figure 5-1, a borderless text field is not visually appealing. However, the SWT makes it easy to change the appearance of the text field using additional style attributes. For most applications, you will enhance the text field's appearance by adding a border.

How do I do that?

By now, you should be familiar with how to specify styles for widgets—having used styles for shells, menus, and toolbars. The style that creates a border around a text field is SWT.BORDER, which is passed into the Text constructor in the usual manner:

```
final Text text1 = new Text(s, SWT.SINGLE | SWT.BORDER);
```

If you make this change to the TextFieldExample class, the text field will appear as shown in Figure 5-2, which is a definite improvement over the borderless text field in Figure 5-1.

Positioning the Text Field

When building a GUI, you need to have precise control over the positioning of every widget that makes up the interface. In SWT, there are two ways to specify the size and position of a widget within a container. The first approach is to use the setBounds() or setLocation() methods that are part of the super class for every widget.

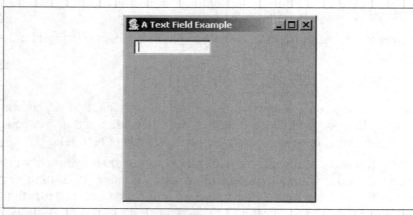

Figure 5-2. Text field with SWT.BORDER specified

How do I do that?

In the TextFieldExample class, the Text widget is positioned with this:

```
text1.setBounds(10,10,100,20);
```

Placing a text field in a particular location on the window is simply a matter of adjusting the first two parameters, which represent the x and y coordinates of the upper lefthand corner of the text field with respect to the upper lefthand corner of the shell's workspace area (the area below the title bar and menu).

The first setBounds( ) parameter moves the text field's position to the right as the parameter's value increases, while the second parameter moves the field's position closer to the bottom of the window as the value increases. Aligning widgets along their lefthand side is a matter of specifying the same value in the first parameter passed to setBounds( ). Example 5-2 demonstrates how to align two Text widgets along their lefthand sides, with the result shown in Figure 5-3.

Example 5-2. Aligning two text widgets

```
public class TextFieldExample {

    Display d;
    Shell s;
    TextFieldExample()    {
        d = new Display();
        s = new Shell(d);
        s.setSize(250,250);
        s.setImage(new Image(d, "c:\\icons\\JavaCup.ico"));
        s.setText("A Text Field Example");
        final Text text1 = new Text(s, SWT.SINGLE | SWT.BORDER);
```

A toolbar that is displayed on the shell takes up room beginning in the upper left-hand corner of the workspace area, so you must account for the height of the toolbar in calculating where to place a widget.

Example 5-2. Aligning two text widgets (continued)

```
    text1.setBounds(100,50,100,20);
    final Text text2 = new Text(s, SWT.SINGLE | SWT.BORDER);
    text2.setBounds(100,75,100,20);
    s.open();
    while(!s.isDisposed()){
        if(!d.readAndDispatch())
            d.sleep();
    }
    d.dispose();
    }
}
```

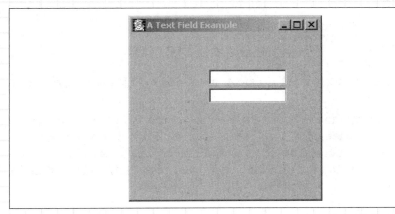

Figure 5-3. Two text fields with positioning

You can also use setLocation() to specify the x and y coordinates of the widget, without specifying its size. This code moves the location of the text1 object in Example 5-2 five pixels toward the bottom of the window:

```
    text1.setLocation(100, 55);
```

In Chapter 9, I demonstrate the second technique for achieving precise designs— the use of layouts.

Precise alignment of widgets that make up the user interface is crucial to achieve the desired effect.

Setting the Tab Order

A critical element of creating a user interface that will be acceptable to your users is getting the *tab order* of the component widgets correct. The tab order is the order in which each widget gains the input focus as the user presses the Tab key. Users expect the tab order to be logical—an order that mirrors the way they interact with the window. For example, consider a window that permits the input of name, address, city, state, and Zip Code information. In such an interface, the user expects to enter the name first, then the address, and so on. If the window opens with the focus in the address field and then shifts to the name field when the user presses the Tab key, the interface does not mirror the manner in which the user expects to enter the information.

In the absence of a specific order, as with the name and address information discussed earlier, the general rule is to have the input focus flow from top to bottom and from left to right.

How do I do that?

The tab order is set by the order in which you create the widgets:

```
final Text text1 = new Text(s, SWT.SINGLE | SWT.BORDER);
text1.setBounds(100,50,100,20);
final Text text2 = new Text(s, SWT.SINGLE | SWT.BORDER);
text2.setBounds(100,75,100,20);
```

In this case, text1 is created before text2 and thus is the first widget in the tab order.

An alternate method that can be used to set the tab order is to call the setTabList() method of the Composite class. Composite is a super class of Shell, so for the Text widgets placed directly on the Shell in the preceding code, adding the following code will cause text2 to be first in the tab order:

```
Control[] c = {text2, text1};
s.setTabList(c);
```

Setting the Text Size Limit

There is one more size attribute for text fields that must be mentioned—the number of characters that the text field can contain. There are two aspects of this size. The first is related to how many characters can appear on-screen within the confines of a text box. Users generally do not like single-line text boxes that do not display all the characters in that box. Although the number of characters that can be seen varies greatly with the font size selected (by default, the operating system settings control this), you should attempt to limit the number of characters to a value that can be reasonably expected to fit within the specified bounds of the text field.

The second, and more programmatically important, reason for setting a character limit on a text field is for data validation purposes. Suppose you are designing a GUI that enables the user to submit data for storage in a database. If your text field accepts values that are to be stored in a particular database column, you can decrease the possibility of a database error by limiting input to only the amount of data that is acceptable.

How do I do that?

Setting the character bounds of a Text widget is done by:

```
text1.setTextLimit(10);
```

If you add that line to TextFieldExample, you see the effect when you attempt to enter more than 10 characters: you won't be permitted to do that.

Proper design consists of determining the number of characters you need to allow in a particular field and then using setBounds( ) to size the field so that that number of characters can be visible, as well as using setTextLimit( ) to limit the number of characters that can be input. This is a complex process when you consider different screen resolutions and font sizes that may be in use on a particular platform. Still, it is a necessary step toward designing a professional-quality user interface.

Interacting with the Text in the Text Widget

If you are building an interface that displays text to the user from some other source—in other words, you're using text fields that are populated with text values when the window is opened or data is retrieved—you must directly interact with the contents of the text field.

How do I do that?

There are two possible interactions with the text in a field—reading the text out of the field and pushing text into the field. The SWT widgets use the getXXX( ) and setXXX( ) methods similar to the JavaBeans Specification.

A call to the setText( ) method of the Text class causes a text value to appear:

```
text1.setText("Some text goes here");
```

The converse operation is to read text out of a text field and store it in a variable for programmatic use. For that task, use the getText( ) method:

```
String contents = text1.getText( );
```

Populating Text Fields from a Database

If you are developing corporate IT applications, you will invariably find a need to populate a series of text fields based upon a database query. To do that, you must understand how to work with the contents of a JDBC ResultSet.

How do I do that?

The code to accomplish this task is straightforward. The following code will connect to the MS Access Northwind sample database, using the JDBC/ODBC Bridge driver:

```
Class.forName("sun.jdbc.odbc.JdbcOdbcDriver");
Connection conn =
DriverManager.getConnection("jdbc:odbc:NorthWind");
Statement stmt = conn.createStatement( );
ResultSet rs = stmt.executeQuery("SELECT * FROM Employees");
if(rs.next( )) {
  text1.setText(rs.getString("FirstName"));
  text2.setText(rs.getString("LastName"));
  }
```

The text fields text1 and text2 are populated with the String values in the FirstName and LastName columns of the result set's first row.

What about...

those times when the column data in the `ResultSet` is not a `String`? For those occasions, use one of the other result set methods, such as `getInt()` to retrieve the data and then convert it to a `String` value to pass to the `setText()` method, like so:

```
text2.setText(Integer.toString(rs.getInteger("EmployeID")
));
```

Appending Text to a Text Field's Contents

Sometimes, you may have a situation that requires you to append text to the end of contents that are already in the text field, or to insert contents into text at some location in the text field.

How do I do that?

To add text to the end of whatever text is already in the text field, you use the `append()` method:

```
text1.append(" This will be added to the end of what's already there");
```

You can also insert text ahead of whatever text is currently displayed:

```
text1.insert("This goes before ");
```

What about...

times when you want to insert text in the middle of text that already appears in the text field? `insert()` can also be used for that purpose when used in combination with the selection methods (discussed shortly). All you must do is select the area of text where you want the insertion to appear prior to calling `insert()`. The inserted text will replace the selected area. If you don't actually want to replace any text, just make the selected area a one-character space between two words.

Creating Multiline Text Fields

Often your interface design mandates that you create a text field that permits a user to enter more data than can be conveniently viewed in a single-line edit type of text field. For these types of applications, such as text editors or database applications that allow the entry of free-form text (perhaps for comment fields), you must use a multiline edit-style text field.

How do I do that?

Creating a multiline text field is easy—just specify the SWT.MULTI style in the Text constructor:

```
Text text1 = new Text(s, SWT.MULTI | SWT.BORDER);
```

Example 5-3 creates the window shown in Figure 5-4, where you see a multiline text field that fills the entire workspace area of the window.

Example 5-3. A multiline text field

```java
public class TextFieldExample {

    Display d;
    Shell s;
    TextFieldExample()    {
        d = new Display();
        s = new Shell(d);
        s.setSize(250,250);
        s.setImage(new Image(d, "c:\\icons\\JavaCup.ico"));
        s.setText("A Text Field Example");
        Text text1 = new Text(s, SWT.MULTI | SWT.BORDER);
        text1.setBounds(0,0,250,250);
        s.open();
        while(!s.isDisposed()){
            if(!d.readAndDispatch())
                d.sleep();
        }
        d.dispose();
    }
}
```

Figure 5-4. A multiline example

Wrapping Text

If you run Example 5-3, you see that entering text in the field does not yield exactly the anticipated results. If you enter more text than can be displayed in the field, the text does not wrap to the next line; it just disappears off somewhere to the right. This continues until you press Enter to drop to the next line.

How do I do that?

As you might expect, creating a field that wraps is just a matter of specifying another style attribute, SWT.WRAP:

```
final Text text1 = new Text(s, SWT.MULTI | SWT.WRAP | SWT.BORDER);
```

Changing Example 5-3 to construct a wrapping text field will result in Figure 5-5.

Users generally expect text to wrap to the next line when one line is filled.

Figure 5-5. Wrapping text

What about...

times when you need to change the style of a text field from wrapping to nonwrapping, or even from single-line to multiline. This isn't possible using the SWT, since those styles are specified at the time the widget is created. A workaround is to create two separate widgets, one with each style, then hide or show them as needed:

```
final Text text1 = new Text(s, SWT.MULTI | SWT.WRAP |SWT.BORDER);
text1.setBounds(100,50,100,100);
text1.setVisible(true);
final Text text2 = new Text(s, SWT.MULTI | SWT.BORDER);
text2.setBounds(100,50,100,100);
```

Most text editors enable the user to specify wrap or nonwrap.

```
text2.setVisible(false);
```

When the nonwrapping version is needed, you do this:

```
text1.setVisible(false);
text2.setVisible(true);
```

Admittedly, this is a hack, but given the style system used by the SWT, it's the best hack available.

Fortunately, times when styles of widgets must be changed are rare, in my experience.

Adding Scrollbars

If you completely fill a text field, the text begins to disappear from the top. It's still there, but it's just not visible—you can access it by using the up arrow on the keyboard to move back toward the top. Still, users expect not to have to resort to the arrow keys to navigate a text field. To cure this problem, you need to add a scrollbar to your text field.

How do I do that?

There are two types of scrollbars—horizontal and vertical. Which type you use depends upon which way you want to allow scrolling. Since a horizontal scrollbar isn't necessary with the WRAP style used in Example 5-3, a vertical scrollbar is what's required.

Specifying a scrollbar is also a matter of passing the correct style attribute. There are two to choose from—SWT.H_SCROLL and SWT.V_SCROLL. To add a vertical scrollbar, just add the SWT.V_SCROLL attribute to the styles passed to the constructor:

```
final Text text1 = new Text(s, SWT.MULTI | SWT.WRAP | SWT.BORDER | SWT.V_
SCROLL);
```

Making this change to the text field created in Example 5-3 yields Figure 5-6 when the field is filled with text.

Reacting to Text Events

Sometimes the underlying business logic of your application requires that you respond to events that occur when the user interacts with a text field. One example is when you must perform validation on the field's contents before you enable the user to move away from the field to another widget on the window. Another example is the popular interface feature that causes text in a field to become selected whenever the field gains focus.

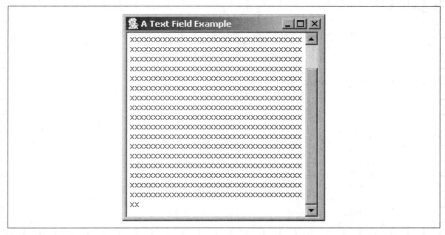

Figure 5-6. Multiline wrapping field with vertical scrollbar

As with the MenuItem and ToolItem classes, for a text field to respond to an event a Listener must be added to the Text object. Text objects can respond to one of three text-specific listener types:

- ModifyListener, which fires whenever the text in the field is altered
- SelectionListener, which fires whenever the text in the field is selected
- VerifyListener, which fires when the text in the field is about to be modified, but before the modification becomes visible to the user

Text fields can also respond to a number of more generic events that are defined as being applicable to all widgets.

One of the more commonly used events for text fields is the *focus* event. Focus events occur whenever the text field gains or loses the input focus. This is most commonly caused by the user tabbing or clicking between fields. The focus event is a good place to perform field-level validation or to select text on entry.

The add() methods for these events are defined in the Control class, which is the ancestor to almost all widgets.

How do I do that?

Select on entry is a feature of text fields that selects the contents of the field whenever the field gains the input focus. Example 5-4 demonstrates how to create this effect using the focus event.

Example 5-4. Performing select on entry

```
import org.eclipse.swt.SWT;
import org.eclipse.swt.events.FocusEvent;
```

Example 5-4. Performing select on entry (continued)

```java
import org.eclipse.swt.events.FocusListener;
import org.eclipse.swt.graphics.Image;
import org.eclipse.swt.widgets.*;

public class TextFieldExample {

    Display d;
    Shell s;
    TextFieldExample()    {
        d = new Display();
        s = new Shell(d);
        s.setSize(250,250);
        s.setImage(new Image(d, "c:\\icons\\JavaCup.ico"));
        s.setText("A Text Field Example");
        Text text1 = new Text(s, SWT.WRAP |SWT.BORDER);
        text1.setBounds(100,50,100,20);
        text1.setTextLimit(5);
        text1.setText("12345");
        Text text2 = new Text(s, SWT.SINGLE | SWT.BORDER);
        text2.setBounds(100,75,100,20);
        text2.setTextLimit(30);

        // add a focus listener
        FocusListener focusListener = new FocusListener() {
            public void focusGained(FocusEvent e) {
                Text t = (Text)e.widget;
                t.selectAll();
            }
            public void focusLost(FocusEvent e) {
                Text t = (Text)e.widget;
                if(t.getSelectionCount() > 0){
                    t.clearSelection();
                }
            }
        };
        text1.addFocusListener(focusListener);
        text2.addFocusListener(focusListener);
        s.open();
        while(!s.isDisposed()){
            if(!d.readAndDispatch())
                d.sleep();
        }
        d.dispose();
    }
}
```

Example 5-4 creates the window shown in Figure 5-7. Notice that when the window first appears and the first text field obtains focus, the text is preselected. When the field loses focus due to clicking away to the second field, the text becomes deselected. You can toggle back and forth between the fields, entering text in both to see the effect.

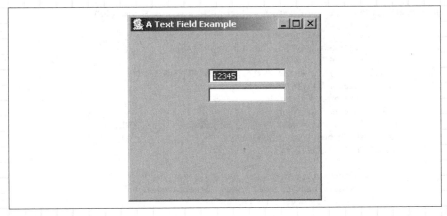

Figure 5-7. Using a focus listener

Performing Field Validation

The focus event can also be used to perform field-level validation. You must perform two tasks when you undertake this type of validation. First, you must compare the text in the field at the time the event occurs with an expected value, such as the length of the entered text compared to a fixed length. Second, you must prevent the focus from leaving the text field in the event that the text entered is not valid.

How do I do that?

To perform field-level validation and prevent the user from switching away from a text field until the contents pass the validation test, you must again use a FocusListener. Example 5-5 demonstrates how to perform validation on text2 by comparing the contents entered by the user with a known value.

Example 5-5. Performing field-level validation in a FocusListener

```
import org.eclipse.swt.SWT;
import org.eclipse.swt.events.FocusEvent;
import org.eclipse.swt.events.FocusListener;
import org.eclipse.swt.graphics.Image;
import org.eclipse.swt.widgets.*;

public class TextFieldExample {
    Display d;
    Shell s;
    TextFieldExample()    {
        d = new Display();
        s = new Shell(d);
```

Example 5-5. Performing field-level validation in a FocusListener (continued)

```
            s.setSize(250,250);
            s.setImage(new Image(d, "c:\\icons\\JavaCup.ico"));
            s.setText("A Text Field Example");
            final Text text1 = new Text(s, SWT.WRAP |SWT.BORDER);
            text1.setBounds(100,50,100,20);
            text1.setTextLimit(5);
            text1.setEchoChar('*');
            final Text text2 = new Text(s, SWT.SINGLE | SWT.BORDER);
            text2.setBounds(100,75,100,20);
            text2.setTextLimit(30);

            // add a focus listener
            FocusListener focusListener = new FocusListener() {
                public void focusGained(FocusEvent e) {
                }
                public void focusLost(FocusEvent e) {
                    Text t = (Text)e.widget;
                    if(t==text2)
                    {
                        if(t.getText().length() < 3)
                        {
                            t.setFocus();
                        }
                    }
                }
            };
            text1.addFocusListener(focusListener);
            text2.addFocusListener(focusListener);
            s.open();
            while(!s.isDisposed()){
                if(!d.readAndDispatch())
                    d.sleep();
            }
            d.dispose();
        }
    }
```

What just happened?

The println( ) call should be replaced with a MessageBox in a production system. See Chapter 17.

The critical code is in the focusLost( ) method of the FocusListener:

```
public void focusLost(FocusEvent e) {
    Text t = (Text)e.widget;
    if(t==text2)
    {
        if(t.getText().length() < 3)
        {
            System.out.println("Data is less than 3 characters");
            t.setFocus();
        }
    }
}
```

Since the validation rule to apply depends upon which text field has the input focus, the first step is to determine which widget is causing the focus event to occur. The SWT makes this task easy. Every Listener type contains an associated *event object*. Encapsulated in the event object is information regarding the status of the application at the time the event occurred. When using FocusListener, the focusLost() method is passed a FocusEvent object. Inside that object is a field—a widget—that contains a reference to the widget that is causing this event to fire. You can compare that reference to your text field using the == operator:

*The actual valida-
tion code you
write in the
focusLost()
method depends
on the business
rules for your
application.*

```
Text t = (Text)e.widget;
if(t==text2)
```

If focus is leaving text2, the equality check in the if statement resolves to true. Code in the if block then checks the length of the String returned from a call to getText() on text2. If that length is less than three characters, a call is made to setFocus() to force focus to remain in text2.

Creating Display-Only Text Fields

At times you may need to display text to the user without permitting the user to modify or otherwise interact with the text—in effect, creating a display-only text field.

How do I do that?

To create a read-only text field, set the text field's enabled attribute to false. This creates a text field that is grayed out as in Figure 5-8.

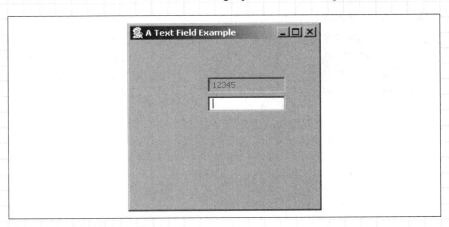

Figure 5-8. Disabled text field

The user may see the text, but may not interact with it in any way. Often, these types of field are referred to as being *disabled*:

```
text1.setEnabled(false);
```

Text fields that aren't editable are grayed out.

What about...

times when you want to prevent the user from editing the text field, but still want to allow the user to select text for copying and pasting to another field or another application? Disabling a text field is not appropriate if you must enable the user to interact with the text. For this task, you use the setEditable( ) method:

```
text1.setEditable(false);
```

This results in a text field that behaves normally in all respects except that the user is not permitted to alter the text.

Creating Password Fields

Sometimes you may want to create fields that allow text to be entered, but that hide that text from onlookers. A password entry field is a typical example. Because it would not be secure to display the text that is entered for all to see, a specific character is displayed to mask that text as it is being entered.

How do I do that?

Notice that you pass a single-quoted character to this method, not a double-quoted string.

To create a password-type field, use the setEchoChar( ) method:

```
text1.setEchoChar('*');
```

This code results in Figure 5-9.

As you can see, SWT provides a very flexible widget for display and entry of text, which is an essential element of almost every GUI. Since you're using SWT, most of the implementation details are hidden from you in the Java classes and native libraries that lie under the hood.

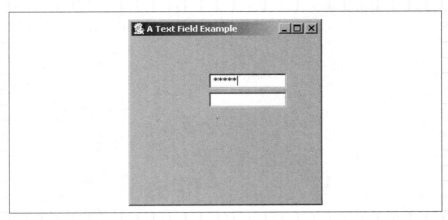

Figure 5-9. A password field using setEchoChar( )

CHAPTER 6

SWT Buttons

This chapter focuses on the SWT Button class. Button is part of the org.eclipse.swt.widgets package. Buttons are a standard part of any GUI and are used to perform a wide variety of tasks.

The most common button style is the push button, which enables the user to click the button to initiate some action. The Yes, No, and Cancel buttons that you often find on message boxes or other dialogs are examples of this button type, which you will sometimes see referred to as a command button.

Another button style is the radio button. A radio button is part of a group of buttons configured so that only one button within the group may be selected at any given time.

Yet a third frequently used button style is a checkbox. A checkbox is a button, or group of buttons, that permits the user to make multiple selections from within the group.

The final button style is the toggle button, which acts very similar to the check ToolItem type used in Chapter 4. In the examples that follow, you will work with each of these button types.

Creating Push-Style Buttons

The most common use of buttons in a GUI is to enable the user to click in order to initiate some action or process. For this purpose, you use the standard SWT.PUSH–style button, often referred to as a command button.

How do I do that?

Example 6-1 creates a window with a standard SWT.PUSH button.

Example 6-1. A standard push button

```
import org.eclipse.swt.SWT;
import org.eclipse.swt.graphics.Image;
import org.eclipse.swt.widgets.*;
public class ButtonExample {

    Display d;
    Shell s;
    ButtonExample()     {
        d = new Display();
        s = new Shell(d);
        s.setSize(150,150);
        s.setImage(new Image(d, "c:\\icons\\JavaCup.ico"));
        s.setText("A Button Example");
        final Button b1 = new Button(s, SWT.PUSH);
        b1.setBounds(50,50,75,40);
        b1.setText("Push Me");
        s.open();
        while(!s.isDisposed()){
            if(!d.readAndDispatch())
                d.sleep();
        }
        d.dispose();
    }
}
```

The default button uses the SWT.BORDER style. You can obtain a different look by specifying SWT.FLAT to remove the border

Creating an instance of ButtonExample results in Figure 6-1.

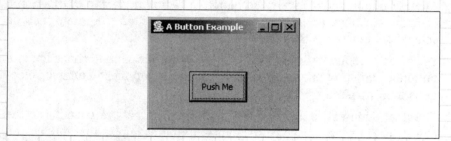

Figure 6-1. A simple push button

What just happened?

The relevant code is in the following three lines:

```
final Button b1 = new Button(s, SWT.PUSH);
b1.setBounds(100,75,75,40);
b1.setText("Push Me");
```

As you see, this code is very similar to the code used to create text fields—you just create an instance of the Button class, passing the constructor the SWT.PUSH style; then you set the button's position and location using setBounds( ), and use setText( ) to specify the text you wish to appear as the button's label. You will see this pattern of code repeated for almost every widget in the SWT.

Responding to Button Clicks

A button is useless unless you provide some mechanism that responds to the user having clicked the button. To do that, you must add a SelectionListener to the button and develop code in the widgetSelected( ) event to accomplish the desired task.

How do I do that?

To respond to the button being clicked by the user, you need to add a SelectionListener to the code shown in Example 6-1:

```
import org.eclipse.swt.events.*;

//then, in the constructor of ButtonExample
b1.addSelectionListener(new SelectionAdapter( ) {
    public void widgetSelected(SelectionEvent e) {
        System.out.println("Push Me Was Pushed");
    }
});
```

This code performs the task of printing to the Console when the button is clicked. This is essentially all you need to know about SWT.PUSH-style buttons and how to use them to permit the user to initiate some action. Whatever action you wish your button to perform, the steps required to develop the code will be the same.

Creating Check Buttons

In the SWT, unlike in SWING and AWT, only a single Button class is used to create buttons of different styles. One such style is the checkbox. Check buttons don't have the appearance of buttons as you usually think of them, and it may take some getting used to the idea of using a single class to represent two vastly different interface elements, especially if you are moving to SWT from AWT or Swing, but once you are accustomed to the concept, it is really convenient.

How do I do that?

The code to create Figure 6-2 is similar to that used to create Figure 6-1, except that the code that creates the buttons has been changed to this:

```
final Button b1 = new Button(s, SWT.CHECK);
b1.setBounds(50,50,75,20);
b1.setText("Check Me");
final Button b2 = new Button(s, SWT.CHECK);
b2.setBounds(50,75,100,20);
b2.setText("No, Check Me");
```

Two buttons with the SWT.CHECK style are shown in Figure 6-2.

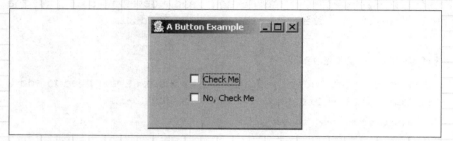

Figure 6-2. Two checkbox-style buttons

Instead of using SWT.PUSH as the button style, you use SWT.CHECK. If you experiment with these SWT.CHECK-style buttons, you see the expected behavior—either button can be checked or unchecked, independently of the other.

TIP

It is possible that this implementation may change in future releases of SWT. The SWT API documentation notes that the Button class is not intended to be subclassed, except within the SWT implementation.

Although this would seem to preclude your creating a subclass of Button for each type and setting the style attribute in the subclasses constructor, it doesn't preclude the SWT developers from doing that, which is exactly the way Swing is implemented.

Determining CHECK Button Status

Proper interface design sometimes requires you to programmatically interact with the state of a button. An example is when you need to set a button's state to checked, depending upon a value retrieved from a database or upon the occurrence of some other condition in the application

How do I do that?

The properties of Button are accessible using get and set methods in the JavaBeans paradigm. To programmatically cause a button to be checked, use this code:

```
b1.setSelection(true);
```

Use getSelection( ) to determine the current state of a variable:

```
boolean selected = b1.getSelection( );
```

Adding Listeners to CHECK Buttons

On a few occasions it will be necessary to add a Listener to an SWT.CHECK-style button. One instance when this is required is when you want to populate a List or Combo with items depend on which button is checked.

How do I do that?

The following code adds a SelectionListener to the SWT.CHECK buttons created in the section "Creating Check Buttons" and, in the widgetSelected( ) method, determines the state of the button at the time the button is clicked:

```
b1.addSelectionListener(new SelectionAdapter( ) {
    public void widgetSelected(SelectionEvent e) {
        System.out.println(b1.getSelection( ));
    }
});
b2.addSelectionListener(new SelectionAdapter( ) {
    public void widgetSelected(SelectionEvent e) {
        System.out.println(b2.getSelection( ));
    }
});
```

Pass false to setSelection( ) to uncheck the button.

In the widgetSelected( ) method of these Listeners, determine the selection state of the button, then take any action required based on that state. This code will be executed each time the button's state changes.

Using Radio-Style Buttons

Radio buttons are similar to Check buttons, except that only one button of a group of buttons may be selected at any given time. You use Radio buttons to enable the user to select one, and only one, of a group of options.

How do I do that?

You create Radio buttons simply by specifying the SWT.RADIO style:

```
final Button b1 = new Button(s, SWT.RADIO);
b1.setBounds(100,50,75,20);
b1.setText("Check Me");
final Button b2 = new Button(s, SWT.RADIO);
b2.setBounds(100,75,100,20);
b2.setText("No, Check Me");
```

Changing the ButtonExample code to include the preceding code will display Figure 6-3.

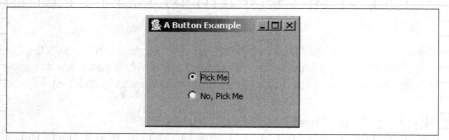

Figure 6-3. Radio buttons

What just happened?

In addition to the Radio button look and feel, you see that it is no longer possible to check both buttons at the same time. Checking one will cause the other to automatically become unchecked. For this reason, radio buttons must belong to a group. A *group* is all buttons with the RADIO style that are placed within the same container. In ButtonExample the container is a Shell, which means that all radio buttons placed on the shell belong to the same group and will share mutually exclusive selectability.

You may foresee a problem. What if you need to create two different groups to enable the user to specify one option from two sets of options? In this case, the solution is to place the buttons on two separate containers—Composites or Groups work nicely for this. See Chapter 10 for details.

Causing No Radio Button to beSelected

In a group of Radio buttons, one button must be selected at all times. In Figure 6-3, when the window opens, Check Me is checked by default.

Yet, proper functioning of your user interface may require that a window open with no button currently selected.

How do I do that?

To cause a group of buttons to have no default option, simply create a hidden button and set its selection property to true:

```
final Button fake = new Button(s, SWT.RADIO);
fake.setSelection(true);
```

Do not make the fake button visible, to preserve the group you wish the user to see on-screen.

WARNING

Interestingly, on Windows XP, explicitly making the fake button invisible causes it not to count as part of the group.

Creating Toggle Buttons

SWT.TOGGLE-style buttons look like push buttons, but behave like checkbox buttons in that they stay pushed when clicked. This enables you to create buttons that provide the user with the same look as SWT.PUSH buttons, but provide them with a visual indication that the button has been clicked.

How do I do that?

Creating an SWT.TOGGLE button is, once again, just a matter of specifying the correct style:

```
final Button toggle = new Button(s, SWT.TOGGLE);
```

A button with the SWT.TOGGLE style appears as shown in Figure 6-4 until the button is clicked, when it appears as shown in Figure 6-5. Clicking the button again will return it to the Figure 6-4 state.

Determining the State of a Toggle Button

If you're using SWT.TOGGLE buttons at all, you're interested in determining their states at different points in the application.

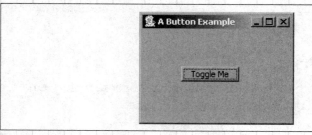

Figure 6-4. Untoggled button

Figure 6-5. A toggled button

How do I do that?

You determine the toggled/untoggled state of the button using:

```
boolean state = b1.getSelection( );
```

This is no different than determining the state of an SWT.CHECK- or an SWT.RADIO-style button.

Creating Arrow Buttons

The final style attribute that you can apply to the Button class is SWT. ARROW. SWT.ARROW buttons, as the name implies, display an arrow graphic indicating the direction in which something that will occur when the button is pressed. SWT.ARROW style buttons also need to specify an additional style that determines in which direction the arrow graphic points. Possibilities are SWT.UP, SWT.DOWN, SWT.LEFT, and SWT.RIGHT.

A common use for arrow buttons is to enable the user to increment a value in an associated text box.

How do I do that?

Example 6-2 demonstrates how to use the SWT.ARROW button style in association with a Text field to permit the user to increment a value.

Example 6-2. Using SWT arrow buttons

```
import org.eclipse.swt.SWT;
import org.eclipse.swt.events.SelectionAdapter;
import org.eclipse.swt.events.SelectionEvent;
import org.eclipse.swt.graphics.Image;
import org.eclipse.swt.widgets.*;
public class ArrowButtonExample {
    Display d;
    Shell s;
    ArrowButtonExample( )     {
        d = new Display( );
        s = new Shell(d);
        s.setSize(250,250);
        s.setImage(new Image(d, "c:\\icons\\JavaCup.ico"));
        s.setText("A Button Example");
        final Button b1 = new Button(s, SWT.ARROW | SWT.UP);
        b1.setBounds(100,55,20,15);
        final Button b2 = new Button(s, SWT.ARROW | SWT.DOWN);
        b2.setBounds(100,70,20,15);
        final Text t1 = new Text(s, SWT.BORDER | SWT.SINGLE | SWT.CENTER);
        t1.setBounds(80, 55, 20, 30);
        t1.setText("1");
        t1.selectAll( );
        b1.addSelectionListener(new SelectionAdapter( ) {
            public void widgetSelected(SelectionEvent e) {
                int n = new Integer(t1.getText()).intValue( );
                n++;
                t1.setText(new Integer(n).toString( ));
                t1.selectAll( );
            }
        });
        b2.addSelectionListener(new SelectionAdapter( ) {
            public void widgetSelected(SelectionEvent e) {
                int n = new Integer(t1.getText()).intValue( );
                n--;
                t1.setText(new Integer(n).toString( ));
                t1.selectAll( );
            }
        });
        s.open( );
        while(!s.isDisposed( )){
            if(!d.readAndDispatch( ))
                d.sleep( );
        }
        d.dispose( );
    }
}
```

ArrowButtonExample creates Figure 6-6. Clicking the up arrow increases the number in the text field, while clicking the down arrow decreases it.

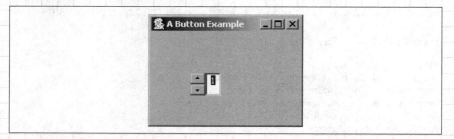

Figure 6-6. Using Arrow buttons

What just happened?

The crucial code is in the widgetSelected() method of the SelectionListener attached to each button:

```
b1.addSelectionListener(new SelectionAdapter() {
        public void widgetSelected(SelectionEvent e) {
            int n = new Integer(t1.getText()).intValue();
            n++;
            t1.setText(new Integer(n).toString());
            t1.selectAll();
        }
});
b2.addSelectionListener(new SelectionAdapter() {
        public void widgetSelected(SelectionEvent e) {
            int n = new Integer(t1.getText()).intValue();
            n--;
            t1.setText(new Integer(n).toString());
            t1.selectAll();
        }
});
```

When the up arrow button is selected, the code in the widgetSelected() method of the SelectionListener attached to Button b1 executes. In that code, the current contents of Text t1 is obtained using getText() and converted to an int value for mathematical operations. The int value is then incremented by one, and the result is converted to a String that is then displayed in Text t1 using setText().

Using Images with Buttons

Buttons can use more than text to explain to the user the purpose of the button—images can also be used. Those of you familiar with Borland's

C++ development environment may recall the popularity of the OK button that displayed a green checkmark image. You can use images associated with buttons to achieve a similar effect in your SWT applications.

How do I do that?

You have already used images in association with ToolItem buttons in Chapter 4. The techniques are the same when using images with the Button class:

```
final Button b1 = new Button(s, SWT.PUSH);
b1.setBounds(100,55,75,50);
b1.setImage(new Image(d, "c:\\icons\\check.jpg"));
```

This code creates the button shown in Figure 6-7.

Figure 6-7. Push button with image

You can also use images with SWT.CHECK and SWT.RADIO button styles to good effect in the appropriate application. Regardless of button style, the code to create an image button is the same.

Setting Tool-Tip Text

As with ToolItem buttons, it is possible to assign tool-tip text to an instance of the Button class.

How do I do that?

The code required to create a tool tip for a button is identical to that used to create tool-tip text for a ToolItem:

```
b1.setToolTipText("Help");
```

There does not appear, at this time, to be a way to use both text labels and images on the same button—something you can, however, accomplish with ToolItems.

Enabling and Disabling Buttons

It is often useful to "disable" a button when it is not appropriate for the user to initiate the action to be taken upon a button click, or when the option represented by a check or radio button is not available. In fact, users expect this behavior. It is disconcerting for the user to click an enabled button, only to have no action take place. To prevent discomforting your users, you must enable and disable buttons depending upon program conditions.

How do I do that?

A button is disabled by:

```
b1.setEnabled(false);
```

Conversely, a button is enabled by:

```
b1.setEnabled(false);
```

Figure 6-8 shows the effect of disabling an SWT.PUSH-style button:

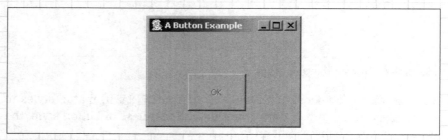

Figure 6-8. Disabled push button

The techniques discussed in this chapter are useful when creating and working with Button widgets, which form a central part of many user interfaces.

CHAPTER 7

SWT Lists

List widgets are used to present information to the user and allow selection of an item or items for further action (when processing is initiated by a command button, for example). List is similar in concept to the Combo, or drop-down, list, which is the subject of Chapter 8. The choice between using a List or a Combo is simple: use a List when it is either important for the user to have some or all of the items to choose from visible at all times, or when screen real estate is not an important design consideration.

A single SWT class is used to construct all lists—the List class—located in the org.eclipse.swt.widgets package.

Creating a List

A typical list is shown in Figure 7-1.

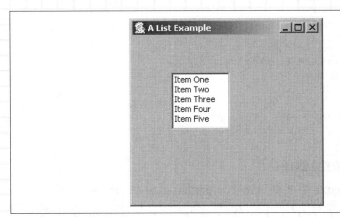

Figure 7-1. A simple list

As with all widgets, the first step in using a list is to create the List object—an instance of the List class—then position the list within the container as desired. Once a List object has been created, it can be populated with items.

How do I do that?

To create a list you must create an instance of the List class, passing the constructor a reference to a shell or other container, and specifying the style of list you wish to create. The list in Figure 7-1 is created using the code in Example 7-1.

Example 7-1. Creating a list

```
import org.eclipse.swt.SWT;
import org.eclipse.swt.graphics.Image;
import org.eclipse.swt.widgets.*;

public class ListExample {

    Display d;
    Shell s;
    ListExample( )    {
        d = new Display( );
        s = new Shell(d);
        s.setSize(250,250);
        s.setImage(new Image(d, "c:\\icons\\JavaCup.ico"));
        s.setText("A List Example");
        final List l = new List(s, SWT.SINGLE | SWT.BORDER);
        l.setBounds(50, 50, 75, 75);
        l.add("Item One");
        l.add("Item Two");
        l.add("Item Three");
        l.add("Item Four");
        l.add("Item Five");
        s.open( );
        while(!s.isDisposed( )){
            if(!d.readAndDispatch( ))
                d.sleep( );
        }
        d.dispose( );
    }
}
```

What just happened?

The code in Example 7-1 should be familiar due to its similarity to the code required to create the examples from earlier chapters. As with all widgets, you first create an instance of List, passing a reference to the container and the desired style attributes. The following creates a single selection list with a border:

```
final List l = new List(s, SWT.SINGLE | SWT.BORDER);
```

Two styles apply specifically to lists—SWT.SINGLE and SWT.MULTI. These styles control whether the user can select one item or more than one item from the list. No additional coding is needed to cause highlighting of the selected items, a function handled by the native code. The list displayed in Figure 7-1 uses SWT.BORDER to create the 3D look. A "flat" look would be achieved by omitting that style attribute.

Positioning of the list is accomplished, as with Text and Button widgets, using the setBounds() method:

```
l.setBounds(50, 50, 75, 75);
```

It is important to set the bounds of the list correctly. Proper sizing depends partly on the contents of the list. The list should be sized so that its width allows each item in the list to be completely visible but the height of the list is more flexible, since scrollbars enable you to create workable lists in which not all items are visible.

Users don't like horizontal scrollbars on lists, so setting the width correct is very important.

After the List object is created, you must add the items you wish to appear in the list. These items can either be hardcoded into the application (for static lists), or retrieved from a database (for dynamic lists). Either way, the process of actually adding an item to the list is the same.

To add an item to the list, you call the List class's add() method. The following code adds five items to a List object represented by the variable l:

```
l.add("Item One");
l.add("Item Two");
l.add("Item Three");
l.add("Item Four");
l.add("Item Five");
```

Adding Items to a List

You can use the setItems() method to add items to a list with only a single method call. This keeps code clutter to a minimum and makes for cleaner implementation.

How do I do that?

To populate the list with only a single method call, you must first create an array of String objects that hold the items to be added:

```
String items[] = {"Item One", "Item Two", "Item Three",
    "Item Four", "Item Five"};
```

You then call the setItems( ) method, passing it the String array:

```
l.setItems(items);
```

Changing ListExample to use this approach will result in a window identical to Figure 7-1, as shown in Example 7-2.

Example 7-2. Using setItems( ) to populate a list

```
import org.eclipse.swt.SWT;
import org.eclipse.swt.graphics.Image;
import org.eclipse.swt.widgets.*;

public class ListExample {
    Display d;
    Shell s;
    ListExample()    {
        d = new Display();
        s = new Shell(d);
        s.setSize(250,250);
        s.setImage(new Image(d, "c:\\icons\\JavaCup.ico"));
        s.setText("A List Example");
        String items[] = {"Item One", "Item Two", "Item Three", "Item Four",
            "Item Five"};
        final List l = new List(s, SWT.SINGLE | SWT.BORDER);
        l.setBounds(50, 50, 75, 75);
        l.setItems(items);
        s.open();
        while(!s.isDisposed()){
            if(!d.readAndDispatch())
                d.sleep();
        }
        d.dispose();
    }
}
```

If you have large lists, this method will result in code that is more readable than will using an add( ) call for each item.

Inserting Items in the Middle of a List

Sometimes it is necessary to add items to a list that has already been populated. At such times, you often need to cause new items to appear in the middle of the list, instead of adding them to the end.

How do I do that?

There are two versions of the add( ) method. As you saw in Example 7-1, the first version appends items to the list in the order in which the method is called. Each successive add causes the item to appear at the bottom of the list.

It is possible to insert an item at any position in the list using the second form of add( ), which accepts a second parameter to specify the index location after which the item should appear. Consider the following code:

```
l.add("Item One");
l.add("Item Two");
l.add("Item Three");
l.add("Item Four");
l.add("Item Five");
l.add("Three and a Half", 3);
```

Changing ListExample to use this code will result in Figure 7-2.

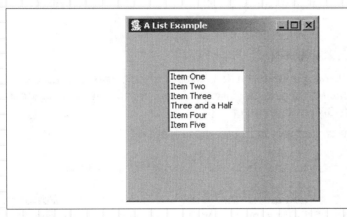

Figure 7-2. Results of inserting an item in the middle of a list

---

T I P

Although indexing of the list begins with zero, which is the Java convention, if you consider the second parameter of the add( ) method to be the index number of the item after which you want to insert the item, you will not need to mentally perform the calculation of counting by zero. Otherwise, you must think of the parameter as the index of the item before which you want to insert the item, or as the index that will be taken by the inserted item.

Populating a List from a Database

In the previous examples, the list was populated from items that were known at development time. It is more often the case in business IT development that you must populate the list based on the contents of a database or some other source outside your program code. The goal is to prevent the need to rewrite, recompile, and redeploy in the event that there is a change to the items that populate the list.

How do I do that?

This code populates a list based on the contents of a database it connects to via JDBC:

```
Class.forName("sun.jdbc.odbc.JdbcOdbcDriver");
Connection conn =
DriverManager.getConnection("jdbc:odbc:NorthWind");
Statement stmt = conn.createStatement();
ResultSet rs = stmt.executeQuery("SELECT * FROM Employees");
while(rs.next()) {
    l.add(rs.getString("FirstName") + " " + rs.getString("LastName"));
}
```

What just happened?

The preceding code populates a list with the first and last names of employees in the MS Access Northwind database, to which it connects using the JDBC/ODBC bridge driver.

The list-relevant code appears in the while loop:

```
while(rs.next()) {
    l.add(rs.getString("FirstName") + " " + rs.getString("LastName"));
}
```

The loop iterates for as long as the ResultSet contains rows. For each row, the contents of the first-name and last-name columns are concatenated, with the result being passed to the add() method for appending to the list.

Removing Items from a List

Just as you must add items to the list, it is often necessary to remove items from the list while the application is running. This is most often done to remove a selection that is no longer valid given program conditions.

How do I do that?

To remove an item from the list, you use the appropriate version of the remove() method, or you use removeAll() to clear the contents of the list.

To remove a single item, use this:

```
l.remove(3);
```

This removes the item that resides at index 3, or the fourth item in the list.

You can also use a version of remove( ) to eliminate more than one item from a list. One way to code for that task is to specify a range of items to remove. Figure 7-3 results from adding the following line to the code that created Figure 7-2:

```
l.remove(1,3);
```

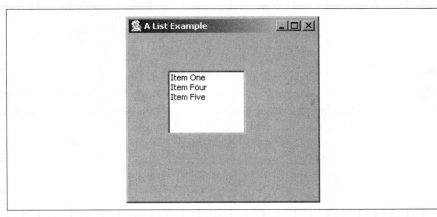

Figure 7-3. Results of removing a range of items

You can also use a version of remove( ) that accepts an array of integers that instruct the method which items to remove:

```
int n[] = {1,3,5};
l.remove(n);
```

This yields Figure 7-4 when added to ListExample, shown in Example 7-2, after the code in which the list is initially populated.

Figure 7-4. Removing items using an int array

Finally, you can remove a single item by referencing it by its String value:

```
l.remove("Item One");
```

This version of remove( ) starts at the beginning of the list, searches the list item by item, then removes the first item that exactly matches the String value passed.

Finally, removeAll( ) operates exactly as the name implies and merits no discussion. Use it to clear the list prior to repopulating with fresh data.

What about...

altered index positions? You must take care when removing items from the list, as the index positions upon which other code may rely can be altered. Consider what happens with the following code:

```
l.add("Item One");
l.add("Item Two");
l.add("Item Three");
l.add("Item Four");
l.add("Item Five");
l.add("Three and a Half", 3);
int i = l.indexOf("Item One");
int x = l.indexOf("Item Two");
int y = l.indexOf("Item Three");
l.select(y);
l.select(x);
l.remove(i);
```

The preceding code results in Figure 7-5, in which Item Two and Item Three are selected and Item One is removed.

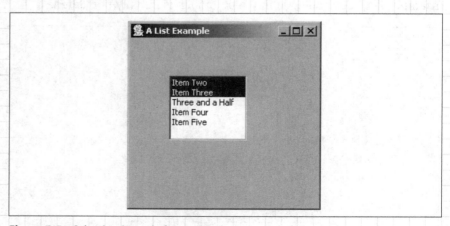

Figure 7-5. Selecting items before removal

Now, examine what happens when you change the order of operations just a tiny bit:

```
l.add("Item One");
l.add("Item Two");
l.add("Item Three");
l.add("Item Four");
l.add("Item Five");
l.add("Three and a Half", 3);
int i = l.indexOf("Item One");
int x = l.indexOf("Item Two");
int y = l.indexOf("Item Three");
l.remove(i);
l.select(y);
l.select(x);
```

Execution of this code results in Figure 7-6 being displayed.

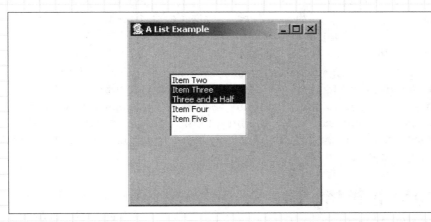

Figure 7-6. Selecting items after removal

Notice that different items are now selected. This is because removing items causes the index numbers of other items in the list to change. Given the fact that code often resides in different Listeners, which can execute in any order, care must be taken when working with items by index value, lest you obtain unfortunate results.

Determining the Selected Items

As you can see, adding a list to a window and populating it with items is a fairly simple exercise, requiring mastery of only a few simple methods. Most of the methods of the List class deal with interacting with the list and its items in some meaningful fashion. The interaction that we will

This is what lists are all about, after all is said and done.

almost always need to perform is to obtain the item or items that the user has selected from the list.

How do I do that?

Consider the following code:

```
l.addSelectionListener(new SelectionListener() {
    public void widgetSelected(SelectionEvent e) {
        String selected[] = l.getSelection();
        System.out.println(selected[0]);
    }
    public void widgetDefaultSelected(SelectionEvent e) {
    }
});
```

Here a SelectionListener is created and added to the list. In the widgetSelected() method, which is called each time the user clicks an item in the list, you call getSelection() to print out the item selected to the Console.

Recall that a list may enable the user to select more than one item, if it is an SWT.MULTI-style List. getSelection() returns an array of strings that contain every item that is currently selected. In this example, only the 0 position is referenced when the print to the Console is performed. Why? Since this is a single selection list only one position in the string array is populated—position 0.

Determining the Selected Item with Multiple Selections

More work is required when you deal with a multiple selection list. While you can still use getSelection() to return a string array populated with all the selected items, you must perform more processing to interact with any given single item.

How do I do that?

Example 7-3 demonstrates how to deal with multiple selected items returned from a call to getSelection().

Example 7-3. Working with multiple selection lists

```
import org.eclipse.swt.SWT;
import org.eclipse.swt.events.SelectionAdapter;
import org.eclipse.swt.events.SelectionEvent;
import org.eclipse.swt.graphics.Image;
```

Example 7-3. *Working with multiple selection lists (continued)*

```java
import org.eclipse.swt.widgets.*;

public class ListExample {

    Display d;
    Shell s;
    ListExample()    {
        d = new Display();
        s = new Shell(d);
        s.setSize(250,250);
        s.setImage(new Image(d, "c:\\icons\\JavaCup.ico"));
        s.setText("A List Example");
        final List l = new List(s, SWT.MULTI | SWT.BORDER);
        l.setBounds(50, 50, 75, 75);
        l.add("Item One");
        l.add("Item Two");
        l.add("Item Three");
        l.add("Item Four");
        l.add("Item Five");
        final Button b1 = new Button(s, SWT.PUSH | SWT.BORDER);
        b1.setBounds(150, 150, 50, 25);
        b1.setText("Click Me");
        b1.addSelectionListener(new SelectionAdapter() {
                public void widgetSelected(SelectionEvent e) {
                    String selected[] = l.getSelection();
                    for(int i = 0; i< selected.length; i++)
                    {
                        System.out.println(selected[i]);
                    }
                }
        });
        s.open();
        while(!s.isDisposed()){
            if(!d.readAndDispatch())
                d.sleep();
        }
        d.dispose();
    }
}
```

In Example 7-3, a button is added to the window to simulate the user taking some action after selecting items from the list.

What just happened?

The relevant code is found in the widgetSelected( ) method for the Listener attached to the Button b1:

```
b1.addSelectionListener(new SelectionAdapter( ) {
    public void widgetSelected(SelectionEvent e) {
        String selected[] = l.getSelection( );
        for(int i = 0; i< selected.length; i++)
        {
            System.out.println(selected[i]);
        }
    }
});
```

When the user clicks the button, the widgetSelected( ) method of the selectionListener is fired. Then a call is made to the getSelection( ) method to return an array of selected items. Since you no longer know the bounds of the array (which will depend on how many items the user selects prior to clicking the button), you must construct a loop that avoids an ArrayOutOfBounds exception.

At times, especially for large lists, the overhead associated with creating and carrying around an array of strings representing the selected items may be a bit large. In those cases, you can use an alternate technique to obtain only the index numbers of items that are selected, and then you can obtain each selected item by index number only when needed. This technique is also used when the text of the item is not necessary for further program execution. This code will have the same effect as the preceding code:

```
b1.addSelectionListener(new SelectionAdapter( ) {
    public void widgetSelected(SelectionEvent e) {
        int selected[] = l.getSelectionIndices( );
        for(int i = 0; i< selected.length; i++)
        {
            System.out.println(l.getItem(selected[i]));
        }
    }
});
```

Causing an Item to Appear Selected

The List class also provides methods that enable you to cause an item or items to become selected without user interaction with the list.

How do I do that?

You can use two methods when you need to programmatically select an item before the user selects items using a mouse click. To cause an item at a specified index position to become selected, use the select() method:

```
l.select(1);
```

TIP

Remember that lists are zero-indexed.

You can also select a range of items, by using another version of select(), one that accepts two int values—one to specify where to start selecting and the other to specify where to stop. This code selects the second through fifth:

```
l.select(1,4);
```

What about...

the times when you want to select an item by the String display value? There isn't a direct method for that purpose, but you can always combine methods to accomplish the task. In this code, you use the indexOf() method to search the list for the first item that matches the passed String, then pass the index returned to the select() method to perform the selection:

```
l.select(l.indexOf("Item Two"));
```

TIP

In a single selection listbox, a call to select() causes any items that are already selected to become deselected, even if the previously selected items were selected via user input. Programmatically selecting items takes a bit of thought as to how the user will perceive the action.

You can also select items using another method—setSelection( ). setSelection( ) provides functional equivalents to the select( ) methods discussed earlier, with perhaps a bit more ease of use. For example, it enables you to select multiple items that are not consecutively arranged:

```
int n[] = {1,3,5};
l.setSelection(n);
```

You can select items by String value:

```
String sel[] = {"Item One","Item Three","Item Five"};
l.setSelection(sel);
```

You can also select a single item using setSelection( ) if you pass in a one-element array:

```
String sel[] = {"Item One "};
l.setSelection(sel);
```

Changing an Item's Text Value

Occasionally, you will need to alter the text of a particular item. For example, you may need to change the text of the item to reflect that the user has taken some action elsewhere in the interface.

How do I do that?

You can always accomplish this task by removing the item and adding a new item with the new text using the techniques discussed previously. However, if the position of the item in the list is important, you would have to take additional coding steps to ensure that the new item is added at the proper location.

The List class provides an easier mechanism. When you need to change the text of an item, while preserving its index value, all you need to do is this:

```
l.setItem(2, "New Item");
```

This is the functional equivalent of removing the old item at index position 2 and inserting "New Item" at that index position.

Adding Scrollbars to a List

Scrollbars are necessary when the list is longer than the space available to view all the items. This is often the case, given that there is almost never enough room in a window for all interface elements. Scrollbars are added as a style attribute to the list at the time it is created.

How do I do that?

As with Text widgets, there are two scrollbar styles—SWT.V_SCROLL and SWT.H_SCROLL. For proper interface design, the scrollbar type you want to use most often is SWT.V_SCROLL:

```
final List l = new List(s, SWT.MULTI | SWT.BORDER | SWT.V_SCROLL);
```

You can specify SWT.H_SCROLL in all occasions, since it, too, will not appear unless needed.

And that's a wrap on this discussion of the SWT List class, one of the major widgets provided for building your user interfaces. In the next chapter, you will learn how to use the Combo class, which is closely related to, and shares much functionality with, List.

The scrollbar will appear only when there are more items than can be seen in the list.

The SWT Combo

The last of the four basic SWT widget classes is the Combo. Combos are used to gather information by enabling the user to choose from a list of items *or* to enter text not in the list. It combines the functionality of the List class with functionality from the Text class, hence the name combo. In other toolkits, you may find the combo box referred to by an older name—the drop-down listbox.

Since the Combo is a combination of two classes, you must consider each aspect of the class separately. This chapter begins with an examination of the List aspects of Combo, and then continues with the Text aspects. You will find much of this material familiar after having read the chapters that cover Text and List.

Creating a Combo List

As with all widgets, you must add a Combo to a Shell or other container by creating an instance of the Combo class and passing it the parameters required to create the desired style effects.

How do I do that?

By this stage of the process of learning SWT programming, you should be proficient in the code needed to add a widget to a shell and to specify the style of the widget. For Combo, there are three basic styles—SWT.DROP_DOWN, SWT.READ_ONLY, and SWT.SIMPLE. This code, which creates, sizes, and positions a Combo, should be familiar:

```
final Combo c = new Combo(s, SWT.READ_ONLY);
c.setBounds(50, 50, 150, 65);
```

In this chapter:
- *Creating a Combo List*
- *Adding Items to a Combo List*
- *Creating a Working Combo List*
- *Getting the Value of the Selected Item*
- *Programmatically Selecting an Item*
- *Removing Items from a Combo List*
- *Adding Events to Combo Widgets*
- *Allowing Additions to the Combo List*
- *Getting and Setting Text in the Text Portion of the Combo*
- *Setting the Maximum Length for Entries*
- *Deselecting Text*

The preceding code creates a Combo that has the SWT.READ_ONLY style. The SWT.READ_ONLY style is used to enable the user to select only an item that appears in the list portion of the combo, and prohibits them from entering in the text portion of the combo anything that does not appear on the list.

Adding Items to a Combo List

In keeping with the List nature of a Combo, the next step you must take when creating a Combo is to add items to the list.

All this is identical to the way List works.

How do I do that?

As with List objects, you can use two mechanisms to add items to a Combo. The first is to use the add( ) method:

```
c.add("Item One");
c.add("Item Two");
c.add("Item Three");
c.add("Item Four");
c.add("Item Five");
```

You can also create an array of String objects to hold the items, then make a single call to setItems( ):

```
String items[] = {"Item One", "Item Two", "Item Three", "Item Four",
    "Item Five"};
c.setItems(items);
```

Creating a Working Combo List

Knowing how to create a Combo object and add items to it makes it easy to create a functional ComboExample class.

How do I do that?

Example 8-1 creates a Combo object with five items added to the list.

Example 8-1. A Combo example class

```
import org.eclipse.swt.SWT;
import org.eclipse.swt.graphics.Image;
import org.eclipse.swt.widgets.*;

public class ComboExample {
    Display d;
    Shell s;
    ComboExample()    {
```

Example 8-1. A Combo example class (continued)

```
    d = new Display();
    s = new Shell(d);
    s.setSize(250,250);
    s.setImage(new Image(d, "c:\\icons\\JavaCup.ico"));
    s.setText("A Combo Example");
    final Combo c = new Combo(s, SWT.READ_ONLY);
    c.setBounds(50, 50, 150, 65);
    String items[] = {"Item One", "Item Two", "Item Three", "Item Four",
                      "Item Five"};
    c.setItems(items);
    s.open();
    while(!s.isDisposed()){
        if(!d.readAndDispatch())
            d.sleep();
    }
    d.dispose();
    }
}
```

The setItems( ) method of adding items to the list is used here. The add( ) method could have been used just as easily, although with a net increase in the number of lines of code required.

Everything you learned about creating, sizing, positioning, and adding items to an instance of the List class applies to the Combo class as well, without change. In fact, if you compare this code to the code that created the initial ListExample class in the previous chapter, you see that they are identical. Creating an instance of ComboExample displays Figure 8-1.

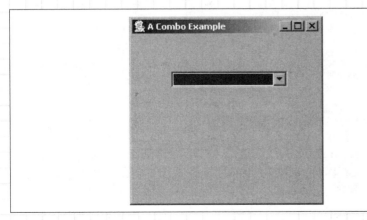

Figure 8-1. A Read_Only Combo

The combo box has a real advantage over the listbox. As you see, the combo box consumes much less space than a listbox of similar proportions. The "list" portion of the combo box is hidden until the user clicks the arrow button, at which time Figure 8-2 is revealed.

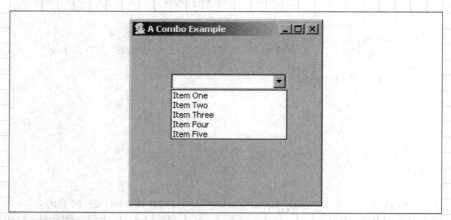

Figure 8-2. The "list" portion of the combo box

When the user selects an item from the list, the drop-down portion is again hidden and the item is displayed in the text portion of the combo, as in Figure 8-3.

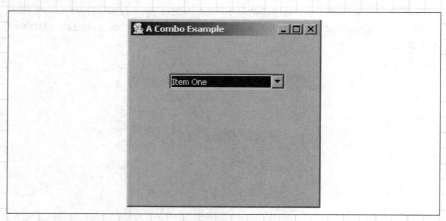

Figure 8-3. Selecting an item in the combo box

Chapter 8: The SWT Combo

Getting the Value of the Selected Item

The main programmatic interaction you must have with a Combo, once created, is in the realm of determining which item the user has selected.

How do I do that?

Obtaining the selected item is much easier with a Combo than it is with a List, for a couple of reasons. First, since all combos are single-selection, you need not worry about parsing multiple selection arrays to determine the item(s) selected.

The second reason stems from the combo's dual use of a text field in conjunction with the list. When the user selects an item from the list, the text portion of the Combo changes to show the item selected. To determine what that item is, use this:

```
String item = c.getText();
```

This returns the String value of the selected item. If you need the index value, you use this:

```
int i = c.getSelectionIndex();
```

getSelectionIndex() returns the index value (zero-referenced) of the selected item, or -1 if no item has been selected.

Programmatically Selecting an Item

As with List, it's useful sometimes to programmatically cause an item in a Combo to be selected without user interaction. Suppose, for example, you want the window to open with a default item already selected, as in Figure 8-4. In that case, you need to force the selection to the proper item.

How do I do that?

Programmatically selecting an item is a Combo is done in the same manner as selecting an item in a List—by making a call to the select() method. This line causes the item in the first position to become selected:

```
c.select(0);
```

Since a Combo consists of a text portion in addition to a list portion, you can also cause an item to be selected by setting the text for the item into the

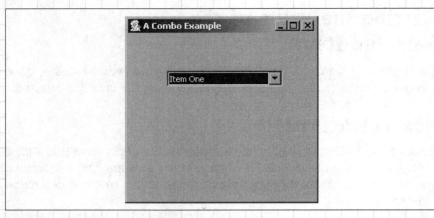

Figure 8-4. Opening a window with a selected item

text field. This works for Combo objects created with the SWT.READ_ONLY style, but does not work for those created with the SWT.DROP_DOWN style:

```
c.setText("Item One");
```

Adding either of these lines of code to Example 8-1 will result in the window opening in the Figure 8-4 state.

Removing Items from a Combo List

As with List, you must sometimes remove items from the list portion of a Combo at runtime.

How do I do that?

Combo contains a set of remove( ) methods that behave almost exactly as did those of the List.

To remove an item from the list, you use the appropriate version of the remove( ) method, or you use removeAll( ) to clear the contents of the list.

To remove a single item:

```
c.remove(3);
```

This removes the item that resides at index 3, or the fourth item in the list.

You can also use a version of remove( ) to eliminate more than one item from a list. One way to code for that task is to specify a range of items to remove:

```
c.remove(1,3);
```

`remove( )` can also accept an array of integers that tell the method which nonconsecutive items should be removed:

```
int n[] = {1,3,5};
c.remove(n);
```

Finally, you can remove a single item by referencing it by its `String` value:

```
c.remove("Item One");
```

This version of `remove` will begin at the beginning of the list, search the list item by item, and then remove the first item that exactly matches the `String` value passed. After finding a matching item, the search is abandoned.

Finally, `removeAll( )` operates exactly as the name implies and merits no discussion. Use it to clear the list prior to repopulating with fresh data.

What about...

index values of items that remain in the list after an item is removed? As with `List`, care must be taken when working with `Combo` items by index value, lest you obtain unfortunate results. This is as true of `Combo` as it was of `List`, as demonstrated in Chapter 7.

Adding Events to Combo Widgets

There are times when you must take an action immediately after the user selects something in a `Combo`. Perhaps the most frequent example is when you want to populate a second `Combo` (or `List`) based on the selection the user makes in the first `Combo`.

This is something a lot of user interfaces require.

How do I do that?

Like `List`, the `Combo` can listen for and respond to an event fired when the user makes a selection from the list. To accomplish this task, you use a `SelectionListener`. Consider Example 8-2, which creates two `Combo` objects, then populates the second based upon the item selected by the user in the first.

Example 8-2. Adding a SelectionListener to a Combo

```
import org.eclipse.swt.SWT;
import org.eclipse.swt.events.*;
import org.eclipse.swt.graphics.Image;
import org.eclipse.swt.widgets.*;

public class ComboExample {
```

Example 8-2. *Adding a SelectionListener to a Combo (continued)*

```
Display d;
Shell s;
ComboExample()    {
    d = new Display();
    s = new Shell(d);
    s.setSize(250,250);
    s.setImage(new Image(d, "c:\\icons\\JavaCup.ico"));
    s.setText("A Combo Example");
    final Combo c1 = new Combo(s, SWT.READ_ONLY);
    c1.setBounds(50, 50, 150, 65);
    final Combo c2 = new Combo(s, SWT.READ_ONLY);
    c2.setBounds(50, 85, 150, 65);
    c2.setEnabled(false);
    String items[] = {"Item One", "Item Two", "Item Three", "Item Four",
                      "Item Five"};
    c1.setItems(items);
    c1.addSelectionListener(new SelectionAdapter() {
        public void widgetSelected(SelectionEvent e) {
            if (c1.getText().equals("Item One"))
            {
              String newItems[] = {"Item One A", "Item One B", "Item One C"};
                c2.setItems(newItems);
                c2.setEnabled(true);
            }
            else if (c1.getText().equals("Item Two"))
            {
              String newItems[] = {"Item Two A", "Item Two B", "Item Two C"};
                c2.setItems(newItems);
                c2.setEnabled(true);
            }
            else
            {
                c2.add("Not Applicable");
                c2.setText("Not Applicable");
            }

        }
    });
    s.open();
    while(!s.isDisposed()){
        if(!d.readAndDispatch())
            d.sleep();
    }
    d.dispose();
}
}
```

What just happened?

The key section of code is in the widgetSelected() method of the
SelectionListener that is added to Combo c1:

```
public void widgetSelected(SelectionEvent e) {
    if (c1.getText().equals("Item One"))
    {
        String newItems[] = {"Item One A", "Item One B", "Item One C"};
        c2.setItems(newItems);
        c2.setEnabled(true);
    }
    else if (c1.getText().equals("Item Two"))
    {
        String newItems[] = {"Item Two A", "Item Two B", "Item Two C"};
        c2.setItems(newItems);
        c2.setEnabled(true);
    }
    else
    {
        c2.add("Not Applicable");
        c2.setText("Not Applicable");
    }
}
```

This code is executed whenever the user selects an item from the c1 list.
The code determines what item has been selected by making a call to
getText(), then compares the selected item against a known value:

```
if (c1.getText().equals("Item One"))
```

Based upon the c1 selection, items are then added to combo c2.

Allowing Additions to the Combo List

Up until now, the examples have contained only a READ_ONLY-style
combo. In that mode, the text field portion of the combo cannot be
directly edited by the user. The user must select an item from the list, at
which time that item will be displayed in read-only mode in the text
field. However, the combo can also be configured to enable the user to
enter text in the text portion that is not represented by a corresponding
item on the list.

How do I do that?

To permit the user to enter text in the text portion of the combo that does not directly correspond to an item in the list portion, just use the SWT.DROP_DOWN style when you create the combo:

```
final Combo c1 = new Combo(s, SWT.DROP_DOWN);
```

As seen in Figure 8-5, drop-down-style combos have a slightly different look on the Windows platform. When the text portion has focus, you see a different mouse cursor, usually an I-beam, which indicates that the text field is editable.

Figure 8-5. The DROP_DOWN style

Since the combo now has a completely functional text field, the user can enter any text in the combo and is not limited to simply choosing an item on the list. This also opens up your code for the use of some text-field-specific methods, many of which will be familiar from the Chapter 5 discussion of the Text class.

Getting and Setting Text in the Text Portion of the Combo

You have already worked with getText( ) and setText( ) in the preceding sections, but that was in the context of an SWT.READ_ONLY combo. In an SWT.DROP_DOWN style combo, setText( ) works a little differently and bears re-examination.

In the preceding examples, setText( ) was used as a method of selecting an item in the list portion of the combo. With a SWT.READ_ONLY combo, that approach works fine, but in an SWT.DROP_DOWN-style combo, that approach no longer works. When you perform a setText( ) action on an SWT.DROP_DOWN combo, the text portion of the combo will reflect the change, but you must take an additional action to force an item to actually become selected.

How do I do that?

As shown earlier, the following code can be used in a READ_ONLY combo to force an item to become selected:

```
final Combo c = new Combo(s, SWT.READ_ONLY);
c.setBounds(50, 50, 150, 65);
String items[] = {"Item One", "Item Two", "Item Three", "Item Four", "Item
Five"};
c.setItems(items);
c.setText("Item One");
System.out.println(c.getSelectionIndex( ));
```

Executing this code will cause Item One to be selected in the list. The call to getSelectionIndex( ) will cause the index value 0 (remember the list is zero-indexed) to be printed to the Console.

Contrast that code with this:

```
final Combo c = new Combo(s, SWT.DROP_DOWN);
c.setBounds(50, 50, 150, 65);
String items[] = {"Item One", "Item Two", "Item Three", "Item Four", "Item
Five"};
c.setItems(items);
c.setText("Item One");
System.out.println(c.getSelectionIndex( ));
```

If this code is executed, it causes -1 to be printed to the Console, indicating that no item has been selected from the list. The only difference is the style of the combo. With the SWT.DROP_DOWN style, another step is necessary to force selection:

```
c.select(0);
```

Care must obviously be taken when working with setText( ) among different styles of combos. Of course, getText( ) will always return what text is visible in the text portion, whether or not it matches any item in the list.

What difference does it make, as long as the item appears in the text portion? It matters if you use a method that returns the index value of the selected item.

Setting the Maximum Length for Entries

Since the SWT.DROP_DOWN-style combo has an editable text field into which the user can enter data, it is useful to be able to set a limit on the number of characters of text that may be entered. As discussed in the context of the Text class in Chapter 5, this is sometimes necessary to prevent database errors if the text entered is used to insert or update records in a database.

How do I do that?

As with the Text class, the following code will set a limit on entry:

```
c.setTextLimit(25);
```

Deselecting Text

If the user has entered text in the text field, or has selected an item causing it to be entered in the text field, he may need to remove that text or de-select the item.

How do I do that?

Deselecting an item can be done programmatically by:

```
c.deselectAll();
```

In the case of an SWT.DROP_DOWN-style combo, you may also need to call setText() to remove any text from the text portion of the combo:

```
c.setText("");
```

This is the brute force approach, but it works well since Combo objects are single-selection.

Responding to Item Changes in the Combo

With the editable text field of the SWT.DROP_DOWN combo style, it may be necessary to listen for the event that is fired when the user has modified the text in the field.

How do I do that?

To respond to the event that occurs when the user enters text in the Combo object's text field, you must add a ModifyListener to the combo:

```
c.addModifyListener(new ModifyListener() {
    public void modifyText(ModifyEvent e) {
        System.out.println("Text Changed");
    }
});
```

WARNING

Planning code for the modifyText( ) method of ModifyListener requires a bit of thought. This is because the method is called for every text change. If, for example, the user enters "A New Item" in the text field, the modifyText( ) method will be called 10 times, once for each letter and space entered. This may work, but often all you care about is when the user is finished entering text. In that event, using a FocusListener as discussed in Chapter 5 might be a better approach.

Using the SIMPLE Style

The final style for Combo objects is the seldom-used SWT.SIMPLE style. The SIMPLE style is used to create a combo in which the list portion of the combo is always visible.

How do I do that?

SIMPLE Combo objects are created simply by changing the style passed in at the time the Combo object is created:

```
final Combo c = new Combo(s, SWT.SIMPLE);
c.setBounds(50, 50, 150, 65);
String items[] = {"Item One", "Item Two", "Item Three", "Item Four", "Item Five"};
```

This code causes Figure 8-6 to be displayed. As you can see, the list portion of the combo appears in its dropped-down state. Of course, this negates much of the space savings that serve as the primary reason for use of Combo over List. It is appropriate, however, when you want to enable the user to add items not in the list while having the advantage of an always-visible list.

In all respects, a SIMPLE-style combo will work like a DROP_DOWN-style combo, including the ability to edit the text portion.

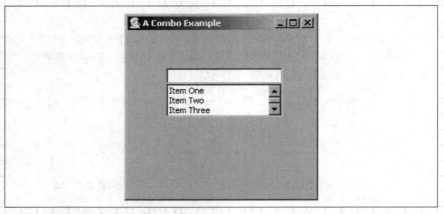

Figure 8-6. A SIMPLE-style combo

This chapter completes our look at the four main SWT widget types—Text, Button, List, and Combo. These four widgets comprise the major user-interface elements that are used to construct graphical applications. But there is more to designing a user interface than knowing which widget to use and how to use them. You also need to consider matters related to complex designs of widget locations and sizing.

To this point, the examples have been limited to those in which a widget, or widgets, was placed directly upon an instance of Shell. The next chapter will begin to examine methods of building more complex interfaces through the use of Layout, Composite, and Group classes.

CHAPTER 9

SWT Layouts

Up until this point, the examples have constructed simple user interfaces that consisted of one, or maybe two, widgets, which were placed directly on the Shell. setBounds() was used to control the size and positioning of each widget.

Although this approach works well, it does have its deficiencies. If you run one of the earlier examples and resize the window, you will uncover one of these—the widgets remain fixed in location with respect to the upper lefthand corner of the window and remain the same size. Even if the window is resized so as to cover up essential widgets, they remain fixed in position. This is not how windows usually behave, and your users will expect your programs to behave differently. This has been an issue with graphical environments since inception, and is not confined to SWT. Over the years, there have been many solutions.

Layouts were the solution devised by Java and have been a part of the Java SDK since the earliest versions. The SWT also uses the layout approach and the effect is very similar to the layouts found in the Java SDK, with perhaps more ease of use.

What Are the SWT Layouts?

Layouts are a solution that has been part of the Java platform since the earliest versions. A layout controls both placement and sizing of components within a container, according to the rules governing that particular layout type. SWT has four layout types:

- FillLayout
- GridLayout
- RowLayout
- FormLayout

Choosing the proper layout for a container depends in large part upon the type of widgets that will be placed in the container and what design effect you are seeking. The sections that follow discuss each layout in turn and demonstrate the effect each has on widget placement as well as what happens to the widgets when the window is resized.

Attaching a Layout to a Container

The first step in using the layout that you have chosen is to attach that layout to a container class (one of the classes that contains other widgets such as Shell, Composite, or Group).

How do I do that?

No matter which layout you choose to use, the same two steps are required to attach it to a container:

1. Create an instance of the layout class you wish to use (i.e., FillLayout).

2. Call the setLayout( ) method on the container instance to attach the layout.

Example 9-1 creates an instance of FillLayout and attaches it to a Shell.

Example 9-1. Using FillLayout

```
import org.eclipse.swt.graphics.Image;
import org.eclipse.swt.layout.*;
import org.eclipse.swt.widgets.*;

public class LayoutExample {
    Display d;
    Shell s;
    LayoutExample()    {
        d = new Display();
        s = new Shell(d);
        s.setSize(500,500);
        s.setImage(new Image(d, "c:\\icons\\JavaCup.ico"));
        s.setText("A Shell Menu Example");
        s.setLayout(new FillLayout());
        s.open();
        while(!s.isDisposed()){
            if(!d.readAndDispatch())
                d.sleep();
        }
        d.dispose();
    }
}
```

The shell in this example is now configured to use FillLayout. Widgets added to the shell will be positioned and sized according to the rules governing FillLayout, with no further programming required to control their position or size.

Filling the Entire Container with Widgets

The first of the layout classes to master is the simplest—FillLayout. As the name implies, FillLayout causes widgets to completely fill the working area of the container within which they are placed. The code developed earlier demonstrated how to create an instance of FillLayout and attach it to a Shell instance:

```
s.setLayout(new FillLayout());
```

FillLayout causes widgets added to the container to expand so as to fill the entire container. When the container is resized, the widget is resized so as to continue to fill the container. The preceding LayoutExample provides a platform for experimenting with FillLayout; all that remains is to add widgets and observe the effect.

How do I do that?

Example 9-2 is identical to Example 9-1 except that it adds a multiline text field to demonstrate the effect that FillLayout has upon widget placement and size.

Example 9-2. FillLayout with Widgets

```
import org.eclipse.swt.*;
import org.eclipse.swt.graphics.Image;
import org.eclipse.swt.layout.*;
import org.eclipse.swt.widgets.*;

public class FillLayoutExample {
    Display d;
    Shell s;
    FillLayoutExample()    {
        d = new Display();
        s = new Shell(d);
        s.setSize(250,250);
        s.setImage(new Image(d, "c:\\icons\\JavaCup.ico"));
        s.setText("A FillLayout Example");
        s.setLayout(new FillLayout());
        final Text t = new Text(s, SWT.MULTI | SWT.BORDER | SWT.WRAP);
        s.open();
```

Example 9-2. FillLayout with Widgets (continued)

```
        while(!s.isDisposed()){
            if(!d.readAndDispatch())
                d.sleep();
        }
        d.dispose();
    }
}
```

Executing this code results in Figure 9-1.

Figure 9-1. FillLayoutExample

What just happened?

Notice that you no longer are required to specify a position or a size for the text field using setBounds() to force it to become visible. Why?

The task of sizing and positioning the text field that was performed by a call to setBounds() is now handled entirely by the FillLayout class under the hood, with no additional coding required. But the benefits of FillLayout extend beyond simply saving a line of code. If you resize the window created by FillLayoutExample, you see the effect that FillLayout provides—no matter what size you make the window, FillLayout automatically handles the resizing of the text field so that it continues to fill the working area of the window.

What about...

adding multiple widgets? If you add multiple widgets to a container using FillLayout, the widgets are sized so that, taken together, they fill the container. If you have two widgets, each will fill 50% of the container; three widgets will fill 33.33% each, and so on. The effect is easily seen by adding additional widgets to FillLayoutExample.

As an example, this code adds a Button to the FillLayoutExample:

```
final Button b = new Button(s, SWT.BORDER);
b.setText("OK");
```

Now, creating an instance of the class causes the window shown in Figure 9-2 to be displayed.

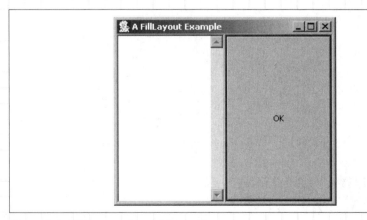

Figure 9-2. FillLayout with multiple widgets

As you resize this window, you see that each widget always maintains a size that causes it to fill its respective percentage of the container (in this case, each gets 50% of the window).

Changing Widget Placement in FillLayouts

The default of FillLayout positions the widgets horizontally so that widgets appear side by side. If you want the widgets to appear top to bottom, you need to change the style type of the FillLayout.

How do I do that?

Whether the widgets are displayed horizontally (side by side) or vertically (top to bottom) is controlled by passing a style attribute to the FillLayout constructor:

```
s.setLayout(new FillLayout(SWT.VERTICAL));
```

If you make this change to FillLayoutExample, it will produce the dialog displayed in Figure 9-3.

Figure 9-3. The FillLayout SWT.VERTICAL style

Lining Up Widgets Using RowLayout

RowLayout, as the name implies, enables you to place widgets in a row on a container. When a row has been completely filled, a new row, with all widgets resized appropriately, will be started.

Since RowLayout is more complex and acts in a different manner than FillLayout, the best way to understand RowLayout is to build an example—set the layout manager of a Shell to RowLayout, add a few widgets, and observe the results.

How do I do that?

The first step to using RowLayout is the same as when using FillLayout—create a Shell and call setLayout( ) to pass an instance of RowLayout. This is demonstrated by Example 9-3.

Example 9-3. Using RowLayout with a shell

```
import org.eclipse.swt.*;
import org.eclipse.swt.graphics.Image;
import org.eclipse.swt.layout.*;
import org.eclipse.swt.widgets.*;

public class RowLayoutExample {
    Display d;
    Shell s;
    RowLayoutExample( )    {
        d = new Display( );
        s = new Shell(d);
        s.setSize(250,250);
        s.setImage(new Image(d, "c:\\icons\\JavaCup.ico"));
        s.setText("A RowLayout Example");
        s.setLayout(new RowLayout( ));
        final Text t = new Text(s, SWT.SINGLE | SWT.BORDER);
        final Button b = new Button(s, SWT.BORDER);
        final Button b1 = new Button(s, SWT.BORDER);
        b.setText("OK");
        b1.setText("Cancel");
        s.open( );
        while(!s.isDisposed( )){
            if(!d.readAndDispatch( ))
                d.sleep( );
        }
        d.dispose( );
    }
}
```

Execution of Example 9-3 results in Figure 9-4 being displayed.

What about...

the times when the window isn't wide enough to display all the widgets in a row? As you see in the example, the first widget is placed first in the row, then the second, and so on. If a row is filled, the next widget added begins a second row. You can see the effect by resizing the executed RowLayoutExample so that the window's width is too small to display the entire row, as shown in Figure 9-5.

When the width of the window is not sufficient to show all three widgets in a single row, a second row is started with the third widget.

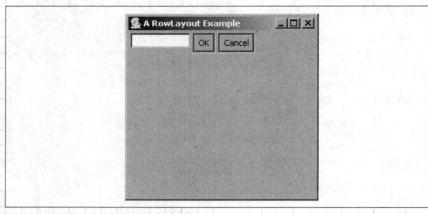

Figure 9-4. RowLayout with defaults

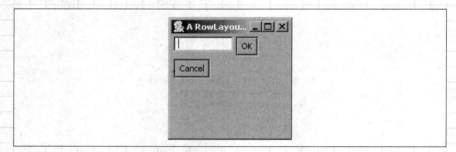

Figure 9-5. Resizing RowLayoutExample

Controlling Wrapping of Widgets with RowLayout

RowLayout is more complex than FillLayout and, consequently, you must manage some additional settings to achieve the desired effect. One such setting—wrap—controls whether widgets will wrap down to a second row if the container is resized so that the widgets no longer fit on a single row. The default behavior, seen in the preceding example, is to wrap widgets; however, there are times when your interface design won't permit wrapping and you must then alter the default RowLayout behavior.

How do I do that?

The row-wrapping feature that is the default for RowLayout can easily be switched off if you want a different effect. The following code creates a RowLayout in which wrapping does not take place:

```
RowLayout rl = new RowLayout();
rl.wrap = false;
s.setLayout(rl);
```

To see the effect, change RowLayoutExample to substitute the previous three lines with this line:

```
s.setLayout(new RowLayout());
```

When you create an instance of the RowLayoutExample class and resize the window, you will notice that the widgets no longer wrap to a second line when the width of the window is not sufficient to display the entire row. Figure 9-6 shows what happens when the window is resized so that the widgets cannot fit across the width of the window.

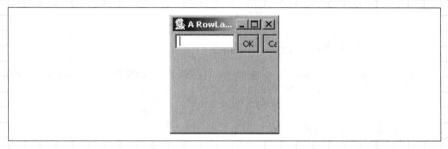

Figure 9-6. Nonwrapping RowLayout

Controlling Sizing of Widgets with RowLayout

Another useful setting of RowLayout is pack. pack controls the initial sizing of widgets placed in the container. A setting of true allows RowLayout to create widgets of different sizes, depending on the widget type and the text setting of the widgets. The effect is seen in Figure 9-4, where each widget has a different size. The size of the Button widgets is controlled by the text each contains, hence the Cancel button is larger than the OK button.

Your interface design may require that you force all widgets in a row to be the same size, no matter what their style or contents.

How do I do that?

As with the wrap setting, you directly access the pack setting field by:

```
rl.pack = false;
```

Adding this line to RowLayoutExample creates Figure 9-7 when executed.

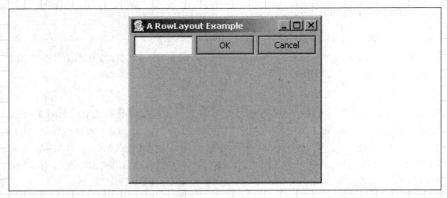

Figure 9-7. RowLayout with pack = false

Creating Vertical Rows

Although the default for RowLayout is to create horizontal rows, you can also create vertical rows when necessary.

How do I do that?

To create a vertical RowLayout, you simply pass the RowLayout constructor the SWT.VERTICAL style when you create an instance of the RowLayout class:

```
RowLayout rl = new RowLayout(SWT.VERTICAL);
```

Creating a GridLayout

GridLayout works somewhat like RowLayout, in that it controls placement of widgets in rows. However, GridLayout provides much more functionality than RowLayout, such as the ability to specify how many widgets wide a row should be, effectively enabling you to create a grid of rows and columns. Along with this extra functionality come even more additional settings that must be managed, making GridLayout much more complex than RowLayout.

The process for creating a GridLayout is slightly different from the process for creating either a RowLayout or a FillLayout. The process begins the same way—with the creation of an instance of the GridLayout class—but an additional setting must be specified: the number of columns in the grid. This setting controls the number of widgets that will make up a single row of the grid.

How do I do that?

The steps used to create a GridLayout are similar to those used to create a RowLayout, with the exception of having to specify the number of columns. Example 9-4 demonstrates how to create a three-column grid.

Example 9-4. Using GridLayout

```
import org.eclipse.swt.*;
import org.eclipse.swt.graphics.Image;
import org.eclipse.swt.layout.*;
import org.eclipse.swt.widgets.*;

public class GridLayoutExample {
    Display d;
    Shell s;
    GridLayoutExample()    {
        d = new Display();
        s = new Shell(d);
        s.setSize(250,250);
        s.setImage(new Image(d, "c:\\icons\\JavaCup.ico"));
        s.setText("A GridLayout Example");
        GridLayout gl = new GridLayout();
        gl.numColumns=3;
        s.setLayout(gl);
        s.open();
        while(!s.isDisposed()){
            if(!d.readAndDispatch())
                d.sleep();
        }
        d.dispose();
    }
}
```

What just happened?

GridLayoutExample creates a window with a grid that is three columns wide. Notice that the number of columns is not set at the time you create the grid, but is specified directly in a separate step:

```
gl.numColumns=3;
```

The number of columns is not a style setting, so it must be specified in this manner.

What about...

the order in which widgets appear in the grid? Widgets are added to the grid in the order in which they are created in the code. The first widget added will be placed in the first cell of the first row, the second in the second cell of the first row, and so on, until the first row is filled. At that point, the next widget added will be placed in the first cell of the second row.

Creating Column Headings

It is possible to create a GridLayout that mimics a table for presentation of data. When this is the design effect you wish to achieve, you must create column headings in the first row of the grid. Text widgets are then used to fill out the additional rows in the table.

How do I do that?

Example 9-5 demonstrates how GridLayout can be used to create a table for presentation of data in text fields aligned in a grid.

Example 9-5. Creating a table effect using GridLayout

```
import org.eclipse.swt.*;
import org.eclipse.swt.graphics.Image;
import org.eclipse.swt.layout.*;
import org.eclipse.swt.widgets.*;

public class GridLayoutExample {
    Display d;
    Shell s;
    GridLayoutExample()    {
        d = new Display();
        s = new Shell(d);
        s.setSize(250,250);
        s.setImage(new Image(d, "c:\\icons\\JavaCup.ico"));
        s.setText("A GridLayout Example");
        GridLayout gl = new GridLayout();
        gl.numColumns=3;
        s.setLayout(gl);
        final Label l1 = new Label(s, SWT.BORDER);
        l1.setText("Column One");
        final Label l2 = new Label(s, SWT.BORDER);
        l2.setText("Column Two");
        final Label l3 = new Label(s, SWT.BORDER);
        l3.setText("Column Three");
        final Text t1 = new Text(s, SWT.SINGLE | SWT.BORDER);
        final Text t2 = new Text(s, SWT.SINGLE | SWT.BORDER);
        final Text t3 = new Text(s, SWT.SINGLE | SWT.BORDER);
        final Text t4 = new Text(s, SWT.SINGLE | SWT.BORDER);
        final Text t5 = new Text(s, SWT.SINGLE | SWT.BORDER);
        final Text t6 = new Text(s, SWT.SINGLE | SWT.BORDER);
        s.open();
        while(!s.isDisposed()){
            if(!d.readAndDispatch())
```

Example 9-5. Creating a table effect using GridLayout (continued)

```
            d.sleep();
        }
        d.dispose();
    }
}
```

Creating an instance of GridLayoutExample now creates Figure 9-8.

Figure 9-8. GridLayoutExample

What just happened?

Creating column headings is just a matter of adding Label widgets to the first row of the grid and setting their text property to that desired for the heading:

```
final Label l1 = new Label(s, SWT.BORDER);
l1.setText("Column One");
final Label l2 = new Label(s, SWT.BORDER);
l2.setText("Column Two");
final Label l3 = new Label(s, SWT.BORDER);
l3.setText("Column Three");
```

Text widgets are then used to complete each row of the grid, to enable the user to interact with data in a tabular form:

```
final Text t1 = new Text(s, SWT.SINGLE | SWT.BORDER);
final Text t2 = new Text(s, SWT.SINGLE | SWT.BORDER);
final Text t3 = new Text(s, SWT.SINGLE | SWT.BORDER);
final Text t4 = new Text(s, SWT.SINGLE | SWT.BORDER);
final Text t5 = new Text(s, SWT.SINGLE | SWT.BORDER);
final Text t6 = new Text(s, SWT.SINGLE | SWT.BORDER);
```

Since the example creates a three-column grid, every three widgets added comprise a single row. To keep the table effect, the number of

Text widgets must be a multiple of three; otherwise, one row is not fully populated, and the table effect is spoiled.

Controlling Widget Sizing and Alignment

If you examine the executing GridLayoutExample, you discover several problems with the default GridLayout settings. First, the widgets are given a default size, which leads to alignment problems if there are widgets of differing types (as with Label and Text widgets). Second, you see that resizing the window does not result in resizing the widgets, which is one of the basic reasons for using a layout in the first place. The use of additional GridLayout settings and another class called GridData helps solve these issues.

How do I do that?

GridData is the class that provides GridLayout with the ability to handle size and position of widgets. Each widget can have a data layout associated with it using the widget's setDataLayout() method. To accomplish this, you must create an instance of the GridData class, then call setLayoutData() on the widget which you are adding to the grid:

```
GridData gd = new GridData();
gd.horizontalAlignment = GridData.CENTER;
l1.setLayoutData(gd);

gd = new GridData();
gd.horizontalAlignment = GridData.CENTER;
l2.setLayoutData(gd);

gd = new GridData();
gd.horizontalAlignment = GridData.CENTER;
l3.setLayoutData(gd);

gd = new GridData(GridData.FILL_HORIZONTAL);
t1.setLayoutData(gd);

gd = new GridData(GridData.FILL_HORIZONTAL);
t2.setLayoutData(gd);

gd = new GridData(GridData.FILL_HORIZONTAL);
t3.setLayoutData(gd);

gd = new GridData(GridData.FILL_HORIZONTAL);
t4.setLayoutData(gd);
```

```
gd = new GridData(GridData.FILL_HORIZONTAL);
t5.setLayoutData(gd);

gd = new GridData(GridData.FILL_HORIZONTAL);
t6.setLayoutData(gd);
```

Try adding the preceding code to GridLayoutExample, just prior to:

```
s.open();
```

Doing so yields Figure 9-9 when an instance of the class is created.

Figure 9-9. Centering widgets using GridData

Notice that the Label objects are now centered. When you resize the window, you see that all widgets are resized and repositioned automatically. This is a distinct improvement over the previous example, but the improvement comes at the cost of having to manage settings not only in the GridLayout class, but also in the GridData class.

What just happened?

The preceding example requires a bit of analysis to foster complete understanding. As you see, it's actually the GridData class that provides most of the magic needed for a fully functional GridLayout. Every widget that participates in a grid should have a GridData object associated with it via its setLayoutData() method. The GridData object's settings control how the widget is positioned in each cell. The relevant settings are:

- GridData.CENTERED
- GridData.BEGINNING
- GridData.END

In the preceding example, the code first specifies the horizontal alignment to apply to the labels:

```
gd.horizontalAlignment = GridData.CENTER;
l1.setLayoutData(gd);
```

When a GridData object with GridData.CENTER specified as the
horizontalAlignment is attached to the Label, it causes the Label to
become centered within the cell in which it is placed. As the cell resizes,
the labels remain centered. But what causes the cells to resize?

Another GridData setting controls how widgets are positioned and
resized within each cell. Examine the GridData object that is attached to
the text fields:

```
gd = new GridData(GridData.FILL_HORIZONTAL);
```

The possibilities here are:

- FILL_HORIZONTAL
- FILL_VERTICAL
- FILL_BOTH

If a GridData object with the FILL_HORIZONTAL setting is specified, it
stretches itself to fill the cell in which it is placed from left to right. What
determines the width of the cell? The GridLayout class fills the container
object by dividing the workspace into cells of equal size. A three-cell grid
sizes itself so that each cell covers one-third of the width of the workspace.
The same is true of the vertical sizing, where a setting of FILL_VERTICAL
causes the widget to fill the cell from top to bottom, with the GridLayout
dividing the workspace according to the number of rows displayed.

Two additional GridData settings that are useful are heightHint and
widthHint, which specify the minimum number of pixels a cell will be
permitted to shrink upon resizing of the window. You use heightHint

and `widthHint` to ensure that a widget in a cell will not shrink so small that its data contents can't be displayed. To set `heightHint` or `widthHint`, just access the field directly:

```
gd.heightHint = 30;
```

Forcing Widgets to Span Multiple Cells

It is possible to make a widget span across multiple cells of the grid, yielding rows that contain fewer widgets than other rows. Likewise, you can cause a widget to span vertically across cells in a column.

How do I do that?

The `GridData` `verticalSpan` and `horizontalSpan` settings control how many cells a widget spans. Consider the following code:

```
gd = new GridData(GridData.FILL_HORIZONTAL);
gd.widthHint=30;
t1.setLayoutData(gd);
gd = new GridData(GridData.FILL_HORIZONTAL);
gd.widthHint=30;
t2.setLayoutData(gd);
gd = new GridData(GridData.FILL_BOTH);
gd.widthHint=30;
gd.verticalSpan = 2;
t3.setLayoutData(gd);
gd = new GridData(GridData.FILL_HORIZONTAL);
gd.widthHint=30;
t4.setLayoutData(gd);
gd = new GridData(GridData.FILL_HORIZONTAL);
gd.widthHint=30;
t5.setLayoutData(gd);
```

Here, one `Text` widget has been removed from `GridLayoutExample` and the `GridData` object that is attached to `Text` `t3` is configured to span two columns vertically:

```
gd.verticalSpan = 2;
```

The style of the `GridData` is also changed to `FILL_BOTH` so that `t3` automatically filsl the entire two-cell span and resizes as the window is resized. The results are shown in Figure 9-10.

As you can see, the combination of `GridData` and `GridLayout` is powerful, but the power comes at the price of having to specify many additional settings. There are easier methods you can use to display data in tables or grids, such as the `Table` widget, which is discussed in Chapter 12.

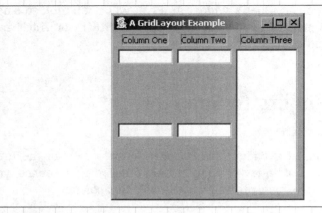

Figure 9-10. Spanning vertical cells

TIP

Table widgets are read-only and do not allow the user to interact with or edit the data. If you are building an editable table, GridLayout may be your only SWT alternative.

The SWT FormLayout

When an interface is designed to allow for data input from a user, it is usually best to design that interface as a *form*. The SWT FormLayout is designed to allow for easy programming of forms. Using FormLayout you pin widgets to a particular position on the window, specifying the height and width of the widget either in pixels or as a percentage of the total container height and width.

FormLayout is the most powerful of the layout classes as far as what it can do for you, but that power comes at the price of having even more classes and settings to deal with when creating the desired physical layout. With FillLayout, you need only manage style settings and no additional supporting classes. RowLayout added new settings and an optional RowData class that is seldom used. With GridLayout comes many additional settings and a GridData class that, although not mandatory, is required to provide a fully functional GridLayout.

With FormLayout there is even more to configure, including two helper classes—FormData and FormAttachment. Unlike with GridLayout, where use of GridData was optional, use of FormData and FormAttachment is mandatory. Failure to use the FormData class, for example, causes all widgets to be stacked on top of each other in the same space on the container.

Creating a Simple Password Entry Form

Figure 9-11 shows a simple form, with two Label widgets and two Text widgets aligned so that each label acts as a text reminder of the contents to input into the corresponding Text widget.

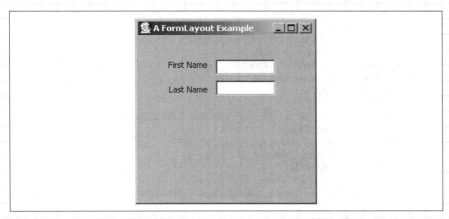

Figure 9-11. FormLayoutExample

How do I do that?

Example 9-6 uses FormLayout to create a simple four-widget form.

Example 9-6. Using FormLayout

```
import org.eclipse.swt.*;
import org.eclipse.swt.graphics.Image;
import org.eclipse.swt.layout.*;
import org.eclipse.swt.widgets.*;

public class FormLayoutExample {
    Display d;
    Shell s;
    FormLayoutExample( )    {
        d = new Display( );
        s = new Shell(d);
        s.setSize(250,250);
        s.setImage(new Image(d, "c:\\icons\\JavaCup.ico"));
        s.setText("A FormLayout Example");
        s.setLayout(new FormLayout( ));

        final Label l1 = new Label(s, SWT.RIGHT);
        l1.setText("First Name");
        FormData fd = new FormData( );
```

Example 9-6. Using FormLayout (continued)

```
            fd.top = new FormAttachment(10, 10);
            fd.left = new FormAttachment(0, 10);
            fd.bottom = new FormAttachment(30,0);
            fd.right = new FormAttachment(40,0);
            l1.setLayoutData(fd);

            final Label l2 = new Label(s, SWT.RIGHT);
            l2.setText("Last Name");
            fd = new FormData();
            fd.top = new FormAttachment(l1, 5);
            fd.left = new FormAttachment(0, 10);
            fd.bottom = new FormAttachment(40,0);
            fd.right = new FormAttachment(40,0);
            l2.setLayoutData(fd);

            final Text t1 = new Text(s, SWT.BORDER | SWT.SINGLE);
            fd = new FormData();
            fd.top = new FormAttachment(l1, 0, SWT.TOP);
            fd.left = new FormAttachment(l1, 10);
            t1.setLayoutData(fd);

            final Text t2 = new Text(s, SWT.BORDER | SWT.SINGLE);
            fd = new FormData();
            fd.top = new FormAttachment(l2, 0, SWT.TOP);
            fd.left = new FormAttachment(l2, 10);
            t2.setLayoutData(fd);

        s.open();
        while(!s.isDisposed()){
            if(!d.readAndDispatch())
                d.sleep();
        }
        d.dispose();
    }
}
```

As you see, even with fewer widgets than were used in
GridLayoutExample, more code is required to control their placement. This
is due to the complex nature of the FormLayout and its supporting classes—
FormData and FormAttachment—as the analysis of the code will show.

What just happened?

To get the most out of FormLayout, you must gain a full understanding of
the FormData and FormAttachment classes. That can be accomplished
within the context of FormLayoutExample by looking at the specific code
segments that deal with each class.

FormData contains the attach points for all four sides of a widget, thus
setting out the position of the widget within the form. The four sides are

left, right, top, and bottom, all of which are instance variables of type FormAttachment within the FormData class. This means that you create up to four instances of FormAttachment, one for each side of the widget to which you are attaching a FormData object.

The FormAttachment class defines the attachment point for a single side of a widget. To define the attachment point, you create an instance of FormAttachment, passing its constructor the desired position as a percentage of the height of the parent. Thus, the following code sets the top position of Label l1 at 10% of the height of the Shell within which the Label is contained, with an offset from the edge of the window of 10%:

```
fd = new FormData();
fd.top = new FormAttachment(10, 10);
l1.setLayoutData(fd);
```

TIP

The first parameter passed into the FormAttachment constructor moves the widget from top to bottom on the window while the second parameter moves the widget from left to right.

Now that Label l1 is positioned, positioning the remaining widgets is easier since they can be positioned in relation to the position of Label l1. This is done by using another form of the FormAttachment constructor—one that permits passing in a widget as an argument. The attachment point is then calculated from the appropriate position of the passed widget. For example, to position Label l2 so that its top is 5 pixels below the bottom of Label l1:

```
final Label l2 = new Label(s, SWT.RIGHT);
l2.setText("Last Name");
fd = new FormData();
fd.top = new FormAttachment(l1, 5);
```

This code causes the top of Label l2 to attach to the bottom of Label l1, always remaining 5 pixels offset from the bottom of l1.

The Text widgets can then be placed in their proper locations, relative to the two Label widgets. To create the form look, the Text widgets must align with the Label widgets so that the left side of each Text widget remains 10 pixels from the right side of the corresponding Label widget.

Start by positioning Text t1:

```
final Text t1 = new Text(s, SWT.BORDER | SWT.SINGLE);
fd = new FormData();
fd.top = new FormAttachment(l1, 0, SWT.TOP);
fd.left = new FormAttachment(l1, 10);
t1.setLayoutData(fd);
```

Here the top of the widget Text t1 is set to align with the top of the widget Label l1, with a 0-pixel offset—meaning the two are (and will remain) perfectly aligned. The left position of t1 is configured so that it remains constantly offset from l1 by 10 pixels.

The form is then completed by positioning the second Text widget in a similar manner:

```
final Text t2 = new Text(s, SWT.BORDER | SWT.SINGLE);
fd = new FormData();
fd.top = new FormAttachment(l2, 0, SWT.TOP);
fd.left = new FormAttachment(l2, 10);
t2.setLayoutData(fd);
```

It takes a great deal of planning and effort to create even this simple form. More complex forms require even more planning and effort.

As demonstrated by these examples, the SWT layout classes are very powerful tools that can assist in widget placement and sizing. However, one shortcoming of the layout approach is the fact that a container can have only one layout manager. This shortcoming is addressed in the next chapter, which covers the Composite and Group container classes, which allow for the creation of windows that use different layout managers for different parts of the window, providing the ability to build very complex user interfaces.

CHAPTER 10

SWT Composites and Groups

Until now, all examples that have been created have included widgets that were added directly to an instance of Shell. This approach works well for simple interfaces, but more complex designs require the use of a different layout manager for different parts of the window. For example, you might want a row of buttons at the bottom of a window—a perfect situation for RowLayout—while data is displayed above the buttons in the form of a grid, a perfect situation for GridLayout.

The SWT provides for these situations with two additional classes that can act as containers for widgets: Composite and Group. These classes are located in the org.eclipse.swt.widgets package.

Before you learn how to use the Composite and Group classes together with layouts to build complex user interfaces for use in your applications, you should first gain a basic understanding of the Composite and Group classes themselves. Since Group is a subclass of Composite, it makes sense to begin this discussion by covering the Composite class.

Composite objects are created simply to contain other widgets. Composite is an ancestor of every SWT class to which you can add widgets, including Shell. For that reason, you can think of a Composite as being simply the working area of a Shell, without the styles associated with the aspects of Shell that make windows—the titlebar, control menu, etc.

Subclassing the Composite Class

One major difference between the Composite and Shell classes is that Composite may be subclassed. Perhaps you have noticed that in every example so far, an instance of Shell was created within another class, and then widgets were added to that instance. The object-oriented purist may have expected to create a subclass of `Shell` and then create widgets within that subclass.

With `Shell` (and many of the SWT widget classes), you are not permitted to create a subclass, so the pure object-oriented approach isn't available. This is not true with `Composite`. With `Composite`, you can create a class that extends `Composite`, add widgets to that class, then add an instance of your custom class to an instance of `Shell`. This enables you to use `Composite` descendants to create reusable custom user-interface elements, such as a standard login prompt, for use in more than one application.

How do I do that?

The code required to subclass `Composite` and add widgets to the subclass is trivial, as shown in Example 10-1.

The code that actually adds the widget looks a lot like the code that adds a widget to a Shell, doesn't it?

Example 10-1. Creating a Composite subclass

```
import org.eclipse.swt.SWT;
import org.eclipse.swt.layout.FillLayout;
import org.eclipse.swt.widgets.*;

public class TextPaneComposite extends Composite {

    public TextPaneComposite(Composite parent)
    {
        super(parent, SWT.BORDER);
        this.setLayout(new FillLayout());
        final Text t = new Text(this, SWT.MULTI | SWT.BORDER
                | SWT.WRAP | SWT.V_SCROLL);

    }
}
```

What just happened?

In keeping with the Java implementation of object orientation, to subclass `Composite` you need only create a class that uses the `extends` keyword:

```
public class TextPaneComposite extends Composite
```

Once that task is accomplished, widgets are added to the subclass in the same manner used to add them directly to instances of `Shell`, except that the reference to a container class passed to the widget constructor uses the `this` keyword:

```
final Text t = new Text(this, SWT.MULTI | SWT.BORDER |
                SWT.WRAP | SWT.V_SCROLL);
```

Using the TextPaneComposite
Class on a Shell

Composite objects themselves cannot be drawn directly on the display, but must be placed within the confines of a Shell or Dialog, the two classes that can be drawn directly on the display.

How do I do that?

Create an instance of the TextPaneComposite class, passing it a reference to the Shell instance that serves as its container. Example 10-2 demonstrates how to use TextPaneComposite on a Shell.

Example 10-2. Using a Composite subclass on a Shell

```
import org.eclipse.swt.SWT;
import org.eclipse.swt.graphics.Image;
import org.eclipse.swt.layout.FillLayout;
import org.eclipse.swt.widgets.*;

public class CompositeShellExample {
    Display d;
    Shell s;
    CompositeShellExample( )    {
        d = new Display( );
        s = new Shell(d);
        s.setSize(500,500);
        s.setImage(new Image(d, "c:\\icons\\JavaCup.ico"));
        s.setText("A Shell Composite Example");
        s.setLayout(new FillLayout( ));
        final TextPaneComposite tpc = new TextPaneComposite(s);
        s.open( );
        while(!s.isDisposed( )){
            if(!d.readAndDispatch( ))
                d.sleep( );
        }
        d.dispose( );
    }
}
```

In this class, you see code that is very familiar from the previous examples, with one difference—instead of creating a Text widget directly on the Shell workspace, you create an instance of TextPaneComposite, passing it a reference to the Shell instance which will be the parent. All other code remains the same. The results are shown in Figure 10-1.

Although this is a pretty simple example, it does serve to illustrate the concept. You can place any combination of widgets in your Composite subclasses, and then you can add them as a unit to any other container class

---

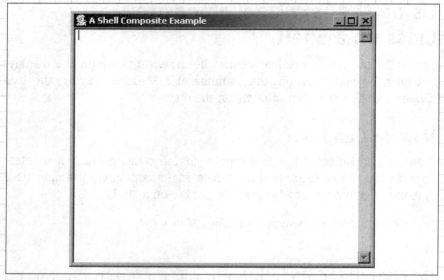

Figure 10-1. A Composite with a Text widget on a Shell

(such as a Shell or even another Composite). The combination of multiple composites within a single window is what enables you to build complex interfaces using different layouts for different sections of the window.

Using Composite Class Styles

Composite will accept several styles. The first is SWT.NO_BACKGROUND, which causes the Composite to be transparent. This is used to allow whatever is underneath the Composite, perhaps a background color or picture, to show through. SWT.NO_FOCUS can be used to prevent the Composite itself from gaining the input focus as the user tabs through controls on the window. Additionally, Composite can accept styles that apply to other widgets, such as SWT.BORDER, as illustrated by the previous example above.

As with all styles, you must experiment with different combinations until you derive the desired effect.

What about...

if you want to enable the end developer—the one who may be using your Composite subclass to develop applications—to specify a style? In TextPaneComposite, from Example 10-1, you see that the class makes a call to the constructor of the Composite class:

```
    super(parent, SWT.BORDER);
```

This is necessary due to a rule of the Java compiler that requires a call to a specific constructor on the super-class whenever the super-class does not contain a default, no-argument, constructor. The Composite class is such a class—all of its constructors require a reference to the parent of the Composite being constructed.

In the case of TextPaneComposite, the style parameter is hardcoded into the call to the parent's constructor. Although this serves the purpose of the example, it does make the resulting class a little inflexible. A much better approach is to enable the ultimate developer, the one who is using the Composite subclass on a Shell, to pass through the desired style attributes.

To enable a developer to specify desired style attributes for TextPaneComposite, add a second parameter to the TextPaneComposite constructor to allow the style to be passed. Then remove the hardcoded style passed in the call to the parent constructor, replacing it with the passed parameter. This is illustrated in Example 10-3:

Example 10-3. Permitting pass-through of styles

```
import org.eclipse.swt.SWT;
import org.eclipse.swt.layout.FillLayout;
import org.eclipse.swt.widgets.*;

public class TextPaneComposite extends Composite {

    public TextPaneComposite(Composite parent, int style)
    {
        super(parent, style);
        this.setLayout(new FillLayout());
        final Text t = new Text(this, SWT.MULTI | SWT.BORDER |
            SWT.WRAP | SWT.V_SCROLL);

    }
}
```

TextPaneComposite is then placed on a Shell by:

```
    final TextPaneComposite tpc = new TextPaneComposite(s, SWT.BORDER);
```

This approach produces maximum flexibility of your Composite subclasses.

Using the Group Class

The SWT Group class extends the Composite class and provides some additional functionality related primarily to the appearance of the group. Group permits you to add a text label as a prompt to the user of group contents and to change the border style of the resulting object, yielding more of a visual indication to the user that the widgets are part of a functional area of the application.

Because the Group class cannot be subclassed, it must be used in a manner similar to Shell—you create an instance of Group within another container class (such as Composite) and then add widgets to that instance.

How do I do that?

The task of creating a Group is very similar to the task of creating a Shell. First, create a Composite that will serve as the container for the Group, as shown in Example 10-4.

Example 10-4. Using a Group

```
import org.eclipse.swt.layout.FillLayout;
import org.eclipse.swt.widgets.*;
import org.eclipse.swt.SWT;

public class GroupExample extends Composite {

    final Button b1;
    final Button b2;
    final Button b3;

    public GroupExample(Composite c, int style)
    {
        super(c, SWT.NO_BACKGROUND );
        this.setSize(110, 75);
        this.setLayout(new FillLayout( ));
        final Group g = new Group(this, style);
        g.setSize(110, 75);
        g.setText("Options Group");
        b1 = new Button(g, SWT.RADIO);
        b1.setBounds(10,20,75, 15);
        b1.setText("Option One");
        b2 = new Button(g, SWT.RADIO);
        b2.setBounds(10,35,75, 15);
        b2.setText("Option Two");
        b3 = new Button(g, SWT.RADIO);
        b3.setBounds(10,50,80, 15);
        b3.setText("Option Three");
    }

    public String getSelected(){
        if(b1.getSelection( )) return "Option One";
        if(b2.getSelection( )) return "Option Two";
        if(b3.getSelection( )) return "Option Three";
        return "None Selected";
```

Example 10-4. Using a Group (continued)

```
      }
}
```

In this class, an instance of Group is created, and Button widgets are added and positioned to achieve the desired effect. The next step is to use the Composite subclass created in GroupExample in a Shell, as shown in Example 10-5.

Example 10-5. Using GroupExample in a Shell

```
import org.eclipse.swt.SWT;
import org.eclipse.swt.graphics.Image;
import org.eclipse.swt.widgets.*;

public class GroupShellExample {
    Display d;
    Shell s;
    GroupShellExample()     {
        d = new Display();
        s = new Shell(d);
        s.setSize(200,200);
        s.setImage(new Image(d, "c:\\icons\\JavaCup.ico"));
        s.setText("A Shell Composite Example");
        final GroupExample ge = new GroupExample(s, SWT.SHADOW_ETCHED_IN );
        ge.setLocation(20,20);
        s.open();
        while(!s.isDisposed()){
            if(!d.readAndDispatch())
                d.sleep();
        }
        d.dispose();
    }
}
```

If you create an instance of GroupShellExample from Example 10-5, it results in the display of Figure 10-2.

What just happened?

In this example, a descendant of Composite is created, to which a Group is added. To the Group are added three instances of Button of style SWT.RADIO.

The GroupExample constructor accepts a Composite, which will be the parent of this class, and an int, which will be passed through to the parent Group constructor to specify the style. The Composite is created with the forced style of SWT.NO_BACKGROUND, allowing the underlying Shell surface to show through.

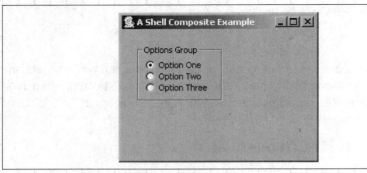

Figure 10-2. GroupShellExample

This is the best approach when the Group must be used in multiple Shell instances.

GroupExample also provides a helper method, getSelected( ), which is used to determine which of the buttons was selected. getSelected( ) is declared public so that it can be called from code within the class in which GroupExample is created.

In GroupShellExample, an instance of GroupExample is created:

```
final GroupExample ge = new GroupExample(s, SWT.SHADOW_ETCHED_IN );
```

The GroupExample constructor is passed a reference to the Shell and the desired style. It is then positioned within the Shell:

```
ge.setLocation(20,20);
```

The results are as shown in Figure 10-2.

What about...

creating a Group inside the Shell class? The approach taken in Example 10-5 is just one of many that can be taken when using the Group class. Although this Group was created in a Composite subclass, that is not always necessary. If, for example, your Group will have no application outside the current Shell, the overhead associated with creating a Composite is unnecessary. In that case, the Group can be created directly within the Shell, as in Example 10-6.

Example 10-6. Creating a Group inside the Shell class

```
import org.eclipse.swt.SWT;
import org.eclipse.swt.graphics.Image;
import org.eclipse.swt.widgets.*;

public class GroupShellExample {
    Display d;
    Shell s;
    GroupShellExample()    {
```

Example 10-6. Creating a Group inside the Shell class (continued)

```
        d = new Display( );
        s = new Shell(d);
        s.setSize(200,200);
        s.setImage(new Image(d, "c:\\icons\\JavaCup.ico"));
        s.setText("A Group Example");
        final Group g = new Group(s, SWT.SHADOW_ETCHED_IN);
        g.setSize(110, 75);
        g.setText("Options Group");
        final Button b1;
        final Button b2;
        final Button b3;
        b1 = new Button(g, SWT.RADIO);
        b1.setBounds(10,20,75, 15);
        b1.setText("Option One");
        b2 = new Button(g, SWT.RADIO);
        b2.setBounds(10,35,75, 15);
        b2.setText("Option Two");
        b3 = new Button(g, SWT.RADIO);
        b3.setBounds(10,50,80, 15);
        b3.setText("Option Three");
        g.pack( );
        g.setLocation(20,20);
        s.open( );
        while(!s.isDisposed( )){
            if(!d.readAndDispatch( ))
                d.sleep( );
        }
        d.dispose( );
    }
}
```

This is the best approach when the Group will not be used in multiple Shell instances.

This example creates the same window as Example 10-5; however, the need for the Composite subclass is eliminated.

Creating Multiple Instances of a Composite Subclass

Of course, the main reason for choosing to create a Group as part of a Composite subclass is that when you want to create multiple instances of the Group on the same window or to use the Group on multiple windows.

How do I do that?

Create an instance of the subclass for each time you wish it to appear, as shown in Example 10-7.

Example 10-7. Creating multiple instances of a Composite subclass

```java
import org.eclipse.swt.SWT;
import org.eclipse.swt.graphics.Image;
import org.eclipse.swt.widgets.*;

public class GroupShellExample {
    Display d;
    Shell s;
    GroupShellExample( )     {
        d = new Display( );
        s = new Shell(d);
        s.setSize(250,250);
        s.setImage(new Image(d, "c:\\icons\\JavaCup.ico"));
        s.setText("A Shell Composite Example");
        final GroupExample ge1 = new GroupExample(s, SWT.SHADOW_ETCHED_IN,
                            "Option Group One" );
        ge1.setLocation(10,10);
        final GroupExample ge2 = new GroupExample(s, SWT.SHADOW_ETCHED_IN,
                            "Option Group Two" );
        ge2.setLocation(100,100);
        s.open( );
        while(!s.isDisposed( )){
            if(!d.readAndDispatch( ))
                d.sleep( );
        }
        d.dispose( );
    }
}
```

Now, if you create an instance of GroupShellExample, from Example 10-7, you cause Figure 10-3 to be displayed.

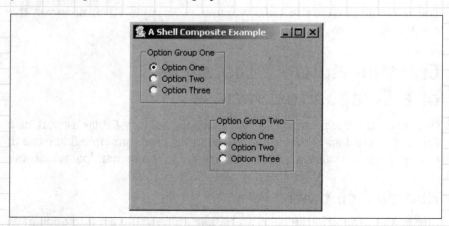

Figure 10-3. Reusing GroupExample

You can create as many instances of a Composite subclass as required for your interface.

Using Composites to Achieve Complex Designs

It is possible to use combinations of Composites or Groups together with layouts to your advantage when you need to construct more complex user interfaces than are possible with the single-container, single-layout approach. You can, for example, design a Shell that utilizes one type of layout and add to it Composite or Group objects that use a different type of layout. Using this combination approach, you can achieve almost any user interface design.

How do I do that?

Example 10-8 consists of three classes. The first is a Composite that makes use of RowLayout to display two SWT.PUSH-style Button objects:

Example 10-8. Using RowLayout on a Composite

```
import org.eclipse.swt.events.*;
import org.eclipse.swt.SWT;
import org.eclipse.swt.layout.RowLayout;
import org.eclipse.swt.widgets.*;

public class RowComposite extends Composite {

    final Button okBtn;
    final Button cancelBtn;

    public RowComposite(Composite c)
    {
        super(c, SWT.NO_FOCUS);
        RowLayout rl = new RowLayout( );
        rl.wrap = false;
        rl.pack = false;
        this.setLayout(rl);
        okBtn = new Button(this, SWT.BORDER | SWT.PUSH);
        okBtn.setText("OK");
        okBtn.setSize(30, 20);
        cancelBtn = new Button(this, SWT.BORDER | SWT.PUSH);
        cancelBtn.setText("Cancel");
        cancelBtn.setSize(30, 20);
        cancelBtn.addSelectionListener(new SelectionAdapter( ) {
            public void widgetSelected(SelectionEvent e) {
                System.out.println("Cancel was clicked");
            }
        });
    }
}
```

RowLayout is perfect for this composite, since the desired effect is that the Button objects be displayed side by side, in a row, and that they be aligned across the top of each button.

TIP

RowComposite also demonstrates how to handle event Listeners inside your Composite classes—exactly as you would attach a Listener to any other widget. The SWT will handle firing off the event to the proper handler.

The next class, in Example 10-9, is another Composite. This object uses GridLayout to create an effect similar to the GridExample program developed in Chapter 9:

Example 10-9. Using GridLayout on a Composite

```
import org.eclipse.swt.SWT;
import org.eclipse.swt.widgets.*;
import org.eclipse.swt.layout.*;

public class GridComposite extends Composite {

    public GridComposite(Composite c)
    {
        super(c, SWT.BORDER);
        GridLayout gl = new GridLayout();
        gl.numColumns=3;
        this.setLayout(gl);
        final Label l1 = new Label(this, SWT.BORDER);
        l1.setText("Column One");
        final Label l2 = new Label(this, SWT.BORDER);
        l2.setText("Column Two");
        final Label l3 = new Label(this, SWT.BORDER);
        l3.setText("Column Three");
        final Text t1 = new Text(this, SWT.SINGLE | SWT.BORDER);
        final Text t2 = new Text(this, SWT.SINGLE | SWT.BORDER);
        final Text t3 = new Text(this, SWT.SINGLE | SWT.BORDER);
        final Text t4 = new Text(this, SWT.SINGLE | SWT.BORDER);
        final Text t5 = new Text(this, SWT.SINGLE | SWT.BORDER);
        final Text t6 = new Text(this, SWT.SINGLE | SWT.BORDER);

        GridData gd = new GridData();
        gd.horizontalAlignment = GridData.CENTER;
        l1.setLayoutData(gd);

        gd = new GridData();
        gd.horizontalAlignment = GridData.CENTER;
        l2.setLayoutData(gd);
```

Example 10-9. Using GridLayout on a Composite (continued)

```
        gd = new GridData( );
        gd.horizontalAlignment = GridData.CENTER;
        l3.setLayoutData(gd);

        gd = new GridData(GridData.FILL_HORIZONTAL);
        t1.setLayoutData(gd);

        gd = new GridData(GridData.FILL_HORIZONTAL);
        t2.setLayoutData(gd);

        gd = new GridData(GridData.FILL_HORIZONTAL);
        t3.setLayoutData(gd);

        gd = new GridData(GridData.FILL_HORIZONTAL);
        t4.setLayoutData(gd);

        gd = new GridData(GridData.FILL_HORIZONTAL);
        t5.setLayoutData(gd);

        gd = new GridData(GridData.FILL_HORIZONTAL);
        t6.setLayoutData(gd);
    }

}
```

Finally, the two Composite classes can be used on a Shell to achieve a multi-layout design for the resulting window, as shown in Example 10-10.

Example 10-10. Using multiple layouts on a Shell

```
import org.eclipse.swt.graphics.Image;
import org.eclipse.swt.layout.*;
import org.eclipse.swt.widgets.*;

public class ComplexShellExample {
    Display d;
    Shell s;
    ComplexShellExample( )    {
        d = new Display( );
        s = new Shell(d);
        s.setSize(250,275);
        s.setImage(new Image(d, "c:\\icons\\JavaCup.ico"));
        s.setText("A Shell Composite Example");

        GridLayout gl = new GridLayout( );
        gl.numColumns=4;
        s.setLayout(gl);
        s.setLayout(gl);

        GridComposite gc = new GridComposite(s);
```

Example 10-10. Using multiple layouts on a Shell (continued)

```
            GridData gd = new GridData(GridData.FILL_BOTH);
            gd.horizontalSpan = 4;
            gc.setLayoutData(gd);
            gd = new GridData();

            RowComposite rc = new RowComposite(s);
            gd = new GridData(GridData.FILL_HORIZONTAL);
            rc.setLayoutData(gd);
            s.open();
            while(!s.isDisposed()){
                if(!d.readAndDispatch())
                    d.sleep();
            }
            d.dispose();
        }
}
```

This code yields Figure 10-4 when executed with your runner program.

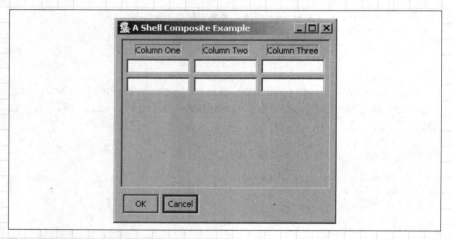

Figure 10-4. Complex layouts using Composites

An Alternate Approach

For any given design, there are usually multiple approaches that will achieve the desired effect (or come close). For example, it's possible to rewrite the code from the ComplexShellExample to utilize one less class and achieve a slightly different object alignment.

How do I do that?

The version of `ComplexShellExample` created by Example 10-11 eliminates the `RowComposite` class in favor of placing the `Button` widgets in a `Composite` created directly on the `Shell`.

Example 10-11. An alternate method for using multiple layouts—inline coding of Composites

```
import org.eclipse.swt.SWT;
import org.eclipse.swt.graphics.Image;
import org.eclipse.swt.layout.*;
import org.eclipse.swt.widgets.*;

public class CompositeShellExample {
    Display d;
    Shell s;
    CompositeShellExample()    {
        d = new Display();
        s = new Shell(d);
        GridLayout gl = new GridLayout();
        gl.numColumns=4;
        s.setLayout(gl);
        s.setSize(250,275);
        s.setImage(new Image(d, "c:\\icons\\JavaCup.ico"));
        s.setText("A Shell Composite Example");
        s.setLayout(gl);
        GridComposite gc = new GridComposite(s);
        GridData gd = new GridData(GridData.FILL_BOTH);
        gd.horizontalSpan = 4;
        gc.setLayoutData(gd);
        gd = new GridData();

        Composite c1 = new Composite(s, SWT.NO_FOCUS);
        gd = new GridData(GridData.FILL_HORIZONTAL);
        c1.setLayoutData(gd);
        Composite c2 = new Composite(s, SWT.NO_FOCUS);
        gd = new GridData(GridData.FILL_HORIZONTAL);
        c2.setLayoutData(gd);

        Composite c = new Composite(s, SWT.NO_FOCUS);
        c.setLayout(new RowLayout());
        Button b1 = new Button(c, SWT.PUSH | SWT.BORDER);
        b1.setText("OK");
        Button b2 = new Button(c, SWT.PUSH | SWT.BORDER);
        b2.setText("Cancel");
        gd = new GridData(GridData.FILL_HORIZONTAL);
        c.setLayoutData(gd);

        s.open();
        while(!s.isDisposed()){
            if(!d.readAndDispatch())
                d.sleep();
```

Example 10-11. *An alternate method for using multiple layouts—inline coding of Composites (continued)*

```
        }
        d.dispose();
    }
}
```

Although you're still using the GridComposite, as in the previous example, the instance of RowComposite has been removed. Instead, an "inline" Composite is created—one where an instance of Composite is created within the class that creates the Shell. Widgets are then added to that Composite. This approach works when you don't plan on reusing the Composite in another Shell.

The ComplexShellExample, from Example 10-11, demonstrates another technique—using empty Composite objects to fill in blank areas of a GridLayout. The results are displayed in Figure 10-5.

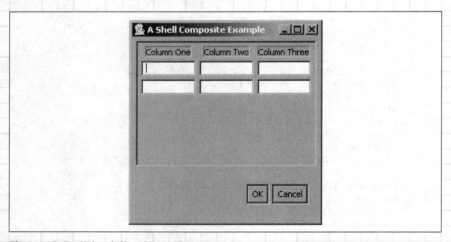

Figure 10-5. *Using inline Composites*

As you see, any look and feel can be created using Composites and layouts. As a fallback, you can always directly position widgets within your Shell, Composite, and Group objects using setBounds().

CHAPTER 11

SWT Tabbed Folders

A very common user interface construct is one in which a window is divided using a notebook format, with tabs allowing easy access to widgets on each page of the notebook. This construct is usually referred to as a *tabbed folder interface*. The SWT provides classes that make developing such an interface a simple task. The two classes used for this purpose are TabFolder and TabItem, both from the org.eclipse.swt.widgets package.

An example of a tabbed interface is shown in Figure 11-1.

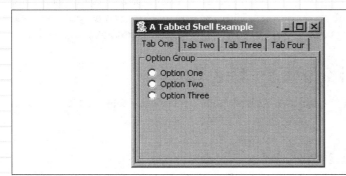

Figure 11-1. A simple tabbed interface

Clicking each tab reveals a separate page of the notebook, each with its own set of widgets.

Creating an Instance of TabFolder

First, create an instance of the TabFolder class that will act as a container for the tabs.

How do I do that?

Create an instance of TabFolder just as you do any other widget:

```
TabFolder tf = new TabFolder(s, SWT.NONE);
```

The TabFolder is added to another container class—either a Composite or a Shell. In the preceding code, it has been added to a Shell object (s). TabFolder has no styles intrinsic to itself, but you must still pass in a placeholder for a style. SWT.NONE is used for this purpose.

Creating the Individual Tabs

Each individual tab is represented by an instance of the TabItem class. You create a new instance of TabItem for each folder and add it to the TabFolder instance previously created.

How do I do that?

Adding tabs is a matter of creating an instance of the TabItem class:

```
TabItem ti1 = new TabItem(tf, SWT.NONE);
ti1.setText("Tab One");
```

The first parameter passed to the TabItem constructor is a reference to the TabFolder that will hold the tabs. Like TabFolder, TabItem accepts no style attributes, so SWT.NONE is again used to placehold the second parameter.

Adding Widgets to the Tabs

The final step in creating a tabbed folder interface is to add controls to the tab pages.

How do I do that?

Use setControl( )to add a control to a tab page:

```
ti1.setControl(new GroupExample(tf, SWT.SHADOW_ETCHED_IN, "Option Group"));
```

Each TabItem page can be assigned only one control. This means that you almost certainly will create a Composite for each page, add widgets to that Composite to achieve the desired user interface, and then add the Composite to the page.

Creating a Complete Tabbed Folder Example

A good way to learn how to work with tab folders is to create a simple example, using multiple techniques to create each TabItem page.

How do I do that?

Let's look at an example that displays controls on every page, using multiple techniques to create each page. Consider Example 11-1.

Example 11-1. A complete TabFolder Example

```
import org.eclipse.swt.SWT;
import org.eclipse.swt.layout.*;
import org.eclipse.swt.graphics.Image;
import org.eclipse.swt.widgets.*;

public class TabbedShellExample {

    Display d;
    Shell s;
    TabbedShellExample( )    {
        d = new Display( );
        s = new Shell(d);

        s.setSize(250,200);
        s.setImage(new Image(d, "c:\\icons\\JavaCup.ico"));
        s.setText("A Tabbed Shell Example");
        s.setLayout(new FillLayout( ));

        TabFolder tf = new TabFolder(s, SWT.BORDER);

        TabItem ti1 = new TabItem(tf, SWT.BORDER);
        ti1.setText("Option Group");
        ti1.setControl(new GroupExample(tf, SWT.SHADOW_ETCHED_IN,
          "Option Group"));
```

Example 11-1. A complete TabFolder Example (continued)

```
TabItem ti2 = new TabItem(tf, SWT.BORDER);
ti2.setText("Grid");
ti2.setControl(new GridComposite(tf));

TabItem ti3 = new TabItem(tf, SWT.BORDER);
ti3.setText("Text");
Composite c1 = new Composite(tf, SWT.BORDER);
c1.setLayout(new FillLayout());
Text t = new Text(c1, SWT.BORDER | SWT.MULTI | SWT.WRAP | SWT.V_SCROLL);
ti3.setControl(c1);

TabItem ti4 = new TabItem(tf, SWT.BORDER);
ti4.setText("Settings");
Composite c2 = new Composite(tf, SWT.BORDER);
c2.setLayout(new RowLayout());
Text t2 = new Text(c2, SWT.BORDER | SWT.SINGLE |
  SWT.WRAP | SWT.V_SCROLL);
Button b = new Button(c2, SWT.PUSH |SWT.BORDER);
b.setText("Save");
ti4.setControl(c2);

s.open();
while(!s.isDisposed()){
    if(!d.readAndDispatch())
        d.sleep();
}
d.dispose();
    }
}
```

This creates the set of tabs shown in Figures 11-2 through 11-4.

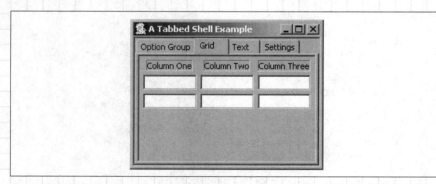

Figure 11-2. A grid Composite on a tab

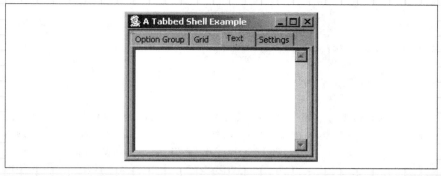

Figure 11-3. An inline Composite with a Text widget

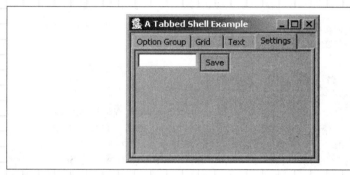

Figure 11-4. AAn inline Composite with multiple widgets

What just happened?

The controls that are added to TabItem ti1 and ti2 are instances of the GroupExample and GridExample from earlier chapters. Each is created and added using a single line of code:

```
ti1.setControl(new GroupExample(tf, SWT.SHADOW_ETCHED_IN, "Option Group"));

ti2.setControl(new GridComposite(tf));
```

This demonstrates the standard technique of creating a Composite subclass, adding widgets to that class, then using the subclass on a TabItem. However, you can use another technique, as illustrated by the creation of ti3 and ti4:

```
TabItem ti3 = new TabItem(tf, SWT.BORDER);
ti3.setText("Text");
Composite c1 = new Composite(tf, SWT.BORDER);
c1.setLayout(new FillLayout());
Text t = new Text(c1, SWT.BORDER | SWT.MULTI | SWT.WRAP | SWT.V_SCROLL);
ti3.setControl(c1);
```

```
TabItem ti4 = new TabItem(tf, SWT.BORDER);
ti4.setText("Settings");
Composite c2 = new Composite(tf, SWT.BORDER);
c2.setLayout(new RowLayout( ));
Text t2 = new Text(c2, SWT.BORDER | SWT.SINGLE | SWT.WRAP | SWT.V_SCROLL);
Button b = new Button(c2, SWT.PUSH |SWT.BORDER);
b.setText("Save");
ti4.setControl(c2);
```

For tab pages ti3 and ti4, an "inline" Composite is being used. Recall that an inline Composite is one created on the fly inside the same class that creates an instance of Shell. For each, you create an instance of Composite, then set its layout as appropriate and add widgets. When the Composite is configured as desired, call setControl( ) to bind it to a tab page, just as if that Composite were created in a separate class.

As you can see, this approach is quite flexible and creates a professional-quality user interface.

Setting a Default Tab

Since the SWT does a good job of hiding the inner workings of the tab folder and tab pages, handling the task of making controls visible and invisible as the user navigates the tabs, you won't frequently use many methods on TabFolder. The ones that are useful deal with determining which tab page is selected. As you might guess, there are methods that enable you to force a tab page to the front without the user having clicked the tab, while other methods that enable you to determine which page currently has the focus.

How do I do that?

To force a tab to the front, add the following:

```
tf.setSelection(1);
```

This results in the second tab (tabs are zero-indexed) coming to the front.

To determine which tab is currently selected:

```
tf.getSelectionIndex( );
```

To set a default, just force a tab to the front when the window is first displayed.

Tabs are a wonderful way to spruce up your user interface. Most applications today make liberal use of this construct. Fortunately, SWT makes creating tabbed folders a snap.

CHAPTER 12

SWT Tables

Chapter 9 introduced the GridLayout as a method of designing user interfaces in which data was displayed in tables. Although GridLayout can be used to perform this task, the SWT provides a simpler mechanism for displaying data in tabular format—the SWT Table class, part of the org. eclipse.swt.widgets package. A simple table is shown in Figure 12-1.

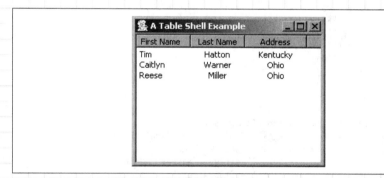

Figure 12-1. A simple table

Creating a Simple Table

The first step in creating a table such as the one shown in Figure 12-1 is to create an instance of the Table class, passing it the parent container and any style attributes. To that object, add instances of the TableColumn class that represent the columns you wish to appear in your table.

How do I do that?

The code to create a Table looks complex, but for the simple table shown in Figure 12-1, it's straightforward, as shown in Example 12-1.

Example 12-1. Creating a simple table

```
import org.eclipse.swt.SWT;
import org.eclipse.swt.layout.*;
import org.eclipse.swt.graphics.Image;
import org.eclipse.swt.widgets.*;

public class TableShellExample {

    Display d;
    Shell s;
    TableShellExample()    {
        d = new Display();
        s = new Shell(d);

        s.setSize(250,200);
        s.setImage(new Image(d, "c:\\icons\\JavaCup.ico"));
        s.setText("A Table Shell Example");
        s.setLayout(new FillLayout());

        Table t = new Table(s, SWT.BORDER);

        TableColumn tc1 = new TableColumn(t, SWT.CENTER);
        TableColumn tc2 = new TableColumn(t, SWT.CENTER);
        TableColumn tc3 = new TableColumn(t, SWT.CENTER);
        tc1.setText("First Name");
        tc2.setText("Last Name");
        tc3.setText("Address");
        tc1.setWidth(70);
        tc2.setWidth(70);
        tc3.setWidth(80);
        t.setHeaderVisible(true);

        TableItem item1 = new TableItem(t,SWT.NONE);
        item1.setText(new String[] {"Tim","Hatton","Kentucky"});
        TableItem item2 = new TableItem(t,SWT.NONE);
        item2.setText(new String[] {"Caitlyn","Warner","Ohio"});
        TableItem item3 = new TableItem(t,SWT.NONE);
        item3.setText(new String[] {"Reese","Miller","Ohio"});

        s.open();
        while(!s.isDisposed()){
            if(!d.readAndDispatch())
                d.sleep();
        }
        d.dispose();
    }
}
```

What just happened?

When the code required to create the table in Example 12-1 is broken into segments, it is easy to understand. The first segment creates the Table object:

```
Table t = new Table(s, SWT.BORDER);
```

As you see, this is nothing more than creating an instance of the Table class and passing it a reference to the parent container and a style attribute—a task you have performed with every widget type throughout this book.

The next code segment is used to create and configure the columns that the table is to contain:

```
TableColumn tc1 = new TableColumn(t, SWT.CENTER);
TableColumn tc2 = new TableColumn(t, SWT.CENTER);
TableColumn tc3 = new TableColumn(t, SWT.CENTER);
tc1.setText("First Name");
tc2.setText("Last Name");
tc3.setText("Address");
tc1.setWidth(70);
tc2.setWidth(70);
tc3.setWidth(80);
t.setHeaderVisible(true);
```

Three steps are required to create table columns:

1. Create an instance of the TableColumn class for each column.

2. Set the header text for each column (if headers are to be shown) using the setText( ) method.

3. Set the width of the column using the setWidth( ) method.

To create an instance of TableColumn, pass the constructor a reference to the Table object that is to contain the column and the desired style of the column:

```
TableColumn tc1 = new TableColumn(t, SWT.CENTER);
```

The TableColumn class supports three styles:

- SWT.CENTER
- SWT.RIGHT
- SWT.LEFT

These styles determine how text is displayed in each column.

To set the header text that will appear for the column, use the setText( ) method:

```
tc1.setText("First Name");
```

There doesn't appear to be any approach that permits you to create a column in which the header is SWT.CENTER and the items added to the column are SWT.RIGHT or SWT.LEFT. It's an all or nothing proposition.

Specify the width of the TableColumn using the setWidth() method:

```
tc1.setWidth(70);
```

TIP

The width is specified in pixels rather than number of characters.

The next task is to add your data to the table. Table data is represented by instances of the TableItem class:

```
TableItem item1 = new TableItem(t,SWT.NONE);
item1.setText(new String[] {"Tim","Hatton","Kentucky"});
TableItem item2 = new TableItem(t,SWT.NONE);
item2.setText(new String[] {"Caitlyn","Warner","Ohio"});
TableItem item3 = new TableItem(t,SWT.NONE);
item3.setText(new String[] {"Reese","Miller","Ohio"});
```

Each TableItem object represents a single row of the table and must contain a value for every column in the row. Data is passed to the TableItem in a String array.

Even the most complex tables, those with many columns, are developed using the techniques shown by this example.

What about...

the column headers and grid lines? They can be made visible or invisible with a single method call each. For column headers:

```
t.setHeaderVisible(true);
```

Displaying grid lines is easily accomplished by:

```
t.setLinesVisible(true);
```

The result of adding this line to the example is shown in Figure 12-2.

Grid lines and column headers enable you to change the appearance of the table, perhaps to mimic a spreadsheet.

Highlighting Rows upon Selection

When you execute the example and click a cell, you see that the cell becomes selected.

You also see that the text in that column is highlighted, but is not editable. To create an editable table, you must resort to developing your own code, likely using a Composite and GridLayout. For now, Table is read-only.

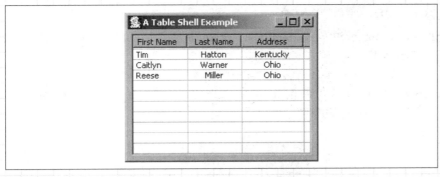

Figure 12-2. Showing grid lines

It is more common to give the user a visual indication that an entire row is selected, by causing the highlight bar to extend across all columns in the row when any column in the row has been clicked.

How do I do that?

To highlight an entire row in the Table when the user clicks any column in the row, you use the SWT.FULL_SELECTION style:

```
Table t = new Table(s, SWT.BORDER | SWT.FULL_SELECTION);
```

The result of this change is shown in Figure 12-3.

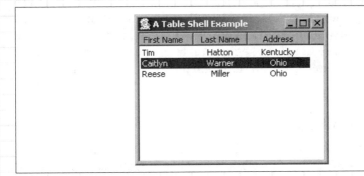

Figure 12-3. FULL_SELECTION table

Allowing Multiple-Row Selection

The Table default is to allow only one row to be selected at a time. This is equivalent to a setting of SWT.SINGLE. To allow more than one row to be selected, you must use the SWT.MULTI style.

How do I do that?

To allow for multiple selection of rows, add SWT.MULTI to the styles list passed to the Table constructor:

```
Table t = new Table(s, SWT.BORDER | SWT.MULTI | SWT.FULL_SELECTION);
```

The result of this change is shown in Figure 12-4, when the user has selected more than one row.

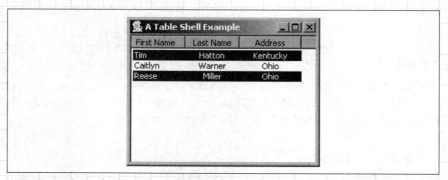

Figure 12-4. Multiple-selection table

Selecting Items Programmatically

Of course, if table items are selectable, there must be a way to programmatically determine which item is selected, or to cause it to be selected without user intervention. For example, when a Table is first displayed, no items are selected but it is often desirable to cause the table to open with the first item highlighted, or to highlight some other item based on program conditions.

How do I do that?

When it comes to working with selected items, Table generally works like lists, and as with the List class, a number of methods are provided that enable you to perform this task.

The getSelection() method will return an array of TableItem objects that are currently selected:

```
TableItems[] t = t.getSelection();
```

This is particularly useful if the table is of the multiple-selection type, since it enables you to get all selected items in a single method call.

Also, for multiple-selection tables, getSelectionIndices() returns an array of int values that specify which TableItems are selected, based on a zero index:

```
int[] selected = t.getSelectionIndices();
```

Calling getSelectionIndices() against a table in the state shown in Figure 12-4 will return 0 and 2 in the int array.

For single-selection tables, you can use getSelectionIndex() to return the index of the currently selected item:

```
int selected = t.getSelectedIndex();
```

Once you have a reference to the item that is selected, you can perform other tasks such as getting values from particular columns. A later section will examine those techniques.

The CHECK Style

The SWT.CHECK style places a checkbox at the beginning of each table item, as in Figure 12-5.

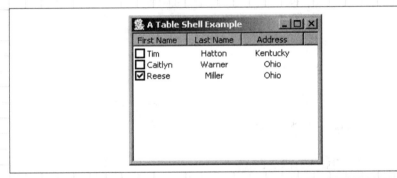

This is another way to allow multiple selection, only without the entire row being highlighted.

Figure 12-5. CHECK-style table

If you use the SWT.CHECK style, you often need to determine or set the state of the checkbox.

How do I do that?

Two methods are provided that allow interaction with the state of the checkbox on a TableItem. These methods follow the familiar JavaBeans get and set pattern.

setChecked() is used to cause the item to become checked:

```
item3.setChecked(true);
```

getChecked( ) is then used to determine the current state of the item:

```
boolean checked = item3.getChecked();
```

Changing the Background Color

A useful technique that enables you to visually delimit data in a table is to change the background color of a TableItem.

How do I do that?

Use setBackground( ) to specify the background color of an individual TableItem:

```
item2.setBackground(new Color(d,127,178,127));
```

Adding this code to the Example 12-1 class results in Figure 12-6.

Figure 12-6. Setting the background color

What just happened?

setBackground( ) accepts a Color object created by passing a reference to the Display in which the table is being managed, as well as three int values representing the Red, Green, and Blue values of the desired color.

This technique is useful in creating alternating "bar paper" looks that visually separate rows of data (the Quicken check register program is an example that uses this technique).

What about...

the times you want to cause a row to be highlighted if a cell in that row contains a particular value? Using the table from TableShellExample as a basis, the following code will cause all rows in which the Address column contains the word "Ohio" to be highlighted by changing the background color to green:

```
TableItem[] tia = t.getItems();

for(int i = 0; i<tia.length;i++)
{
    if (tia[i].getText(2).equals("Ohio"))
    {
        tia[i].setBackground(new Color(d,127,178,127));
    }
}
```

The preceding code retrieves an array of items from the table and then loops through the array. For every item in which the value of the third column is "Ohio," the code calls setBackground() against the current TableItem to set the background color to green, as shown in Figure 12-7.

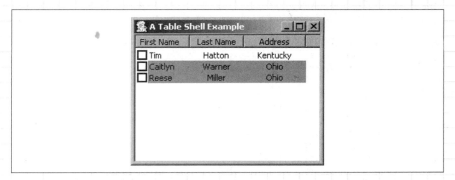

Figure 12-7. Setting the background color for matching records

Creating a Searchable Table

Although the Table class has a built-in ability to find items by typing the first character of the text in a cell, this falls far short of providing a full searchable table. Some interface designs call for the ability of the user to specify search text (using a text field) and have the table searched for matching items (perhaps by clicking a button). Providing this functionality for your users is fairly easy.

How do I do that?

This version of TableShellExample, shown in Example 12-2, adds in the ability to search a table based upon user-supplied search text.

Example 12-2. A searchable table

```java
import org.eclipse.swt.SWT;
import org.eclipse.swt.layout.*;
import org.eclipse.swt.events.SelectionAdapter;
import org.eclipse.swt.events.SelectionEvent;
import org.eclipse.swt.graphics.Color;
import org.eclipse.swt.graphics.Image;
import org.eclipse.swt.widgets.*;

public class TableShellExample {

    Display d;
    Shell s;
    TableShellExample()    {
        d = new Display();
        s = new Shell(d);

        s.setSize(250,200);
        s.setImage(new Image(d, "c:\\icons\\JavaCup.ico"));
        s.setText("A Table Shell Example");
        GridLayout gl = new GridLayout();
        gl.numColumns = 2;
        s.setLayout(gl);

        final Table t = new Table(s, SWT.BORDER | SWT.CHECK |
            SWT.MULTI | SWT.FULL_SELECTION);
        final GridData gd = new GridData(GridData.FILL_BOTH);
        gd.horizontalSpan = 2;
        t.setLayoutData(gd);
        t.setHeaderVisible(true);
        final TableColumn tc1 = new TableColumn(t, SWT.LEFT);
        final TableColumn tc2 = new TableColumn(t, SWT.CENTER);
        final TableColumn tc3 = new TableColumn(t, SWT.CENTER);
        tc1.setText("First Name");
        tc2.setText("Last Name");
        tc3.setText("Address");
        tc1.setWidth(70);
        tc2.setWidth(70);
        tc3.setWidth(80);
        final TableItem item1 = new TableItem(t,SWT.NONE);
        item1.setText(new String[] {"Tim","Hatton","Kentucky"});
        final TableItem item2 = new TableItem(t,SWT.NONE);
        item2.setText(new String[] {"Caitlyn","Warner","Ohio"});
        final TableItem item3 = new TableItem(t,SWT.NONE);
        item3.setText(new String[] {"Reese","Miller","Ohio"});

        final Text input = new Text(s, SWT.SINGLE | SWT.BORDER);
        final Button searchBtn = new Button(s, SWT.BORDER | SWT.PUSH);
        searchBtn.setText("Search");
        searchBtn.addSelectionListener(new SelectionAdapter() {
            public void widgetSelected(SelectionEvent e) {
                TableItem[] tia = t.getItems();
```

Example 12-2. A searchable table (continued)

```
            for(int i = 0; i<tia.length;i++)
            {
                if (tia[i].getText(2).equals(find.getText()))
                {
                    tia[i].setBackground(new Color(d,127,178,127));
                }

            }
        }
    });

    s.open();
    while(!s.isDisposed()){
        if(!d.readAndDispatch())
            d.sleep();
    }
    d.dispose();
    }
}
```

Figure 12-8 results from execution of the new example. When you enter the word "Ohio" in the text field and click Search, the appropriate rows become highlighted.

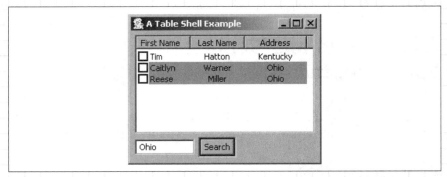

This is pretty neat functionality to provide your users.

Figure 12-8. Implementing search in a table

Setting the Background of a Single Cell

It's also possible to set the background color for only a single cell in a column. This technique is useful for highlighting cells when they contain certain values (such as number ranges).

How do I do that?

To change the background color of a single cell only, use a version of setBackground( ) that accepts a new parameter in the first position. This int value specifies the zero-indexed number of the column that will receive the new background:

```
item3.setBackground(0, new Color(d,127,178,127));
```

Adding this line of code changes the background of the first column in the third row to green, as shown in Figure 12-9.

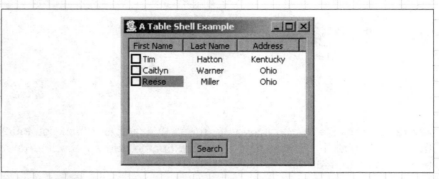

Figure 12-9. Setting background color for a single cell

Although TableItem cells are not editable, you can allow the user to change data in a cell simply by providing a text field for the entry of data. In fact, this is the approach taken by many spreadsheet programs.

Adding Find-and-Replace Functionality

It is also possible to interact with the text in a TableItem using the getText( ) and setText( ) methods. One such use of setText( ) and getText( ) is to build a find-and-replace capability into your tables.

How do I do that?

Example 12-3 incorporates find-and-replace functionality into the TableShellExample.

Example 12-3. A Table with find-and-replace

```
import org.eclipse.swt.SWT;
import org.eclipse.swt.layout.*;
import org.eclipse.swt.events.SelectionAdapter;
import org.eclipse.swt.events.SelectionEvent;
import org.eclipse.swt.graphics.Color;
import org.eclipse.swt.graphics.Image;
import org.eclipse.swt.widgets.*;
```

Example 12-3. A Table with find-and-replace (continued)

```java
public class TableShellExample {

    Display d;
    Shell s;
    TableShellExample()    {
        d = new Display();
        s = new Shell(d);

        s.setSize(250,200);
        s.setImage(new Image(d, "c:\\icons\\JavaCup.ico"));
        s.setText("A Table Shell Example");
        GridLayout gl = new GridLayout();
        gl.numColumns = 4;
        s.setLayout(gl);

        final Table t = new Table(s, SWT.BORDER | SWT.CHECK |
            SWT.MULTI | SWT.FULL_SELECTION);
        final GridData gd = new GridData(GridData.FILL_BOTH);
        gd.horizontalSpan = 4;
        t.setLayoutData(gd);
        t.setHeaderVisible(true);
        final TableColumn tc1 = new TableColumn(t, SWT.LEFT);
        final TableColumn tc2 = new TableColumn(t, SWT.CENTER);
        final TableColumn tc3 = new TableColumn(t, SWT.CENTER);
        tc1.setText("First Name");
        tc2.setText("Last Name");
        tc3.setText("Address");
        tc1.setWidth(70);
        tc2.setWidth(70);
        tc3.setWidth(80);
        final TableItem item1 = new TableItem(t,SWT.NONE);
        item1.setText(new String[] {"Tim","Hatton","Kentucky"});
        final TableItem item2 = new TableItem(t,SWT.NONE);
        item2.setText(new String[] {"Caitlyn","Warner","Ohio"});
        final TableItem item3 = new TableItem(t,SWT.NONE);
        item3.setText(new String[] {"Reese","Miller","Ohio"});

        final Text find = new Text(s, SWT.SINGLE | SWT.BORDER);
        final Text replace = new Text(s, SWT.SINGLE | SWT.BORDER);
        final Button replaceBtn = new Button(s, SWT.BORDER | SWT.PUSH);
        replaceBtn.setText("Replace");
        replaceBtn.addSelectionListener(new SelectionAdapter() {
            public void widgetSelected(SelectionEvent e) {
                TableItem[] tia = t.getItems();

                for(int i = 0; i<tia.length;i++)
                {
                    if (tia[i].getText(2).equals(find.getText()))
                    {
                        tia[i].setText(2, replace.getText());
                    }
```

Example 12-3. A Table with find-and-replace (continued)

```
            }
        }
    });

    s.open();
    while(!s.isDisposed()){
        if(!d.readAndDispatch())
            d.sleep();
    }
    d.dispose();
    }
}
```

What just happened?

When first executed, this code results in Figure 12-10.

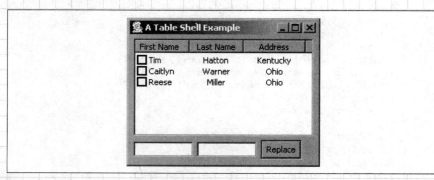

Figure 12-10. Adding find-and-replace

If you enter "Kentucky" in the first field and "Ohio" in the second, then click Replace, Figure 12-11 results, demonstrating find-and-replace functionality.

The relevant code is all in the widgetSelected() method of the SelectionListener attached to replaceBtn:

```
public void widgetSelected(SelectionEvent e) {
    TableItem[] tia = t.getItems();

    for(int i = 0; i<tia.length;i++)
    {
        if (tia[i].getText(2).equals(find.getText()))
        {
            tia[i].setText(2, replace.getText());
        }
    }
}
```

Figure 12-11. After replacing text

The code first calls getItems() to return an array of all items in the Table, and then loops through that array looking for a match to the value entered in the text field:

```
if (tia[i].getText(2).equals(find.getText()))
```

If a match is found, the new value is substituted for the old:

```
tia[i].setText(2, replace.getText());
```

What about...

the times when you want to replace an entire row in a table with new values? There is a version of setText() that accepts an array of String objects. Each element of the array is used to replace a single cell in the TableItem against which setText() is called:

```
String[] newText = {"Nikki","Miller","Ohio"};
item2.setText(newText);
```

As you have seen, tables can be quite useful and flexible when it is appropriate to display data in tabular format. tables would be even more useful if the user were permitted to edit the values in the cells. Perhaps that will be included in a future version.

CHAPTER 13

SWT Trees

Since the early days of the GUI a common element of interface design has been to present hierarchical information in a *tree* format. The grand-father of these interface types is the old Windows File Manager, which has evolved into Windows Explorer in today's versions of Windows. Even Unix-based systems recognize the necessity for providing a tree control.

The SWT contains a set of classes that assist in the development of tree interfaces. These classes are part of the org.eclipse.swt.widgets pack-age. The two classes examined in this chapter are Tree and TreeItem. The Tree class represents the trunk of the tree, to which other items will be attached. TreeItem objects represent individual items (branches) of the tree.

Creating the Tree

The trunk of the tree is represented by the Tree class. To begin program-ming a tree interface, you must create an instance of the Tree class and add it to your Shell or Composite.

How do I do that?

You create the Tree object and add it to a Shell in the same manner as any other widget:

```
Tree t = new Tree(s, SWT.SINGLE | SWT.BORDER);
```

In addition to the common widget styles such as SWT.BORDER, the Tree class supports three additional styles. These are:

- SWT.SINGLE
- SWT.MULTI
- SWT.CHECK

The preceding line of code creates a Tree that supports single selection of items. Later examples examine the SWT.MULTI and SWT.CHECK tree styles.

Adding Items to the Tree

Items within the tree are represented by instances of the TreeItem class. You must create one TreeItem object for each item you wish to add to the tree.

How do I do that?

To attach an item directly to the trunk of the tree, you pass the TreeItem constructor the reference to the Tree object you have created, along with a style and the position in which you want the item to appear:

```
TreeItem child1 = new TreeItem(t, SWT.NONE, 0);
child1.setText("1");
TreeItem child2 = new TreeItem(t, SWT.NONE, 1);
child2.setText("2");
TreeItem child3 = new TreeItem(t, SWT.NONE, 2);
child3.setText("3");
```

This code creates three items, all directly attached to the trunk of the Tree.

Adding Items to Other Items

If you think of the Windows Explorer interface as the design you are mimicking, you know that there are two types of items—those attached directly to the tree and those that appear beneath other items when the higher-level items are expanded. These subitems in the tree hierarchy are created with additional TreeItem objects that are attached to the higher-level TreeItem that serves as the parent.

How do I do that?

To create items that are children of another item, pass the TreeItem constructor a reference to the TreeItem that you wish to serve as the parent item, a style, and the position in which you want the child item to appear:

```
TreeItem child2a = new TreeItem(child2, SWT.NONE, 0);
child2a.setText("2A");
TreeItem child2b = new TreeItem(child2, SWT.NONE, 0);
child2b.setText("2B");
```

Creating a Full Tree Example

Using the preceding techniques, it's possible to create an example of a Tree placed on a Shell and populated with a few items.

How do I do that?

Example 13-1 demonstrates the creation of a complete Tree.

Example 13-1. Creating a simple tree

```
import org.eclipse.swt.SWT;
import org.eclipse.swt.layout.*;
import org.eclipse.swt.events.*;
import org.eclipse.swt.graphics.Image;
import org.eclipse.swt.widgets.*;

public class TreeShellExample {
        Display d;
        Shell s;
        TreeShellExample()    {
            d = new Display();
            s = new Shell(d);

            s.setSize(250,200);
            s.setImage(new Image(d, "c:\\icons\\JavaCup.ico"));
            s.setText("A Table Shell Example");
            s.setLayout(new FillLayout());
            Tree t = new Tree(s, SWT.SINGLE | SWT.BORDER);
            TreeItem child1 = new TreeItem(t, SWT.NONE, 0);
            child1.setText("1");
            TreeItem child2 = new TreeItem(t, SWT.NONE, 1);
            child2.setText("2");
            TreeItem child2a = new TreeItem(child2, SWT.NONE, 0);
            child2a.setText("2A");
            TreeItem child2b = new TreeItem(child2, SWT.NONE, 1);
            child2b.setText("2B");
            TreeItem child3 = new TreeItem(t, SWT.NONE, 2);
            child3.setText("3");
            s.open();
            while(!s.isDisposed()){
                if(!d.readAndDispatch())
                    d.sleep();
            }
            d.dispose();
        }
}
```

What just happened?

Example 13-1 creates the simple tree shown in Figure 13-1, consisting of three items attached directly to the Tree.

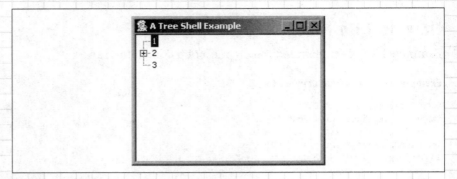

Figure 13-1. Tree example

Since item 2 has two children added to it, you see a + mark. Clicking that mark will expand 2 to show its children, as shown in Figure 13-2.

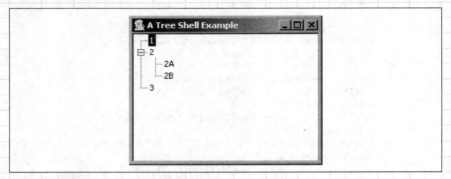

Figure 13-2. Expanded tree with children

The code used to create this Tree is simple. First, the Tree object itself is constructed:

```
Tree t = new Tree(s, SWT.SINGLE | SWT.BORDER);
```

This creates a Tree that permits single selection of items, with a border.

Next, TreeItem objects are created to serve as the highest-level items attached directly to the Tree:

```
TreeItem child1 = new TreeItem(t, SWT.NONE, 0);
child1.setText("1");
TreeItem child2 = new TreeItem(t, SWT.NONE, 1);
child2.setText("2");
TreeItem child3 = new TreeItem(t, SWT.NONE, 2);
child3.setText("3");
```

These items are given the text labels 1, 2, and 3.

Finally, TreeItem objects are created and attached to child2 to create the subitems that are visible when item 2 is expanded:

```
TreeItem child2a = new TreeItem(child2, SWT.NONE, 0);
child2a.setText("2A");
TreeItem child2b = new TreeItem(child2, SWT.NONE, 1);
child2b.setText("2B");
```

These items are given the text labels 2A and 2B.

This example demonstrates everything you need to know about creating Tree objects. No matter how complex or how many layers, creating a Tree is just a matter of repeating this basic code.

Using Images with TreeItem

Most Trees will use an image to show the user the type of item that is represented by an item in the tree. Windows Explorer, for example, uses a closed folder to represent folders that are closed and an open folder to represent the folder that is currently open. Some file management systems that use trees will show files at the lowest level of the tree and will use an icon that depicts the file type to the user.

You want to use an image in almost all cases. It just looks better than the default tree. To the user, looks are everything.

How do I do that?

An image can be associated with a TreeItem by using setImage( ):

```
child1.setImage(new Image(d, "c:\\icons\\folder.gif"));
child2.setImage(new Image(d, "c:\\icons\\folder.gif"));
child3.setImage(new Image(d, "c:\\icons\\folder.gif"));
```

If you add the preceding lines to the example you get the results shown in Figure 13-3.

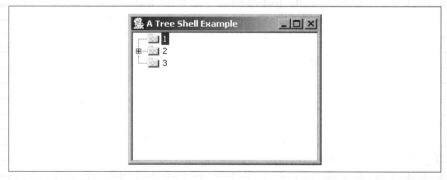

Figure 13-3. Using images with TreeItem

Changing the Image When the Item Is Expanded

Of course, to mimic Windows Explorer you need to change the image when an item with children is expanded: the "Closed" folder should be displayed when the tree is collapsed and the "Open" folder displayed when the tree is expanded.

How do I do that?

To use an image with a collapsed node that's different from images used with expanded nodes, you need a mechanism to determine the state of the item. You must also capture the event that occurs when the item changes state. Fortunately, the SWT provides a listener type designed specially for these events—the TreeListener.

Consider the following code:

```
t.addTreeListener(new TreeListener() {
    public void treeExpanded(TreeEvent e) {
        TreeItem ti = (TreeItem)e.item;
        ti.setImage(new Image(d, "c:\\icons\\open.gif"));
    }

    public void treeCollapsed(TreeEvent e) {
        TreeItem ti = (TreeItem)e.item;
        ti.setImage(new Image(d, "c:\\icons\\folder.gif"));
    }
});
```

If you add this code to Example 13-1, it results in the display of Figure 13-4, shown after item 2 has been expanded:

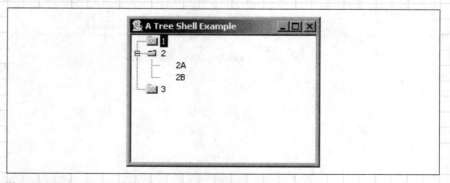

Figure 13-4. Using a different image for expanded items

What just happened?

The example now includes a TreeListener to respond to the event that occurs whenever an item in the tree is expanded or collapsed. There are two TreeListener methods—treeExpanded( ) and treeCollapsed( )—in which you develop the code that changes the image depending upon whether the item is expanded or collapsed.

The code in treeExpanded( ) changes the image to the one desired for expanded objects:

```
TreeItem ti = (TreeItem)e.item;
ti.setImage(new Image(d, "c:\\icons\\open.gif"));
```

Conversely, the code in treeCollapsed( ) changes the image to the one desired for collapsed items

```
TreeItem ti = (TreeItem)e.item;
ti.setImage(new Image(d, "c:\\icons\\folder.gif"));
```

Using Trees with Other Widgets

While Tree is, in and of itself, a massively useful construct, it gains power when used in conjunction with the List widget. Windows Explorer itself is one of these half tree–half list constructs, where the tree view on the left drives the contents of the list on the right.

How do I do that?

Build the same type of interface in the SWT using FillLayout with a Tree and List. Example 13-2 demonstrates the techniques required.

Example 13-2. Building an Explorer-style interface

```
import org.eclipse.swt.SWT;
import org.eclipse.swt.layout.*;
import org.eclipse.swt.events.*;
import org.eclipse.swt.graphics.Image;
import org.eclipse.swt.widgets.*;

public class TreeShellExample {
        Display d;
        Shell s;
        TreeShellExample()    {
            d = new Display();
            s = new Shell(d);

            s.setSize(250,200);
            s.setImage(new Image(d, "c:\\icons\\JavaCup.ico"));
            s.setText("A Tree Shell Example");
```

Example 13-2. Building an Explorer-style interface (continued)

```
s.setLayout(new FillLayout(SWT.HORIZONTAL));
final Tree t = new Tree(s, SWT.SINGLE | SWT.BORDER);
final TreeItem child1 = new TreeItem(t, SWT.NONE, 0);
child1.setText("1");
child1.setImage(new Image(d, "c:\\icons\\folder.gif"));
final TreeItem child2 = new TreeItem(t, SWT.NONE, 1);
child2.setText("2");
child2.setImage(new Image(d, "c:\\icons\\folder.gif"));
final TreeItem child2a = new TreeItem(child2, SWT.NONE, 0);
child2a.setText("2A");
final TreeItem child2b = new TreeItem(child2, SWT.NONE, 1);
child2b.setText("2B");
final TreeItem child3 = new TreeItem(t, SWT.NONE, 2);
child3.setText("3");
child3.setImage(new Image(d, "c:\\icons\\folder.gif"));

final List l = new List(s, SWT.BORDER | SWT.SINGLE);

t.addTreeListener(new TreeListener() {
    public void treeExpanded(TreeEvent e) {
        TreeItem ti = (TreeItem)e.item;
        ti.setImage(new Image(d, "c:\\icons\\open.gif"));
    }

    public void treeCollapsed(TreeEvent e) {
        TreeItem ti = (TreeItem)e.item;
        ti.setImage(new Image(d, "c:\\icons\\folder.gif"));
    }
});

t.addSelectionListener(new SelectionAdapter() {
    public void widgetSelected(SelectionEvent e) {
        TreeItem ti = (TreeItem)e.item;
        populateList(ti.getText());
    }

    private void populateList(String type){
        if(type.equals("1"))
        {
            l.removeAll();
            l.add("File 1");
            l.add("File 2");
        }
        if(type.equals("2"))
        {
            l.removeAll();
        }
        if(type.equals("2A"))
        {
            l.removeAll();
            l.add("File 3");
            l.add("File 4");
```

Example 13-2. Building an Explorer-style interface (continued)

```
                    }
                    if(type.equals("2B"))
                    {
                        l.removeAll();
                        l.add("File 5");
                        l.add("File 6");
                    }
                    if(type.equals("3"))
                    {
                        l.removeAll();
                        l.add("File 7");
                        l.add("File 8");
                    }

                }
            });
            s.open();
            while(!s.isDisposed()){
                if(!d.readAndDispatch())
                    d.sleep();
            }
            d.dispose();
        }
}
```

Example 13-2 yields Figure 13-5 when executed and is an example of how to populate a list depending on which item in a tree is selected.

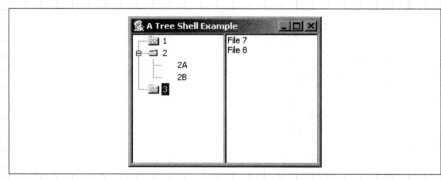

Figure 13-5. An Explorer-style interface

What just happened?

Creating the user interface for an Explorer-type interface is done using a few simple techniques, all of which you have learned in earlier chapters of this book. First, create a FillLayout using the SWT.HORIZONTAL style to provide the side-by-side split-screen look. Then add a Tree to the left side and a List to the right. The layout manager handles all widget positioning and sizing, keeping each sized to 50% of the window size.

The code that makes the interface actually perform as intended is in the SelectionListener added to the Tree object:

```
t.addSelectionListener(new SelectionAdapter() {
    public void widgetSelected(SelectionEvent e) {
        TreeItem ti = (TreeItem)e.item;
        populateList(ti.getText());
    }

    private void populateList(String type){
        if(type.equals("1"))
        {
            l.removeAll();
            l.add("File 1");
            l.add("File 2");
        }
        if(type.equals("2"))
        {
            l.removeAll();
        }
        if(type.equals("2A"))
        {
            l.removeAll();
            l.add("File 3");
            l.add("File 4");
        }
        if(type.equals("2B"))
        {
            l.removeAll();
            l.add("File 5");
            l.add("File 6");
        }
        if(type.equals("3"))
        {
            l.removeAll();
            l.add("File 7");
            l.add("File 8");
        }

    }
});
```

SelectionListener is used for this purpose since it will be notified whenever the user makes a selection in the Tree, exactly the event you need to capture. In the SelectionListener, you first determine which of the items in the tree has been selected, then call a populateList() method to perform the action of generating the list contents.

In a real-world application, code in populateList( ) could go to a database and make a retrieval based on the item selected, but here the list items are simply hardcoded to demonstrate the technique.

Working with Other Tree Styles

So far, the examples have used just the SWT.SINGLE tree style. The Tree class also supports other styles. SWT.MULTI creates a tree that enables the user to make multiple selections. This is of limited use in Tree-type interfaces, which normally permit only one item in the tree to be active at a time (again, Windows Explorer is an example; you can work only in one folder at a time).

SWT.CHECK-style Tree objects are another matter. SWT.CHECK creates a Tree whose items have a checkbox incorporated, as in Figure 13-6.

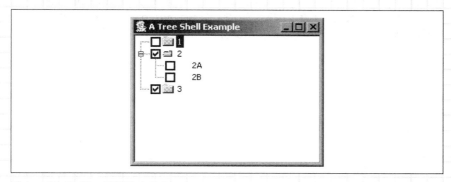

Figure 13-6. The CHECK-style tree

Determining the Checked Item(s)

If you use the SWT.CHECK style, you need to determine what item or items have been checked by the user.

How do I do that?

You can determine whether a particular item is checked or unchecked by calling the TreeItem getChecked( ) method. The following code loops through the Tree and determines the status of each TreeItem it finds:

```
TreeItem[] tia = t.getItems( );
for(int i=0; i<tia.length;i++){
    if(tia[i].getChecked( )){
```

```
            // take some action
            System.out.println("Checked");
        }
        TreeItem[] children = tia[i].getItems();
        for(int n=0; n<children.length;n++){
            if(children[i].getChecked()){
                // take some action
                System.out.println("Checked");
        }
        }
    }
```

Admittedly, this code is specific to our tree, which has only one level of children. Multiple layers of children would require recursion to avoid multiple nested if statements and for loops.

SWT.CHECK-style Tree objects are very useful when you need to allow the user to make multiple selections from the tree, but don't want the extra overhead associated with the SWT.MULTI mode (which wouldn't be appropriate if using the selected TreeItem to take some action such as populating a list).

As with all the SWT widgets, Tree is very simple to create and use, especially if you compare it to the SWING JTree, which has a reputation for being very hard to configure and use.

CHAPTER 14

Other SWT Listeners

In many of the examples so far you have seen that to respond to user events such as button clicking, you develop code using a listener. Until now, these listeners have been specific to the widget to which they were attached (i.e., attaching a SelectionListener to a button to respond to the click event). The SWT provides other Listener classes that are useful in making our user interfaces respond to other types of user actions. To understand event types, you must begin with the proposition that for every action a user can take in your application, an event will be generated by the operating system. This means that each time the user moves the mouse, or presses a mouse button or a key on the keyboard, an event, or multiple events, will occur.

Most of these events go unhandled by your application. After all, for most applications do you really need to know that the user moved the mouse from point A to point B within a window? Probably not. You need only know whether the user moved the mouse into a critical area or whether the user pressed a mouse button while pointing at a widget.

For those events which you do need to capture and take action on, you must add a Listener to your code. A Listener must be attached to some user interface element—the Shell, MenuItem, or Composite, or one of the widgets placed in one of the container-type classes. There is no such thing as a "free-standing" Listener.

Earlier, you were exposed to how to add the most common listeners to widgets that have been added to your user interfaces—MenuItem, ToolItem, Button, Text, List, and so on. Next, you need to learn how to attach some of the less common Listener classes to widgets, for times when your program must respond to some of the lesser-used events. The following sections examine each such Listener type, with examples of how they can be used to perform some useful tasks in your user interface.

In this chapter:
- *Using KeyListener*
- *Using MouseListener*
- *Working with the MouseEvent Class*
- *Responding to Shift-Click Events*
- *Working with the MouseMove-Listener*
- *Using the MouseTrack-Listener*

Using KeyListener

KeyListener is attached to a widget to listen for the events that occur when the user presses a keyboard key. These events are going to occur most often when the user is interacting with a widget that permits text entry, such as Text or Combo.

One task associated with Combo is a good way to demonstrate the KeyListener. Some user interfaces that use Combo permit the user to enter text in the text portion of the Combo. As the user types, the list portion of the Combo is searched for an item that matches the text that has been entered. If an item is found, it is automatically selected.

How do I do that?

Creating a searching Combo is a matter of attaching a KeyListener to the Combo, then developing the search and selection code in the KeyListener methods. Example 14-1 demonstrates this.

Example 14-1. A searching Combo

```
import org.eclipse.swt.SWT;
import org.eclipse.swt.layout.*;
import org.eclipse.swt.events.*;
import org.eclipse.swt.graphics.Image;
import org.eclipse.swt.widgets.*;

public class KeyListenerExample {

        Display d;
        Shell s;

        KeyListenerExample()    {

                d = new Display();
                s = new Shell(d);

                s.setSize(250,200);
                s.setImage(new Image(d, "c:\\icons\\JavaCup.ico"));
                s.setText("A KeyListener Example");
                s.setLayout(new RowLayout());

                final Combo c = new Combo(s, SWT.DROP_DOWN | SWT.BORDER);
                c.add("Lions");
                c.add("Tigers");
                c.add("Bears");
                c.add("Oh My!");
```

Example 14-1. A searching Combo (continued)

```
    c.addKeyListener(new KeyListener() {
        String selectedItem = "";
        public void keyPressed(KeyEvent e) {
            if(c.getText().length() > 0)
            {
                return;
            }
            String key = Character.toString(e.character);
            String[] items = c.getItems();
            for(int i =0;i<items.length;i++)
            {
                if(items[i].toLowerCase().startsWith(key.toLowerCase()))
                {
                    c.select(i);
                    selectedItem = items[i];
                    return;
                }
            }
        }
        public void keyReleased(KeyEvent e) {
            if(selectedItem.length() > 0)
            c.setText(selectedItem);
            selectedItem = "";
        }
    });
    s.open();
    while(!s.isDisposed()){
        if(!d.readAndDispatch())
            d.sleep();
    }
    d.dispose();
    }
}
```

What just happened?

The class in Example 14-1 creates a simple Shell with a Combo widget.
The Combo is of the SWT.DROP_DOWN style, so it is editable—the user isn't
limited to selecting items from the list. However, as a convenience to the
user, when text is entered in the text field portion of the Combo, the first
item that begins with that letter is selected. For example, if the user
presses the "L" key, the "Lion" item is selected and the text field automatically contains the full word "Lion."

The relevant code is, of course, in the KeyListener:

```
c.addKeyListener(new KeyListener() {
    String selectedItem = "";
    public void keyPressed(KeyEvent e) {
        if(c.getText().length() > 0)
        {
            return;
        }
        String key = Character.toString(e.character);
        String[] items = c.getItems();
        for(int i =0;i<items.length;i++)
        {
            if(items[i].toLowerCase().startsWith(key.toLowerCase()))
            {
                c.select(i);
                selectedItem = items[i];
                return;
            }
        }
    }
    public void keyReleased(KeyEvent e) {
        if(selectedItem.length() > 0)
            c.setText(selectedItem);
            selectedItem = "";
    }
});
```

KeyListener has two methods—keyPressed() and keyReleased(). keyPressed() will be called when the user presses a key, but before that key is released. keyReleased() will be called when the key is released.

In the example, the code in keyPressed( ) first determines which key the user has pressed to cause this event. This is accomplished by examining the KeyEvent object that is passed to the keyPressed( ) method. KeyEvent encapsulates several fields that tell you what caused the event and what conditions prevailed when the event occurred. One of these fields, character, tells you what key was pressed:

```
String key = Character.toString(e.character);
```

The character is converted to a String for ease of comparison in the later code.

The code next loops through the array of items in the Combo, comparing the first letter of each item with the key that was pressed. If a match occurs, the item test is stored in an instance variable for later use. The keyPressed( ) method then issues a return to halt processing after the first match is located:

```
String[] items = c.getItems( );
for(int i =0;i<items.length;i++)
{
    if(items[i].toLowerCase().startsWith(key.toLowerCase( )))
    {
        c.select(i);
        selectedItem = items[i];
        return;
    }
}
```

When the user releases the key, the operating system calls the keyReleased( ) method. In that method the code determines whether any item matched in the keyPressed( ) method and, if so, sets the text in the Combo to the selected item:

```
if(selectedItem.length( ) > 0)
    c.setText(selectedItem);
    selectedItem = "";
}
```

It's possible, but more difficult, to write code only in the keyReleased( ) method that accomplishes this task, but this code better demonstrates the interaction between the two methods—which is the purpose of this example.

This example gives a complete workout to the KeyListener. As demonstrated, KeyListener permits you to build sophisticated keyboard interactions into your applications. You need to be careful when developing code in the KeyListener methods, as this may slow the user's interaction with the system. Remember that the KeyListener methods are called each time a key is pressed. If long-running code is placed in either or both of the methods, a delay between the key press and the results of the key press (something showing up in the text field) will occur. This may prove disconcerting to users and must be avoided.

Using MouseListener

MouseListener is used to respond to events that occur when a mouse button is pressed. MouseListener responds to three distinct mouse events:

MouseButtonPressed
> When a mouse button is pressed, but not yet released

MouseButtonReleased
> When a mouse button that has been pressed is released

MouseDoubleClick
> When a mouse button is double-clicked

Each event has a corresponding method in the MouseListener class that is called at the occurrence of the event. The developer's task when using MouseListener is to determine which event is appropriate for the desired action and to develop code in the corresponding method. An example to consider is an interface that displays the mouse location in a Label whenever a mouse button is pressed.

How do I do that?

Example 14-2 demonstrates a possible use of MouseListener.

Example 14-2. Using MouseListener

```
import org.eclipse.swt.SWT;
import org.eclipse.swt.events.*;
import org.eclipse.swt.graphics.Image;
import org.eclipse.swt.widgets.*;
public class MouseListenerExample {
    final Display d;
    final Shell s;
    public MouseListenerExample()
    {
        d = new Display();
        s = new Shell(d);

        s.setSize(250,200);
        s.setImage(new Image(d, "c:\\icons\\JavaCup.ico"));
        s.setText("A MouseListener Example");
        s.open();

        s.addMouseListener(new MouseListener() {
            public void mouseDown(MouseEvent e) {
                Label l = new Label(s, SWT.FLAT);
                l.setText("Mouse Button Down at:" + e.x + " " + e.y);
                l.setBounds(e.x,e.y, 150,15);

            }
```

Example 14-2. Using MouseListener (continued)

```
        public void mouseUp(MouseEvent e) {
            Label l = new Label(s, SWT.FLAT);
            l.setText("Mouse Button up at:" + e.x + " " + e.y);
            l.setBounds(e.x,e.y, 150,15);
        }
        public void mouseDoubleClick(MouseEvent e) {

        }
    });

    while(!s.isDisposed( )){
        if(!d.readAndDispatch( ))
            d.sleep( );
    }
    d.dispose( );
  }
}
```

This example creates a Label and positions it at the location at which any mouse button was pressed and released. When you execute this code, press the left mouse button, drag the mouse, and release, you see something similar to Figure 14-1.

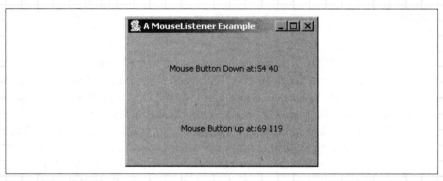

Figure 14-1. Results of MouseListenerExample

What just happened?

The example code implements MouseListener as an anonymous inner class. MouseListener has three methods—mouseDown( ), mouseUp( ), and mouseDoubleClick( ), that correspond to the events that are possible with mouse buttons. It is in the implementation of those methods that you perform the work for this simple example:

```
public void mouseDown(MouseEvent e) {
    Label l = new Label(s, SWT.FLAT);
    l.setText("Mouse Button Down at:" + e.x + " " + e.y);
```

```
        l.setBounds(e.x,e.y, 150,15);
    }
    public void mouseUp(MouseEvent e) {
        Label l = new Label(s, SWT.FLAT);
        l.setText("Mouse Button up at:" + e.x + " " + e.y);
        l.setBounds(e.x,e.y, 150,15);
    }
```

As with KeyListener, you are passed an event object that encapsulates information about exactly what has occurred in the event. In this case, it's the MouseEvent class that contains the types of things you need to know. In mouseDown( ), the code creates a new Label widget, then interrogates the MouseEvent object to determine the current x and y location of the mouse cursor, which is in turn passed to setText( ) to create the label:

```
        l.setText("Mouse Button Down at:" + e.x + " " + e.y);
```

The setBounds( ) method is then passed the x and y coordinates to position the Label at the current mouse position:

```
        l.setBounds(e.x,e.y, 150,15);
```

mouseUp( ) performs the same action as mouseDown( ), except that the Label text indicates that an up event has occurred.

Admittedly, this is an example that won't find much real-world use; however it does demonstrate the technique of using MouseListener.

What about...

when you don't want to go to the trouble of implementing every method in a Listener? In those instances, it is more useful to use an adapter class. An adapter is a class that implements the desired Listener interface and provides the necessary implementation of each method without performing any action. When you add a Listener to a widget, you can use the adapter to sidestep the requirement that every method in an interface must be implemented by the class that implements the interface. The Listener code for the example, rewritten to use an adapter and eliminate the unused mouseDoubleClick( ) method, is:

```
    s.addMouseListener(new MouseAdapter() {
        public void mouseDown(MouseEvent e) {
        Label l = new Label(s, SWT.FLAT);
        l.setText("Mouse Button Down at: " + e.x + " " + e.y);
        l.setBounds(e.x,e.y, 150, 15);
    }
    public void mouseDown(MouseEvent e) {
        Label l = new Label(s, SWT.FLAT);
        l.setText("Mouse Button Up at: " + e.x + " " + e.y);
        l.setBounds(e.x,e.y, 150, 15);
    }
    });
```

When you have more than one or two methods in a Listener that you aren't going to code, an adapter makes sense as a space-saving device. The SWT has adapter classes predefined for many Listener types, but it is possible to write your own for any Listener that does not have an adapter. All you must do is create a class that implements the interface for the Listener and then provide empty method implementations for each method in the interface.

Working with the MouseEvent Class

The MouseEvent class encapsulates a couple of fields other than the x and y coordinates of the mouse to assist in determining exactly what user action has caused the event. If you run our example again, you will notice that it does not differentiate between left-button and right-button clicks, but treats both the same. It is usually advisable to distinguish between a left-button click and a right-button click.

How do I do that?

The following code limits the action taken to left-button clicks only:

```
s.addMouseListener(new MouseAdapter( ) {
        public void mouseDown(MouseEvent e) {
            if(e.button==3)
            {
                Label l = new Label(s, SWT.FLAT);
                l.setText("Mouse Button Down at:" + e.x + " " + e.y);
                l.setBounds(e.x,e.y, 150,15);
            }

        }
        public void mouseUp(MouseEvent e) {
            if(e.button==3)
            {
                Label l = new Label(s, SWT.FLAT);
                l.setText("Mouse Button up at:" + e.x + " " + e.y);
                l.setBounds(e.x,e.y, 150,15);
            }
        }
});
```

This is accomplished by interrogating the MouseEvent to determine the number of the button that has been pressed:

```
if(e.button==3)
```

What about...

all the different types of mice in use? When dealing with the MouseEvent button field, you must remember that not all mice are created equal. Some have two buttons, some three. Some have two buttons and a wheel. For purposes of the MouseEvent, buttons are numbered from left to right, with the wheel, if present, counting as a button. The preceding code, executed with a mouse that has two buttons and a wheel, results in the label being created for right-clicks only. A mouse that has only two buttons would not cause this code to execute.

Responding to Shift-Click Events

Sometimes you must respond to mouse events that occur in combination with keystrokes. For example, some interfaces select text when the user holds the Shift key while dragging the mouse. For these times, there must be a mechanism that enables you to determine if a key is being pressed simultaneously with a mouse button.

When designing code that responds to events depending upon which button is clicked, you must test for the desired result against different hardware combinations.

How do I do that?

For this purpose MouseEvent contains a field known as stateMask. This field is populated only when the user is holding down one of the keyboard keys at the same time the mouse is being clicked. If you want to code some action that occurs only when the user is holding the Shift key while clicking a mouse button:

```
s.addMouseListener(new MouseAdapter() {
        public void mouseDown(MouseEvent e) {
            if(e.stateMask==SWT.SHIFT)
            {
                Label l = new Label(s, SWT.FLAT);
                l.setText("Mouse Button Down at:" + e.x + " " + e.y);
                l.setBounds(e.x,e.y, 150,15);
            }

        }
        public void mouseUp(MouseEvent e) {
            Label l = new Label(s, SWT.FLAT);
            l.setText("Mouse Button up at:" + e.x + " " + e.y);
            l.setBounds(e.x,e.y, 150,15);
        }
    });
```

This code results in the Label being created in the mouseDown( ) method only if the user is also holding down the Shift key. The mouseUp( ) method creates the Label even if the Shift key is not pressed.

Working with the MouseMoveListener

The `MouseMoveListener` responds to events caused when the mouse is moved into, across, or away from a widget. It has only one method—`mouseMove()`. The most common use for the `MouseMoveListener` used to be to provide tool-tip text for users, but that functionality is now encapsulated in the widget classes. `MouseMove()` can be used to create a simple game.

How do I do that?

A good example that demonstrates `MouseMoveListener` is the creation of a simple game consisting of a `Shell` with a single button that displays "Click Me" text. When the user moves the mouse over the button to click, the button is repositioned away from the mouse, making it impossible to click. Example 14-3 does exactly that.

Example 14-3. A simple MouseMove game

```java
import java.util.Random;
import org.eclipse.swt.SWT;
import org.eclipse.swt.events.*;
import org.eclipse.swt.graphics.Image;
import org.eclipse.swt.graphics.Point;
import org.eclipse.swt.widgets.*;

public class MouseListenerExample {
    final Display d;
    final Shell s;
    public MouseListenerExample()
    {
        d = new Display();
        s = new Shell(d);

        s.setSize(250,200);
        s.setImage(new Image(d, "c:\\icons\\JavaCup.ico"));
        s.setText("A MouseListener Example");
        final Button b = new Button(s, SWT.PUSH);
        b.setText("Push Me");
        b.setBounds(20,50, 55, 25);
        s.open();

        b.addMouseMoveListener(new MouseMoveListener() {
            public void mouseMove(MouseEvent e) {
                Random r = new Random(System.currentTimeMillis());
                Point p = s.getSize();
                int newX = r.nextInt(p.y);
                int newY = r.nextInt(p.x);
                b.setBounds(newX-55, newY-25, 55, 25);
```

Example 14-3. A simple MouseMove game (continued)

```
            }

        });

        while(!s.isDisposed()){
            if(!d.readAndDispatch())
                d.sleep();
        }
        d.dispose();
    }
}
```

Creating an instance of this class demonstrates the effect.

What just happened?

The action here is in the mouseMove( ) method, which is called whenever the mouse is positioned anywhere inside the bounds of the button b:

```
public void mouseMove(MouseEvent e) {
    Random r = new Random(System.currentTimeMillis());
    Point p = s.getSize();
    int newX = r.nextInt(p.y);
    int newY = r.nextInt(p.x);
    b.setBounds(newX-55, newY-25, 55, 25);
}
```

The code first creates an instance of the Java Random class that is then used to obtain an int value betweemf 0 and the height of the Shell (determined by calling the getSize( ) method on the Shell). A random int value between 0 and the Shell width is also obtained. The location of the button is then set to those new positions, minus an offset to prevent the button from disappearing off the edge of the window.

It's silly, but it does give the mouseMove( ) method a workout.

Using the MouseTrackListener

MouseTrackListener is similar to MouseMoveListener, but is a little more sophisticated. It also responds when the mouse is moved over a widget to which it is attached, but it gives the developer a little more control. Instead of a single method, there are three methods in MouseTrackListener:

- mouseEnter( )
- mouseExit( )
- mouseHover( )

The names explain the event to which each responds. You can use the breakdown of mouse movement events to gain a little more control than is possible with MouseMoveListener. The main use for MouseTrackListener used to be to provide tool-tip text to the user. The text was displayed when the mouse entered a widget and removed when the mouse exited the widget. Today that functionality is encapsulated in the widgets themselves, leaving MouseTrackListener for other interface designs. Perhaps the most common use is to provide the user with a visual indication that the mouse is over a widget by changing the appearance of the widget in some fashion.

How do I do that?

Example 14-4 changes the color of a button when the mouse enters it and restores the color to the original value when the mouse exits.

Example 14-4. Using MouseTrackListener

```
import org.eclipse.swt.SWT;
import org.eclipse.swt.events.*;
import org.eclipse.swt.graphics.Color;
import org.eclipse.swt.graphics.Image;
import org.eclipse.swt.widgets.*;

public class MouseTrackExample {

    final Display d;
    final Shell s;
    public MouseTrackExample()
    {
        d = new Display();
        s = new Shell(d);

        s.setSize(250,200);
        s.setImage(new Image(d, "c:\\icons\\JavaCup.ico"));
        s.setText("A MouseTrackListener Example");
        final Button b = new Button(s, SWT.PUSH);
        b.setText("Push Me");
        b.setBounds(20,50, 55, 25);
        s.open();
        final Color oldColor = b.getBackground();

        b.addMouseTrackListener(new MouseTrackAdapter() {
            public void mouseEnter(MouseEvent e)
            {
                b.setBackground(new Color(d,0,153,153));

            }

            public void mouseExit(MouseEvent e)
            {
```

Example 14-4. Using MouseTrackListener (continued)

```
                b.setBackground(oldColor);
        }
    });

    while(!s.isDisposed()){
        if(!d.readAndDispatch())
            d.sleep();
    }
    d.dispose();
    }
}
```

If you execute this example, moving the mouse over the button changes the color of the button.

What just happened?

As with all Listener classes, the action resides in the Listener methods—in this case, mouseEnter() and mouseExit():

```
public void mouseEnter(MouseEvent e)
{
    b.setBackground(new Color(d,0,153,153));

}

public void mouseExit(MouseEvent e)
{
    b.setBackground(oldColor);
}
```

In mouseEnter(), the code simply calls the setBackground() method of Button to change to a new color. In mouseExit(), the color is returned to oldColor, which has been stored in oldColor after a call to getBackground() earlier in the code.

TIP

Some platforms don't support dynamically changing colors in this manner. If this example doesn't work for you, try forcing a redraw of the button:

```
        b.redraw();
```

If that doesn't work, you can change the example to see the effect of manipulating the text property of the Button object. Just change the setBackground() calls to setText().

These are a few of the Listener types from the org.eclipse.swt.events package that can be used to respond to user events. Each Listener type will work in the same manner. To use one, just call the appropriate add( ) method to attach the Listener to a widget, and then code the desired Listener method. No matter how complex the user interaction to which you are attempting to respond, it can be reduced to those simple steps.

CHAPTER 15

SWT CoolBars

Chapter 4 demonstrated the creation and use of SWT ToolBars. This chapter examines another set of classes that can be used to create ToolBar-like constructs—the SWT CoolBar and CoolItem classes from the org.eclipse.swt.widgets package.

A CoolBar is like a ToolBar on steroids. Like ToolBar and ToolItems, CoolBar is a container to which you add instances of the CoolItem class. Although a ToolItem object appears as a button on the ToolBar, a CoolItem serves only as a container for other widget types—Combo, Text, or Button. This makes a CoolBar a massively useful interface construct. In fact, the Eclipse toolbar is actually a CoolBar and is a great example of how to leverage the capability of the CoolBar and CoolItem classes to enable the user to customize the user interface.

Creating a CoolBar

The steps required to create a CoolBar are similar to those required to create a ToolBar, except that an instance of CoolBar is created instead of ToolBar and instances of CoolItem are created in place of the ToolItem instances for the individual buttons. The similarity ends there, however.

The CoolItem objects created serve only as containers for other widgets. If you want to create a CoolBar similar in appearance to the ToolBar from Chapter 4, you must create individual Button objects that are added to the corresponding CoolItem. A good understanding of CoolBar can be gained by going through the process of creating a CoolBar similar in appearance to the ToolBar created in Chapter 4.

How do I do that?

1. Create an instance of the CoolBar class and set its initial position and size.

2. Create an instance of the CoolItem class for each widget you wish to appear on the CoolBar.

3. Create a widget and assign it to the corresponding CoolItem.

Consider Example 15-1, which creates a CoolBar similar to the ToolBar created in Chapter 4.

Example 15-1. Creating a CoolBar

```
import org.eclipse.swt.SWT;
import org.eclipse.swt.events.HelpEvent;
import org.eclipse.swt.events.HelpListener;
import org.eclipse.swt.graphics.Image;
import org.eclipse.swt.graphics.Point;
import org.eclipse.swt.widgets.*;

public class CoolbarShellExample {
    Display d;
    Shell s;

    CoolbarShellExample()    {
        d = new Display();
        s = new Shell(d);
        s.setSize(300,300);
        s.setImage(new Image(d, "c:\\icons\\JavaCup.ico"));
        s.setText("A Shell Coolbar Example");

        final CoolBar bar = new CoolBar(s,SWT.BORDER);
        bar.setSize(280,70);
        bar.setLocation(0,0);
        // create images for coolbar buttons
        final Image saveIcon = new Image(d, "c:\\icons\\save.jpg");
        final Image openIcon = new Image(d, "c:\\icons\\open.jpg");
        final Image cutIcon = new Image(d, "c:\\icons\\cut.jpg");
        final Image copyIcon = new Image(d, "c:\\icons\\copy.jpg");
        final Image pasteIcon = new Image(d, "c:\\icons\\paste.jpg");

        // create and add the button for performing an open operation
        final CoolItem openCoolItem = new CoolItem(bar, SWT.NONE);
        final Button openBtn = new Button(bar, SWT.PUSH);
        openBtn.setImage(openIcon);
        openBtn.pack();
        Point size = openBtn.getSize();
        openCoolItem.setControl(openBtn);
        openCoolItem.setSize(openCoolItem.computeSize(size.x, size.y));

        //create and add the button for performing a save operation
        final CoolItem saveCoolItem = new CoolItem(bar, SWT.PUSH);
```

Example 15-1. Creating a CoolBar (continued)

```
        final Button saveBtn = new Button(bar, SWT.PUSH);
        saveBtn.setImage(saveIcon);
        saveBtn.pack();
        size = saveBtn.getSize();
        saveCoolItem.setControl(saveBtn);
        saveCoolItem.setSize(saveCoolItem.computeSize(size.x, size.y));

    //create and add the button for performing a cut operation
        final CoolItem cutCoolItem = new CoolItem(bar, SWT.PUSH);
        final Button cutBtn = new Button(bar, SWT.PUSH);
        cutBtn.setImage(cutIcon);
        cutBtn.pack();
        size = cutBtn.getSize();
        cutCoolItem.setControl(cutBtn);
        cutCoolItem.setSize(cutCoolItem.computeSize(size.x, size.y));

        // create and add the button for performing a copy operation
        final CoolItem copyCoolItem = new CoolItem(bar, SWT.PUSH);
        final Button copyBtn = new Button(bar, SWT.PUSH);
        copyBtn.setImage(copyIcon);
        copyBtn.pack();
        size = copyBtn.getSize();
        copyCoolItem.setControl(copyBtn);
        copyCoolItem.setSize(copyCoolItem.computeSize(size.x, size.y));

        // create and add the button for performing a paste operation
        final CoolItem pasteCoolItem = new CoolItem(bar, SWT.PUSH);
        final Button pasteBtn = new Button(bar, SWT.PUSH);
        pasteBtn.setImage(pasteIcon);
        pasteBtn.pack();
        size = pasteBtn.getSize();
        pasteCoolItem.setControl(pasteBtn);
        pasteCoolItem.setSize(pasteCoolItem.computeSize(size.x, size.y));
        pasteCoolItem.setMinimumSize(size);

    openBtn.addSelectionListener(new SelectionAdapter() {
        public void widgetSelected(SelectionEvent event) {
            System.out.println("Open");
        }
    });

    saveBtn. addSelectionListener(new SelectionAdapter() {
        public void void widgetSelected(SelectionEvent event) {
            System.out.println("Save");
        }
    });

    cutBtn. addSelectionListener(new SelectionAdapter() {
        public void void widgetSelected(SelectionEvent event) {
            System.out.println("Cut");
        }
    });
```

Example 15-1. Creating a CoolBar (continued)

```
copyBtn. addSelectionListener(new SelectionAdapter() {
    public void void widgetSelected(SelectionEvent event) {
        System.out.println("Copy");
    }
});

pasteBtn. addSelectionListener(new SelectionAdapter() {
    public void void widgetSelected(SelectionEvent event) {
        System.out.println("Paste");            }
});

// create the menu
Menu m = new Menu(s,SWT.BAR);

// create a File menu and add an Exit item
    final MenuItem file = new MenuItem(m, SWT.CASCADE);
    file.setText("&File");
    final Menu filemenu = new Menu(s, SWT.DROP_DOWN);
    file.setMenu(filemenu);
    final MenuItem openMenuItem = new MenuItem(filemenu, SWT.PUSH);
    openMenuItem.setText("&Open\tCTRL+O");
    openMenuItem.setAccelerator(SWT.CTRL+'O');
    final MenuItem saveMenuItem = new MenuItem(filemenu, SWT.PUSH);
    saveMenuItem.setText("&Save\tCTRL+S");
    saveMenuItem.setAccelerator(SWT.CTRL+'S');
    final MenuItem separator = new MenuItem(filemenu, SWT.SEPARATOR);
    final MenuItem exitMenuItem = new MenuItem(filemenu, SWT.PUSH);
    exitMenuItem.setText("E&xit");

    // create an Edit menu and add Cut, Copy, and Paste items
    final MenuItem edit = new MenuItem(m, SWT.CASCADE);
    edit.setText("&Edit");
    final Menu editmenu = new Menu(s, SWT.DROP_DOWN);
    edit.setMenu(editmenu);
    final MenuItem cutMenuItem = new MenuItem(editmenu, SWT.PUSH);
    cutMenuItem.setText("&Cut");
    final MenuItem copyMenuItem = new MenuItem(editmenu, SWT.PUSH);
    copyMenuItem.setText("Co&py");
    final MenuItem pasteMenuItem = new MenuItem(editmenu, SWT.PUSH);
    pasteMenuItem.setText("&Paste");

    //create a Window menu and add Child items
    final MenuItem window = new MenuItem(m, SWT.CASCADE);
    window.setText("&Window");
    final Menu windowmenu = new Menu(s, SWT.DROP_DOWN);
    window.setMenu(windowmenu);
    final MenuItem maxMenuItem = new MenuItem(windowmenu, SWT.PUSH);
    maxMenuItem.setText("Ma&ximize");
    final MenuItem minMenuItem = new MenuItem(windowmenu, SWT.PUSH);
    minMenuItem.setText("Mi&nimize");
```

Example 15-1. Creating a CoolBar (continued)

```
// create a Help menu and add an About item
final MenuItem help = new MenuItem(m, SWT.CASCADE);
help.setText("&Help");
final Menu helpmenu = new Menu(s, SWT.DROP_DOWN);
help.setMenu(helpmenu);
final MenuItem abouMenutItem = new MenuItem(helpmenu, SWT.PUSH);
aboutMenuItem.setText("&About");

// add action listeners for the menu items

openMenuItem.addSelectionListener(new SelectionListener() {
    public void widgetSelected(SelectionEvent e) {
        System.out.println("Open");
    }
  public void widgetDefaultSelected(SelectionEvent e) {
  }
  });


saveMenuItem.addSelectionListener(new SelectionListener() {
    public void widgetSelected(SelectionEvent e) {
        System.out.println("Save");
    }
  public void widgetDefaultSelected(SelectionEvent e) {
  }
  });

exitMenuItem.addSelectionListener(new SelectionListener() {
    public void widgetSelected(SelectionEvent e) {
        System.exit(0);
    }
  public void widgetDefaultSelected(SelectionEvent e) {
  }
  });

cutMenuItem.addSelectionListener(new SelectionListener() {
    public void widgetSelected(SelectionEvent e) {
        System.out.println("Cut");
    }
  public void widgetDefaultSelected(SelectionEvent e) {
  }
  });

copyMenuItem.addSelectionListener(new SelectionListener() {
    public void widgetSelected(SelectionEvent e) {
        System.out.println("Copy");
    }
  public void widgetDefaultSelected(SelectionEvent e) {
  }
  });

pasteMenuItem.addSelectionListener(new SelectionListener() {
```

Example 15-1. Creating a CoolBar (continued)

```
                    public void widgetSelected(SelectionEvent e) {
                        System.out.println("Paste");
                    }
                public void widgetDefaultSelected(SelectionEvent e) {
                    }
                });

            maxMenuItem.addSelectionListener(new SelectionListener() {
                public void widgetSelected(SelectionEvent e) {
                    Shell parent = (Shell)maxItem.getParent().getParent();
                    parent.setMaximized(true);
                }
                public void widgetDefaultSelected(SelectionEvent e) {
                    }
                });

            minMenuItem.addSelectionListener(new SelectionListener() {
                public void widgetSelected(SelectionEvent e) {
                    Shell parent = (Shell)minItem.getParent().getParent();
                    parent.setMaximized(false);
                }
                public void widgetDefaultSelected(SelectionEvent e) {
                    }
                });

            aboutMenuItem.addSelectionListener(new SelectionListener() {
                public void widgetSelected(SelectionEvent e) {
                    System.out.println("Help Invoked");
                }
                public void widgetDefaultSelected(SelectionEvent e) {
                    }
                });

        s.setMenuBar(m);

        s.open();
        while(!s.isDisposed()){
            if(!d.readAndDispatch())
                d.sleep();
        }
        d.dispose();
    }
}
```

When executed, CoolbarShellExample, shown in Example 15-1, creates
Figure 15-1.

Chapter 15: SWT CoolBars

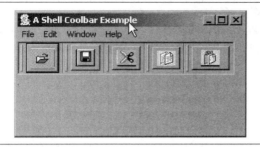

Figure 15-1. CoolbarShellExample

What just happened?

The code that creates the CoolBar itself is straightforward. First, an instance of CoolBar is created, then sized and positioned to fit the Shell:

```
final CoolBar bar = new CoolBar(s,SWT.BORDER);
bar.setSize(280,70);
bar.setLocation(0,0);
```

You can understand the steps required to create and display a complete set of CoolBar buttons by examining of the creation of just one of the CoolItem objects:

```
final CoolItem openCoolItem = new CoolItem(bar, SWT.NONE);
final Button openBtn = new Button(bar, SWT.PUSH);
openBtn.setImage(openIcon);
openBtn.pack();
Point size = openBtn.getSize();
openCoolItem.setControl(openBtn);
openCoolItem.setSize(openCoolItem.computeSize(size.x, size.y));
```

Here, an instance of CoolItem is created. CoolItem serves as the place-holder on the CoolBar to which you attach the widget you wish to place on the CoolBar. In this example, a Button is created and added to the CoolItem using setControl(). The remaining code sets the size of the CoolItem sufficiently to display the Button. The example code repeats this process for all the Button objects on the CoolBar.

Using Events with CoolBars

Unlike ToolItem, no events are associated directly with a CoolItem. Rather, events are associated with the widget that is assigned to the CoolItem.

How do I do that?

Example 15-1 assigns a SelectionListener to each Button to handle the event caused by the user clicking the button:

```
openBtn.addSelectionListener(new SelectionAdapter() {
        public void widgetSelected(SelectionEvent event) {
            System.out.println("Open");
        }
});
```

Adding Widgets Other Than Buttons to the CoolBar

It is possible to add other types of widgets to the CoolBar in the same manner as was done in Example 15-1 with Button. However, it only makes sense to consider a couple widget types for inclusion on a CoolBar. List, for example, is not a good candidate, since the room required for the List would exceed the amount of space available (top to bottom) on the CoolBar.

Not only that, but it would be ugly.

Combo is a good candidate for inclusion on a CoolBar when you must enable your user to select an item from a list.

How do I do that?

You add a Combo to the CoolBar using the same steps that are used to add a Button. Use this code to add a Combo to CoolbarShellExample from Example 15-1:

```
final CoolItem fontCoolItem = new CoolItem(bar, SWT.PUSH);
final Combo fontCombo = new Combo(bar, SWT.READ_ONLY | SWT.BORDER);
String[] items = {"Arial", "Courier", "Times New Roman"};
fontCombo.setItems(items);
fontCombo.pack();
size = fontCombo.getSize();
fontCoolItem.setControl(fontCombo);
fontCoolItem.setSize(fontCoolItem.computeSize(size.x, size.y));
fontCoolItem.setMinimumSize(size);
```

Doing so yields the result shown in Figure 15-2.

A selectionListener can be associated with the Combo to take appropriate action when the user selects an item.

```
fontCombo.addSelectionListener(new SelectionAdapter() {
        public void widgetSelected(SelectionEvent event) {
            System.out.println("Change Font Here");
        }
});
```

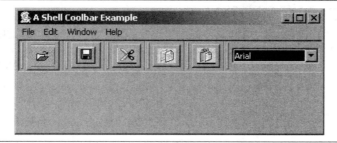

Figure 15-2. Using a Combo on a CoolBar

Preventing the User
from Rearranging the CoolBar

Executing the CoolbarShellExample program demonstrates how the user
can interact with the CoolBar. Each Button can be dragged and dropped
into a new location on the CoolBar in any manner the user sees fit. The
Button objects can also be resized by the user.

There are times when this functionality may not be desirable. In those
situations, you must take steps to prevent the user from rearranging or
resizing the CoolItems.

How do I do that?

Adding this line to the CoolbarShellExample following the code that creates the last CoolItem results in the CoolBar being locked and prevents
the user from rearranging or resizing the CoolItems:

```
bar.setLocked(true);
```

Using ToolBars with CoolBars

A close examination of CoolbarShellExample reveals several issues. First,
Button objects associated with the CoolBar are unable to use both text
and an image, as was the case with ToolBar. Attempting to use both text
and image results in only text being visible. Second, since the user can
move CoolItems around on the CoolBar, you lose the ability to maintain
functional groups of buttons unless you lock the CoolBar (which negates
many of the reasons for using it in the first place).

These issues are easily solved once you realize that it is possible to add a
ToolBar to a CoolBar as a single unit.

How do I do that?

Any ToolBar can be added to a CoolBar. All you must do is create the ToolBar in the normal manner (see Chapter 4), then create a CoolItem to serve as the holder for the ToolBar. Consider the modification to CoolbarShellExample shown in Example 15-2.

Example 15-2. Using a ToolBar with a CoolBar

```java
import org.eclipse.swt.SWT;
import org.eclipse.swt.graphics.Image;
import org.eclipse.swt.graphics.Point;
import org.eclipse.swt.widgets.*;

public class CoolbarShellExample {
    Display d;
    Shell s;

    CoolbarShellExample()    {
        d = new Display();
        s = new Shell(d);
        s.setSize(400,300);
        s.setImage(new Image(d, "c:\\icons\\JavaCup.ico"));
        s.setText("A Shell Coolbar Example");

        final CoolBar coolBar = new CoolBar(s,SWT.BORDER);
        coolBar.setSize(395,70);
        coolBar.setLocation(0,0);
        // create images for toolbar buttons
        final Image saveIcon = new Image(d, "c:\\icons\\save.jpg");
        final Image openIcon = new Image(d, "c:\\icons\\open.jpg");
        final Image childIcon = new Image(d, "c:\\icons\\userH.ico");
        final Image cutIcon = new Image(d, "c:\\icons\\cut.jpg");
        final Image copyIcon = new Image(d, "c:\\icons\\copy.jpg");
        final Image pasteIcon = new Image(d, "c:\\icons\\paste.jpg");

        // create and add the button for performing an open operation
        final CoolItem openCoolItem = new CoolItem(coolBar, SWT.NONE);

        final ToolBar fileToolBar = new ToolBar(coolBar,SWT.HORIZONTAL);
        final ToolItem openToolItem = new ToolItem(fileToolBar, SWT.PUSH);
        openToolItem.setImage(openIcon);
        openToolItem.setText("Open");
        openToolItem.setToolTipText("Open");

        final ToolItem saveToolItem = new ToolItem(fileToolBar, SWT.PUSH);
        saveToolItem.setImage(openIcon);
        saveToolItem.setText("Save");
        saveToolItem.setToolTipText("Save");

        fileToolBar.pack();
        Point size = fileToolBar.getSize();
        openCoolItem.setControl(fileToolBar);
```

Example 15-2. Using a ToolBar with a CoolBar (continued)

```
        openCoolItem.setSize(openCoolItem.computeSize(size.x, size.y));

        final CoolItem editbarCoolItem = new CoolItem(coolBar, SWT.PUSH);
        final ToolBar editToolBar = new ToolBar(coolBar,SWT.HORIZONTAL);

        // create and add the button for performing a cut operation
        final ToolItem cutToolItem = new ToolItem(editToolBar, SWT.PUSH);
        cutToolItem.setImage(cutIcon);
        cutToolItem.setText("Cut");
        cutToolItem.setToolTipText("Cut");

        // create and add the button for performing a copy operation
        final ToolItem copyToolItem = new ToolItem(editToolBar, SWT.PUSH);
        copyToolItem.setImage(copyIcon);
        copyToolItem.setText("Copy");
        copyToolItem.setToolTipText("Copy");

        // create and add the button for performing a paste operation
        final ToolItem pasteToolItem = new ToolItem(editToolBar, SWT.PUSH);
        pasteToolItem.setImage(pasteIcon);
        pasteToolItem.setText("Paste");
        pasteToolItem.setToolTipText("Paste");
        editToolBar.pack();
        size = editToolBar.getSize();
        editbarCoolItem.setControl(editToolBar);
        editbarCoolItem.setSize(editbarCoolItem.computeSize(size.x, size.y));

        final CoolItem fontCoolItem = new CoolItem(coolBar, SWT.PUSH);
        final Combo fontCombo = new Combo(coolBar, SWT.READ_ONLY | SWT.BORDER);
        String[] items = {"Arial", "Courier", "Times New Roman"};
        fontCombo.setItems(items);
        fontCombo.pack();
        size = fontCombo.getSize();
        fontCoolItem.setControl(fontCombo);
        fontCoolItem.setSize(fontCoolItem.computeSize(size.x, size.y));
        fontCoolItem.setMinimumSize(size);


        openToolItem.addListener(SWT.Selection, new Listener() {
            public void handleEvent(Event event) {
                System.out.println("Open");

            }
        });

        saveToolItem.addListener(SWT.Selection, new Listener() {
            public void handleEvent(Event event) {
                System.out.println("Save");

            }
        });

        cutToolItem.addListener(SWT.Selection, new Listener() {
```

Example 15-2. Using a ToolBar with a CoolBar (continued)

```java
        public void handleEvent(Event event) {
            System.out.println("Cut");

        }
    });

    copyToolItem.addListener(SWT.Selection, new Listener() {
        public void handleEvent(Event event) {
            System.out.println("Copy");

        }
    });

    pasteToolItem.addListener(SWT.Selection, new Listener() {
        public void handleEvent(Event event) {
            System.out.println("Paste");

        }
    });



// create the menu
Menu m = new Menu(s,SWT.BAR);

// create a File menu and add an Exit item
    final MenuItem file = new MenuItem(m, SWT.CASCADE);
    file.setText("&File");
    final Menu filemenu = new Menu(s, SWT.DROP_DOWN);
    file.setMenu(filemenu);
    final MenuItem openMenuItem = new MenuItem(filemenu, SWT.PUSH);
    openMenuItem.setText("&Open\tCTRL+O");
    openMenuItem.setAccelerator(SWT.CTRL+'O');
    final MenuItem saveMenuItem = new MenuItem(filemenu, SWT.PUSH);
    saveMenuItem.setText("&Save\tCTRL+S");
    saveMenuItem.setAccelerator(SWT.CTRL+'S');
    final MenuItem separator = new MenuItem(filemenu, SWT.SEPARATOR);
    final MenuItem exitMenuItem = new MenuItem(filemenu, SWT.PUSH);
    exitMenuItem.setText("E&xit");

    // create an Edit menu and add Cut, Copy, and Paste items
    final MenuItem edit = new MenuItem(m, SWT.CASCADE);
    edit.setText("&Edit");
    final Menu editmenu = new Menu(s, SWT.DROP_DOWN);
    edit.setMenu(editmenu);
    final MenuItem cutMenuItem = new MenuItem(editmenu, SWT.PUSH);
    cutMenuItem.setText("&Cut");
    final MenuItem copyMenuItem = new MenuItem(editmenu, SWT.PUSH);
    copyMenuItem.setText("Co&py");
    final MenuItem pasteMenuItem = new MenuItem(editmenu, SWT.PUSH);
    pasteMenuItem.setText("&Paste");
```

Example 15-2. Using a ToolBar with a CoolBar (continued)

```
//create a Window menu and add Child items
final MenuItem window = new MenuItem(m, SWT.CASCADE);
window.setText("&Window");
final Menu windowmenu = new Menu(s, SWT.DROP_DOWN);
window.setMenu(windowmenu);
final MenuItem maxMenuItem = new MenuItem(windowmenu, SWT.PUSH);
maxMenuItem.setText("Ma&ximize");
final MenuItem minMenuItem = new MenuItem(windowmenu, SWT.PUSH);
minMenuItem.setText("Mi&nimize");

// create a Help menu and add an About item
final MenuItem help = new MenuItem(m, SWT.CASCADE);
help.setText("&Help");
final Menu helpmenu = new Menu(s, SWT.DROP_DOWN);
help.setMenu(helpmenu);
final MenuItem abouMenutItem = new MenuItem(helpmenu, SWT.PUSH);
aboutMenuItem.setText("&About");

// add action listeners for the menu items

openMenuItem.addSelectionListener(new SelectionListener() {
    public void widgetSelected(SelectionEvent e) {
        System.out.println("Open");
    }
    public void widgetDefaultSelected(SelectionEvent e) {
    }
    });


saveMenuItem.addSelectionListener(new SelectionListener() {
    public void widgetSelected(SelectionEvent e) {
        System.out.println("Save");
    }
    public void widgetDefaultSelected(SelectionEvent e) {
    }
    });

exitMenuItem.addSelectionListener(new SelectionListener() {
    public void widgetSelected(SelectionEvent e) {
        System.exit(0);
    }
    public void widgetDefaultSelected(SelectionEvent e) {
    }
    });

cutMenuItem.addSelectionListener(new SelectionListener() {
    public void widgetSelected(SelectionEvent e) {
        System.out.println("Cut");
    }
    public void widgetDefaultSelected(SelectionEvent e) {
    }
    });
```

Example 15-2. Using a ToolBar with a CoolBar (continued)

```java
            copyMenuItem.addSelectionListener(new SelectionListener( ) {
                public void widgetSelected(SelectionEvent e) {
                    System.out.println("Copy");
                }
                public void widgetDefaultSelected(SelectionEvent e) {
                }
                });

            pasteMenuItem.addSelectionListener(new SelectionListener( ) {
                public void widgetSelected(SelectionEvent e) {
                    System.out.println("Paste");
                }
                public void widgetDefaultSelected(SelectionEvent e) {
                }
                });

            maxMenuItem.addSelectionListener(new SelectionListener( ) {
                public void widgetSelected(SelectionEvent e) {
                    Shell parent = (Shell)maxItem.getParent().getParent( );
                    parent.setMaximized(true);
                }
                public void widgetDefaultSelected(SelectionEvent e) {
                }
                });

            minMenuItem.addSelectionListener(new SelectionListener( ) {
                public void widgetSelected(SelectionEvent e) {
                    Shell parent = (Shell)minItem.getParent().getParent( );
                    parent.setMaximized(false);
                }
                public void widgetDefaultSelected(SelectionEvent e) {
                }
                });

            aboutMenuItem.addSelectionListener(new SelectionListener( ) {
                public void widgetSelected(SelectionEvent e) {
                    System.out.println("Help Invoked");
                }
                public void widgetDefaultSelected(SelectionEvent e) {
                }
                });

        s.setMenuBar(m);
        s.open( );
        while(!s.isDisposed( )){
            if(!d.readAndDispatch( ))
                d.sleep( );
        }
        d.dispose( );
    }
}
```

Executing the new example will show Figure 15-3.

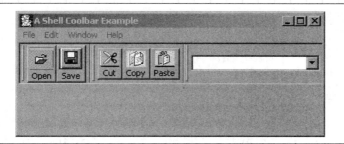

Looks much neater, doesn't it? I always use toolbars when I use a CoolBar

Figure 15-3. CoolBar with ToolBar

What just happened?

Instead of adding `Button` objects to the `CoolItem` objects to create the desired functionality, Example 15-2 creates two `ToolBar` objects—one for the file functions and the other for the editing functions. The relevant changes are found in this section of code:

```
final CoolItem fileCoolItem = new CoolItem(coolBar, SWT.NONE);

final ToolBar fileToolBar = new ToolBar(coolBar,SWT.HORIZONTAL);
final ToolItem openToolItem = new ToolItem(fileToolBar, SWT.PUSH);
openToolItem.setImage(openIcon);
openToolItem.setText("Open");
openToolItem.setToolTipText("Open");

final ToolItem saveToolItem = new ToolItem(fileToolBar, SWT.PUSH);
saveToolItem.setImage(saveIcon);
saveToolItem.setText("Save");
saveToolItem.setToolTipText("Save");

fileToolBar.pack();
Point size = fileToolBar.getSize();
fileCoolItem.setControl(fileToolBar);
fileCoolItem.setSize(fileCoolItem.computeSize(size.x, size.y));

final CoolItem editbarCoolItem = new CoolItem(coolBar, SWT.PUSH);
final ToolBar editToolBar = new ToolBar(coolBar,SWT.HORIZONTAL);

//create and add the button for performing a cut operation
final ToolItem cutToolItem = new ToolItem(editToolBar, SWT.PUSH);
cutToolItem.setImage(cutIcon);
cutToolItem.setText("Cut");
cutToolItem.setToolTipText("Cut");

// create and add the button for performing a copy operation
final ToolItem copyToolItem = new ToolItem(editToolBar, SWT.PUSH);
copyToolItem.setImage(copyIcon);
```

```
copyToolItem.setText("Copy");
copyToolItem.setToolTipText("Copy");

// create and add the button for performing a paste operation
final ToolItem pasteToolItem = new ToolItem(editToolBar, SWT.PUSH);
pasteToolItem.setImage(pasteIcon);
pasteToolItem.setText("Paste");
pasteToolItem.setToolTipText("Paste");
editToolBar.pack();
size = editToolBar.getSize();
editbarCoolItem.setControl(editToolBar);
editbarCoolItem.setSize(editbarCoolItem.computeSize(size.x, size.y));
```

Here, a CoolItem is first instantiated to serve as the holder for the ToolBar that contains the file items ("Open" and "Save"):

```
final CoolItem fileCoolItem = new CoolItem(coolBar, SWT.NONE);
```

The ToolBar is then created and ToolItem objects are added in the same manner as if the ToolBar were to be used directly on the Shell:

```
final ToolBar fileToolBar = new ToolBar(coolBar,SWT.HORIZONTAL);
final ToolItem openToolItem = new ToolItem(fileToolBar, SWT.PUSH);
openToolItem.setImage(openIcon);
openToolItem.setText("Open");
openToolItem.setToolTipText("Open");

final ToolItem saveToolItem = new ToolItem(fileToolBar, SWT.PUSH);
saveToolItem.setImage(saveIcon);
saveToolItem.setText("Save");
saveToolItem.setToolTipText("Save");
```

Finally, the ToolBar is associated with the CoolItem as if it were any other widget:

```
fileToolBar.pack();
Point size = fileToolBar.getSize();
fileCoolItem.setControl(fileToolBar);
fileCoolItem.setSize(fileCoolItem.computeSize(size.x, size.y));
```

The process is then repeated to create a separate ToolBar for the edit functions ("Cut,""Copy," and "Paste"):

```
final CoolItem editbarCoolItem = new CoolItem(coolBar, SWT.PUSH);
final ToolBar editToolBar = new ToolBar(coolBar,SWT.HORIZONTAL);

//create and add the button for performing a cut operation
final ToolItem cutToolItem = new ToolItem(editToolBar, SWT.PUSH);
cutToolItem.setImage(cutIcon);
cutToolItem.setText("Cut");
cutToolItem.setToolTipText("Cut");

// create and add the button for performing a copy operation
final ToolItem copyToolItem = new ToolItem(editToolBar, SWT.PUSH);
copyToolItem.setImage(copyIcon);
copyToolItem.setText("Copy");
```

```
copyToolItem.setToolTipText("Copy");

// create and add the button for performing a paste operation
final ToolItem pasteToolItem = new ToolItem(editToolBar, SWT.PUSH);
pasteToolItem.setImage(pasteIcon);
pasteToolItem.setText("Paste");
pasteToolItem.setToolTipText("Paste");
editToolBar.pack();
size = editToolBar.getSize();
editbarCoolItem.setControl(editToolBar);
editbarCoolItem.setSize(editbarCoolItem.computeSize(size.x, size.y));
```

As the example demonstrates, you can maintain functional groupings using the ToolBar and CoolBar in combination. The issue of the user being able to separate functional groupings is eliminated, as is the issue of proper sizing of individual widgets due to the associated images. Finally, the ability to use text labels together with images is restored.

Coolbars are a great way to easily permit the user to customize the user interface to her taste; however, care must be taken in planning, in order to maintain proper sizing of the individual widgets placed on the CoolBar and in maintaining functional groups as the user rearranges items on the CoolBar.

CHAPTER 16

SWT Slider and ProgressBar

Two useful interface elements are sliders and progress bars. Sliders permit the user to choose a value from within a range of values, simply by dragging the control with the mouse. The volume control found in many sound-enabled applications is an example of a slider.

Progress bars are useful when the user has initiated a long-running process such as a file transfer. The progress meter gives the user the ability to monitor the progress of the operation, to see how much of the operation is complete as well as how much remains.

The SWT provides the classes needed to easily include both sliders and progress bars in your applications.

The SWT Slider Class

The ability to create sliders in the SWT is encapsulated in a single class—Slider, part of the org.eclipse.swt.widgets package. Slider provides the ability to use a single widget to enable the user to specify a range of values, much like was done using the SWT.ARROW style of Button in Chapter 6. In fact, building a similar interface using Slider is a great way to examine the uses of the Slider class.

How do I do that?

To duplicate the SWT.ARROW Button example from Chapter 6, you must create a Shell and add two widgets—a Text to display the data and a Slider to enable the user to alter the data. Example 16-1 demonstrates how to do this.

Example 16-1. Using a Slider to obtain input

```java
import org.eclipse.swt.SWT;
import org.eclipse.swt.events.SelectionAdapter;
import org.eclipse.swt.events.SelectionEvent;
import org.eclipse.swt.graphics.Image;
import org.eclipse.swt.widgets.*;

public class SliderExample {

    Display d;
    Shell s;
    SliderExample()     {
        d = new Display();
         s = new Shell(d);
        s.setSize(250,250);
        s.setImage(new Image(d, "c:\\icons\\JavaCup.ico"));
        s.setText("A Slider Example");
        final Slider slide = new Slider(s, SWT.HORIZONTAL);
        slide.setBounds(115,50, 25, 15);
        slide.setMinimum(0);
        slide.setMaximum(100);
        slide.setIncrement(1);

        final Text t = new Text(s, SWT.BORDER);
        t.setBounds(115, 25, 25, 25);
        t.setText("0");

        slide.addSelectionListener(new SelectionAdapter() {
            public void widgetSelected(SelectionEvent e) {
                t.setText(new Integer(slide.getSelection()).toString());
            }
        });

        s.open();
        while(!s.isDisposed()){
            if(!d.readAndDispatch())
                d.sleep();
        }
        d.dispose();
    }
}
```

If you create an instance of SliderExample, it causes Figure 16-1 to be displayed.

If you click the right arrow, the value in the text field increases, while clicking the left button causes it to decrease.

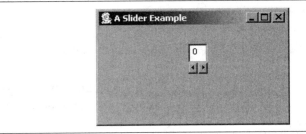

Figure 16-1. A slider

What just happened?

If you compare the code in Example 16-1 with the code that created the SWT.ARROW Button example in Chapter 4, you find that this code is less complex. That's because the Slider already encapsulates most of the code required to achieve the desired effect., so all that is required is to create and configure the Slider:

```
final Slider slide = new Slider(s, SWT.HORIZONTAL);
slide.setBounds(115,50, 25, 15);
slide.setMinimum(0);
slide.setMaximum(100);
slide.setIncrement(1);
```

The crucial methods are setMinimum( ) and setMaximum( ). As their names imply, these methods set the range of values through which the slider will slide. In the example, the slider is configured to slide between 0 and 100:

```
slide.setMinimum(0);
slide.setMaximum(100);
```

The next critical method is setIncrement( ), which determines what value will be added to the slider each time one of the arrows is clicked. In this case, the setting is 1:

```
slide.setIncrement(1);
```

Finally, a SelectionListener is used to interact with the slider as the user clicks the arrows:

```
slide.addSelectionListener(new SelectionAdapter( ) {
      public void widgetSelected(SelectionEvent e) {
        t.setText(new Integer(slide.getSelection()).toString( ));
      }
});
```

In the widgetSelected( ) method, getSelection( ) is called to determine the current value in the slider, which is converted to a String for display in the text widget:

```
t.setText(new Integer(slide.getSelection()).toString( ));
```

What about...

Slider objects that permit you to see the scrollbar portion of the slider? That is what's necessary in some interfaces to create a true "volume control" design.

No additional coding is required to show the scrollbar. You just need to expand the width of the slider so that it shows. This is done by changing the parameters passed to setBounds( ):

```
slide.setBounds(75,50, 100, 15);
```

Using this line in the example creates the display in Figure 16-2.

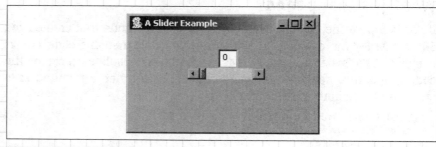

Figure 16-2. A wider slider

When you have a wider slider, you can manipulate a two more settings. The first is PageIncrement, which determines how much the slider will advance when the user clicks in the scrollbar portion rather than on the arrow buttons:

```
slide.setPageIncrement(10);
```

The preceding line means that 10 will be added to the current value of the slider each time the user clicks in the scrollbar.

The second method is used to control the size of the thumb, the button inside the scrollbar. The thumb has a width, a range of values that it covers on the slider. In this case, the width of the thumb is set to 1:

```
slide.setThumb(1);
```

The range that the thumb takes up when it gets to the end of the scrollbar causes a problem. In this case, the thumb has a value of 1, which means that when it gets to the end of the scrollbar it is still taking up one value of the slider. You can see the effect if you slide the slider all the way to the right—the highest value is 99 instead of the expected 100. To correct for this, you must increase the maximum range of the slider by a value equal to the width of the thumb:

A bit of a kludge, but it works.

```
slide.setMaximum(100);
```

Now the slider will slide through the entire range of 100, as expected.

Using the SWT ProgressBar Class

Progress bars are a great way to provide the user with feedback during a long-running process. As a general rule, users don't like clicking a button to begin a process without some visual cue that the process has begun and is continuing. For short processes—those whose time to completion is measured in seconds—displaying an hourglass cursor is sufficient. However, for processes that are measured in tens of seconds, or minutes, a progress bar is required.

The SWT encapsulates all the functionality required to develop progress bars in a single class—ProgressBar. ProgressBar operates much like Slider, as can be demonstrated with a simple example, creating the window shown in Figure 16-3.

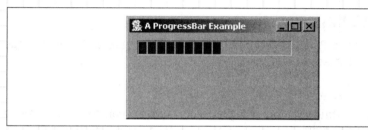

Figure 16-3. A ProgressBar example

How do I do that?

Example 16-2 creates a simple ProgressBar added directly to a Shell, with the progress hardcoded at 50% of completion, as shown in Figure 16-3.

Example 16-2. A ProgressBar example

```
import org.eclipse.swt.SWT;
import org.eclipse.swt.events.SelectionAdapter;
import org.eclipse.swt.events.SelectionEvent;
import org.eclipse.swt.graphics.Image;
import org.eclipse.swt.widgets.*;
public class ProgressBarExample {
    Display d;
    Shell s;
    ProgressBarExample()    {
        d = new Display();
        s = new Shell(d);
        s.setSize(250,250);
        s.setImage(new Image(d, "c:\\icons\\JavaCup.ico"));
        s.setText("A ProgressBar Example");
```

Example 16-2. A ProgressBar example (continued)

```
final ProgressBar pb = new ProgressBar(s,SWT.HORIZONTAL);
pb.setMinimum(0);
pb.setMaximum(100);
pb.setSelection(50);
pb.setBounds(10,10,200,20);

s.open();
while(!s.isDisposed()){
    if(!d.readAndDispatch())
        d.sleep();
}
d.dispose();
    }
}
```

What just happened?

As you can see, a ProgressBar is very similar to a Slider. It has a range of values that are accessed by:

```
pb.setMinimum(0);
pb.setMaximum(100);
```

The current setting of the ProgressBar, which controls how much progress is displayed to the user, is handled by a single method call:

```
pb.setSelection(50);
```

It is usually a good idea to set up a ProgressBar with a range from 0–100 so that you can easily convert the parameter passed to setSelection( ) from a percentage of completion.

Creating a Moving Progress Bar

Example 16-3 doesn't show a moving Progress Bar; it simply hardcodes the progress at 50%. It's easy to create an example that simulates a long-running process, to demonstrate exactly how to create the moving-progress-bar effect.

How do I do that?

In Example 16-3, a button is added to the interface, to simulate the user taking action to initiate some process.

Example 16-3. Simulating a long running process

```
import org.eclipse.swt.SWT;
import org.eclipse.swt.events.SelectionAdapter;
import org.eclipse.swt.events.SelectionEvent;
import org.eclipse.swt.graphics.Image;
import org.eclipse.swt.widgets.*;
public class ProgressBarExample {
    Display d;
    Shell s;
    ProgressBarExample()    {
        d = new Display();
        s = new Shell(d);
        s.setSize(250,250);
        s.setImage(new Image(d, "c:\\icons\\JavaCup.ico"));
        s.setText("A ProgressBar Example");
        final ProgressBar pb = new ProgressBar(s,SWT.HORIZONTAL);
        pb.setMinimum(0);
        pb.setMaximum(100);
        pb.setBounds(10,10,200,20);

        Button b = new Button(s, SWT.PUSH);
        b.setBounds(95, 80, 40, 20);
        b.setText("Start");
        b.addSelectionListener(new SelectionAdapter() {
            public void widgetSelected(SelectionEvent e) {
                int progress = 0;
                for(int n=0; n<=10000000;n++)
                {
                    if((n%100000)==0)
                    {
                        progress++;
                        pb.setSelection(progress);
                    }
                }
            }
        });

        s.open();

        while(!s.isDisposed()){
            if(!d.readAndDispatch())
                d.sleep();
        }
        d.dispose();
    }
}
```

In the `SelectionListener` for the `Button` is placed a loop that counts
from 0 to 80,000,000:

```
b.addSelectionListener(new SelectionAdapter() {
    public void widgetSelected(SelectionEvent e) {
        int progress = 0;
```

```
            for(int n=0; n<=80000000;n++)
            {
                if((n%800000)==0)
                {
                    progress+=10;
                    pb.setSelection(progress);
                }
            }
        }
    });
```

In each iteration of the loop, the code checks for a condition to determine progress:

```
if((n%800000)==0)
```

This is done by dividing the total number of iterations of the loop by a known number, to yield a percentage of completion—in this case, each time the if condition is true, it means that 10% of the process is complete. The ProgressBar is then updated to reflect that situation:

```
progress+=10;
pb.setSelection(progress);
```

Creating an instance of the class in Example 16-3 displays Figure 16-4.

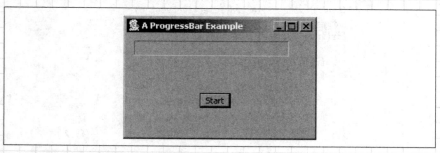

Figure 16-4. A simulated process

Clicking the Start button initiates the loop and starts the Progress Bar.

Both ProgressBar and Slider have uses in a user interface. When the situation calls for them, don't shy away—the user will expect them to be there. Fortunately, as has been shown by the examples, the SWT makes them easy to use.

CHAPTER 17

SWT Standard Dialogs

As GUI users, you are no doubt familiar with some of the complex windows used for common everyday operations such as opening files, choosing fonts or colors, and selecting which printer gets the output. If these windows had to be coded from scratch, the cost in development time would be high.

Recognizing this, the SWT provides us with predeveloped versions of these windows—known collectively as the Standard Dialogs. Six such dialogs are provided for your use:

- MessageBox
- DirectoryDialog
- FileDialog
- ColorDialog
- FontDialog
- PrintDialog

Each of these is represented by a single class that is located in the org.eclipse.swt.widgets package (except for PrintDialog, which resides in org.eclipse.swt.printing). The sections that follow discuss each in turn, showing how to incorporate them into your applications.

Using the SWT MessageBox Class

MessageBox is used to display some information to the user, such as an error condition, or to obtain simple input from the user, or both. The message box is displayed with a series of buttons, such as Yes, No, or Cancel. The program waits until the user makes a selection, then branches execution depending upon which selection was made.

How do I do that?

Perhaps the best example of using a MessageBox is seen when the user attempts to close an application by selecting File → Exit from the program's menu. Often a message box will appear asking the user for confirmation before actually exiting. Example 17-1 demonstrates such a system.

Example 17-1. A message box Confirmation

```java
import org.eclipse.swt.widgets.*;
import org.eclipse.swt.SWT;
import org.eclipse.swt.events.SelectionAdapter;
import org.eclipse.swt.events.SelectionEvent;
import org.eclipse.swt.graphics.Image;

public class MessageBoxExample {

    Display d;
    Shell s;
    MessageBoxExample()    {
        d = new Display();
        s = new Shell(d);
        s.setSize(400,400);
        s.setImage(new Image(d, "c:\\icons\\JavaCup.ico"));
        s.setText("A MessageBox Example");
        // create the menu system
        Menu m = new Menu(s,SWT.BAR);
        // create a File menu and add an Exit item
        final MenuItem file = new MenuItem(m, SWT.CASCADE);
        file.setText("&File");
        final Menu filemenu = new Menu(s, SWT.DROP_DOWN);
        file.setMenu(filemenu);
        final MenuItem exitItem = new MenuItem(filemenu, SWT.PUSH);
        exitItem.setText("E&xit");
        exitItem.addSelectionListener(new SelectionAdapter() {
            public void widgetSelected(SelectionEvent e) {
                MessageBox messageBox = new MessageBox(s, SWT.ICON_QUESTION |
                        SWT.YES | SWT.NO);
                messageBox.setMessage("Do you really want to exit?");
                messageBox.setText("Exiting Application");
                int response = messageBox.open();
                if (response==SWT.YES)
                    System.exit(0);
            }
        });
        s.setMenuBar(m);
        s.open();

        while(!s.isDisposed()){
            if(!d.readAndDispatch())
                d.sleep();
        }
```

Example 17-1. A message box Confirmation (continued)

```
        d.dispose( );
    }
}
```

To see the message box, create an instance of `MessageBoxExample`, shown in Example 17-1, then select File → Exit from the menu. The message box appears as shown in Figure 17-1.

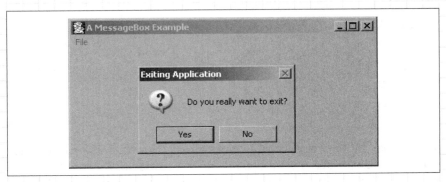

Figure 17-1. A confirmation message box

What just happened?

The code that makes this message box work is all in the `widgetSelected( )` method of the `SelectionListener` attached to the `exitMenuItem`:

```
public void widgetSelected(SelectionEvent e) {
    MessageBox messageBox = new MessageBox(s, SWT.ICON_QUESTION |
            SWT.YES | SWT.NO);
    messageBox.setMessage("Do you really want to exit?");
    messageBox.setText("Exiting Application");
    int response = messageBox.open( );
    if (response==SWT.YES)
        System.exit(0);
}
```

`MessageBox` dialogs are created just like any other widget: by passing the constructor a reference (to the `Shell` that serves as the parent) and the style attribute(s) (to customize the appearance of the resulting dialog):

```
MessageBox messageBox = new MessageBox(s, SWT.ICON_QUESTION |
            SWT.YES | SWT.NO);
```

`MessageBox` styles come in two categories. The first controls the icon displayed in the message box. Possible values are:

- `SWT.ICON_ERROR`
- `SWT.ICON_INFORMATION`

- SWT.ICON_QUESTION
- SWT.ICON_WARNING
- SWT.ICON_WORKING

In the example, the user is being asked a question, so SWT.ICON_QUESTION is appropriate.

The second category of MessageBox style determines which buttons are included in the dialog. Possible values are:

- SWT.YES
- SWT.NO
- SWT.CANCEL
- SWT.ABORT
- SWT.RETRY
- SWT.IGNORE

The proper number and combinations of buttons used depend entirely upon the user input that is sought. In the example, the only possible choices for the question "Do you really want to exit?" are Yes and No.

The next two lines of code specify the message text that's to be displayed to the user and the title bar text for the dialog:

```
messageBox.setMessage("Do you really want to exit?");
messageBox.setText("Exiting Application");
```

Finally, the message box is displayed to the user:

```
int response = messageBox.open();
```

Since MessageBox is a type of dialog, as you learned in Chapter 2, all code execution halts when the dialog is opened, and remains suspended until the user dismisses the dialog. At that time, the result of the dialog is returned to the calling program to be stored—in this case, in the variable response. The value returned depends entirely upon which button is selected by the user.

The next code determines whether the user clicked the Yes button (you don't care if he clicked No, since no action needs be taken in that case):

```
if(response==SWT.YES)
    System.exit(0);
```

If Yes is the button selected, the program exits. Otherwise, nothing happens and the program continues to execute normally.

As you can see, MessageBox is a straightforward way of providing information to the user and obtaining user input. The SWT MessageBox class makes it easy to incorporate that type of functionality in your applications.

Try to avoid overusing MessageBox. It's quite annoying to have things popping up at you all the time. Use it only when it's absolutely necessary to communicate directly with the user.

Using the SWT FileDialog Class

If your application deals with files in any manner, you need a mechanism to ask the user for a filename (to open or save). You have no doubt seen examples of file open dialogs in your favorite development environment or text editor, and you know that they can be fairly complex. A file open dialog will contain many buttons, and a list box or tree view (or both) that enables the user to navigate through the filesystem.

Developing such a dialog from scratch would take many hours of programming time. Fortunately, the SWT `FileDialog` class does all the heavy lifting for you—all you need to do is create an instance of `FileDialog` and specify a few parameters.

How do I do that?

`FileDialog` works almost exactly like `MessageBox`, with just a few different settings to work with. The most logical example of the use of `FileDialog` is to prompt the user for File Open and File Save information, as demonstrated in Example 17-2.

Example 17-2. Using FileDialog

```java
import org.eclipse.swt.widgets.*;
import org.eclipse.swt.SWT;
import org.eclipse.swt.events.SelectionAdapter;
import org.eclipse.swt.events.SelectionEvent;
import org.eclipse.swt.events.SelectionListener;
import org.eclipse.swt.graphics.Image;

public class FileDialogExample {
    Display d;
    Shell s;
    FileDialogExample( )    {
        d = new Display( );
        s = new Shell(d);
        s.setSize(400,400);
        s.setImage(new Image(d, "c:\\icons\\JavaCup.ico"));
        s.setText("A MessageBox Example");
        // create the menu system
        Menu m = new Menu(s,SWT.BAR);
        // create a File menu and add an Exit item
        final MenuItem file = new MenuItem(m, SWT.CASCADE);
        file.setText("&File");
        final Menu filemenu = new Menu(s, SWT.DROP_DOWN);
        file.setMenu(filemenu);
        final MenuItem openItem = new MenuItem(filemenu, SWT.PUSH);
        openItem.setText("&Open\tCTRL+O");
        openItem.setAccelerator(SWT.CTRL+'O');
```

Example 17-2. *Using FileDialog (continued)*

```java
        final MenuItem saveItem = new MenuItem(filemenu, SWT.PUSH);
        saveItem.setText("&Save\tCTRL+S");
        saveItem.setAccelerator(SWT.CTRL+'S');
        final MenuItem separator = new MenuItem(filemenu, SWT.SEPARATOR);
        final MenuItem exitItem = new MenuItem(filemenu, SWT.PUSH);
        exitItem.setText("E&xit");

        class Open implements SelectionListener
        {
            public void widgetSelected(SelectionEvent event) {
                FileDialog fd = new FileDialog(s, SWT.OPEN);
                fd.setText("Open");
                fd.setFilterPath("C:/");
                String[] filterExt = {"*.txt","*.doc", ".rtf", "*.*"};
                fd.setFilterExtensions(filterExt);
                String selected = fd.open();
                System.out.println(selected);
            }
            public void widgetDefaultSelected(SelectionEvent event)
            {
            }
        }

        class Save implements SelectionListener
        {
            public void widgetSelected(SelectionEvent event) {
                FileDialog fd = new FileDialog(s, SWT.SAVE);
                fd.setText("Save");
                fileDialog.setFilterPath("C:/");
                String[] filterExt = {"*.txt","*.doc", ".rtf", "*.*"};
                fd.setFilterExtensions(filterExt);
                String selected = fd.open();
                System.out.println(selected);
            }
            public void widgetDefaultSelected(SelectionEvent event)
            {
            }
        }
        openItem.addSelectionListener(new Open());
        saveItem.addSelectionListener(new Save());

        exitItem.addSelectionListener(new SelectionAdapter() {
            public void widgetSelected(SelectionEvent e) {
                MessageBox messageBox = new MessageBox(s, SWT.ICON_QUESTION |
                        SWT.YES | SWT.NO );
                messageBox.setMessage("Do you really want to exit?");
                messageBox.setText("Exiting Application");
                int response = messageBox.open();
                if (response==SWT.YES)
                    System.exit(0);
            }
        });
```

Example 17-2. Using FileDialog (continued)

```
        s.setMenuBar(m);
        s.open( );

        while(!s.isDisposed( )){
            if(!d.readAndDispatch( ))
                d.sleep( );
        }
        d.dispose( );
    }
}
```

If you create an instance of FileDialogExample, from Example 17-2, and
select File → Open, you see the dialog shown in Figure 17-2.

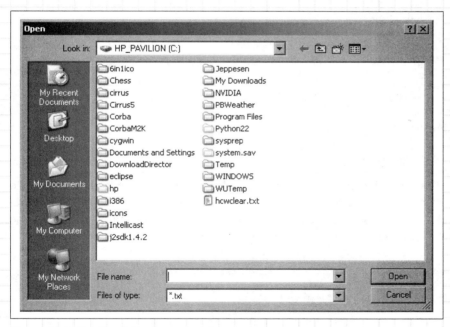

Figure 17-2. The file dialog in open mode

Clicking File → Save displays Figure 17-3—the file dialog in save mode.

In either dialog, navigate the directory structure until you find the desired
file, then click Open (or Save). The name of the file you selected is then
printed to the console.

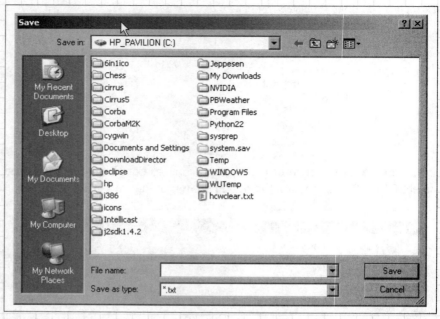

Figure 17-3. File dialog in save mode

What just happened?

The code that creates these two dialogs is identical, except for the style attribute passed to the FileDialog constructor. The relevant code for the FileDialog used to open files is in the widgetSelected() method of the SelectionListener attached to the openMenuItem:

```
public void widgetSelected(SelectionEvent event) {
    FileDialog fd = new FileDialog(s, SWT.OPEN);
    fd.setText("Open");
    fd.setFilterPath("C:/");
    String[] filterExt = {"*.txt","*.doc", ".rtf", "*.*"};
    fd.setFilterExtensions(filterExt);
    String selected = fd.open();
    System.out.println(selected);
}
```

The first line in widgetSelected() creates the FileDialog object. As with all widgets, a reference to the Shell and a style are required parameters. Two styles—SWT.OPEN and SWT.SAVE—control the text on the button the user clicks to perform the intended action.

Next, the FileDialog is configured so that it knows which directory to display initially and which files within that directory will be displayed:

```
fd.setText("Open");
fd.setFilterPath("C:/");
String[] filterExt = {"*.txt","*.doc", ".rtf", "*.*"};
```

Here, the dialog is set to open in the root directory of the C drive (on a Windows XP system; the parameter passed to a non-Windows system will be different). `setFilterExtensions()` is called to specify what files within the directory will be displayed. It accepts an array of `String` objects that contain the extension list.

Finally, the dialog is opened. As with `MessageBox`, processing in the calling code is halted until the user dismisses the dialog, at which time the current selection of the dialog will be returned to the caller:

```
String selected = fd.open();
```

The variable `selected` contains the file that was selected when the dialog was closed. If no file was selected, the variable is `null`.

The same code opens the `FileDialog` in save mode, except that the style passed to the constructor is `SWT.SAVE`.

As you can see, using `FileDialog` takes the complexity out of obtaining a filename selection from the user.

What about...

times when you need to obtain only a directory name, not a complete file name? The SWT provides a similar dialog for that purpose—`DirectoryDialog`. `DirectoryDialog` works almost exactly like `FileDialog`, right down to the types of settings that must be specified:

```
DirectoryDialog dd = new DirectoryDialog(s);
dd.setText("Choose a Directory");
dd.setFilterPath("C:/Program Files");
String selected = dd.open();
System.out.println(selected);
```

As you see, the only difference is that no filter extensions are required. A typical `DirectoryDialog` looks like Figure 17-4 on the Windows XP platform.

Navigating to a directory and clicking OK results in the directory name being printed to the console.

The SWT ColorDialog Class

The SWT `ColorDialog` class permits you to enable the user to easily change the color being used by your application to display widgets or text. The dialog provides a graphical mechanism for choosing the desired color, which can then be passed to the `setBackground()` method of a widget.

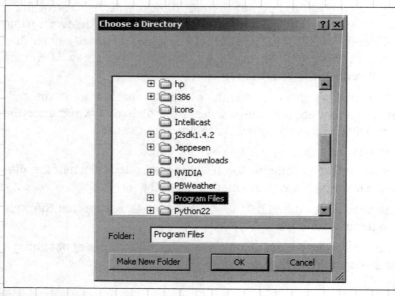

Figure 17-4. DirectoryDialog

How do I do that?

You use the ColorDialog in the same manner as the dialogs that have already been discussed. Example 17-3 demonstrates how to use ColorDialog to change the background color of a Text widget.

Example 17-3. Using ColorDialog

```java
import org.eclipse.swt.widgets.*;
import org.eclipse.swt.SWT;
import org.eclipse.swt.events.SelectionAdapter;
import org.eclipse.swt.events.SelectionEvent;
import org.eclipse.swt.graphics.Color;
import org.eclipse.swt.graphics.Image;
import org.eclipse.swt.graphics.RGB;
import org.eclipse.swt.layout.FillLayout;

public class ColorDialogExample {

    Display d;
    Shell s;
    ColorDialogExample()     {
        d = new Display();
        s = new Shell(d);
        s.setSize(400,400);
        s.setImage(new Image(d, "c:\\icons\\JavaCup.ico"));
        s.setText("A ColorDialog Example");
        s.setLayout(new FillLayout(SWT.VERTICAL));
```

Example 17-3. Using ColorDialog (continued)

```
        final Text t = new Text(s, SWT.BORDER | SWT.MULTI);
        final Button b = new Button(s, SWT.PUSH | SWT.BORDER);
        b.setText("Change Color");
        b.addSelectionListener(new SelectionAdapter() {
            public void widgetSelected(SelectionEvent e) {
                ColorDialog cd = new ColorDialog(s);
                cd.setText("ColorDialog Demo");
                cd.setRGB(new RGB(255,255,255));
                RGB newColor = cd.open();
                if(newColor==null)
                {
                    return;
                }
                t.setBackground(new Color(d, newColor));
            }
        });
        s.open();

        while(!s.isDisposed()){
            if(!d.readAndDispatch())
                d.sleep();
        }
        d.dispose();
    }
}
```

This is a lot of functionality for just a little coding effort. That's a great thing.

If you create an instance of ColorDialogExample, from Example 17-3, Figure 17-5 is displayed. Clicking the Change Color button invokes the color dialog, shown in Figure 17-6. Selecting the color blue from the Basic colors chart, and then clicking OK, results in Figure 17-7.

As you can see, permitting the user to control application colors is very easy when using ColorDialog.

What just happened?

The relevant code is in the widgetSelected() method of the SelectionListener attached to Button b:

```
    public void widgetSelected(SelectionEvent e) {
        ColorDialog cd = new ColorDialog(s);
        cd.setText("ColorDialog Demo");
        cd.setRGB(new RGB(0,0,0));
        RGB newColor = cd.open();
        if(newColor==null)
        {
            return;
        }
        t.setBackground(new Color(d, newColor));
    }
```

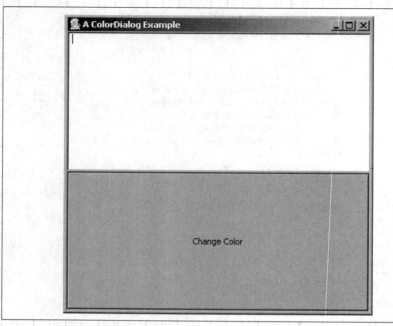

Figure 17-5. ColorDialog example

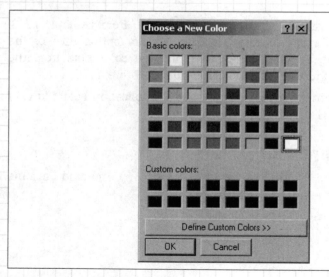

Figure 17-6. The color dialog

The color dialog is first created in the usual manner:

```
ColorDialog cd = new ColorDialog(s);
cd.setText("ColorDialog Demo");
```

Figure 17-7. After changing the color

setRGB( ) is then called to specify the color that will be selected when the dialog opens. Use setRGB( ) to provide a hint to the user as to an appropriate color or to position the dialog on the color that is currently in use. In the example, the dialog is positioned to open on white, the most popular color for Text widgets:

```
cd.setRGB(new RGB(255,255,255));
```

The dialog is then opened, halting the widgetSelected( ) method until the user dismisses the dialog. The color selected is returned into the variable newColor:

```
RGB newColor = cd.open( );
```

Finally, after checking that the user actually selected a color, newColor is passed to the setBackground( ) method of the Text widget:

```
if(newColor==null)
{
    return;
}
t.setBackground(new Color(d, newColor));
```

Permitting the user to change colors is that simple.

Using the SWT FontDialog Class

The FontDialog class is used to present the user with a standard user interface for selecting fonts for Text widgets.

How do I do that?

The use of FontDialog is similar to that of the dialogs previously discussed. Example 17-4 demonstrates a common use of FontDialog—permitting the user to select the font for a Text widget.

Example 17-4. Using the FontDialog

```
import org.eclipse.swt.widgets.*;
import org.eclipse.swt.SWT;
import org.eclipse.swt.events.SelectionAdapter;
import org.eclipse.swt.events.SelectionEvent;
import org.eclipse.swt.graphics.Color;
import org.eclipse.swt.graphics.Font;
import org.eclipse.swt.graphics.FontData;
import org.eclipse.swt.graphics.Image;
import org.eclipse.swt.graphics.RGB;
import org.eclipse.swt.layout.FillLayout;

public class FontDialogExample {

    Display d;
    Shell s;
    FontDialogExample()     {
        d = new Display();
        s = new Shell(d);
        s.setSize(400,400);
        s.setImage(new Image(d, "c:\\icons\\JavaCup.ico"));
        s.setText("A FontDialog Example");
        s.setLayout(new FillLayout(SWT.VERTICAL));
        final Text t = new Text(s, SWT.BORDER | SWT.MULTI);
        final Button b = new Button(s, SWT.PUSH | SWT.BORDER);
        b.setText("Change Font");
        b.addSelectionListener(new SelectionAdapter() {
            public void widgetSelected(SelectionEvent e) {
                FontDialog fd = new FontDialog(s, SWT.NONE);
                fd.setText("Select Font");
                fd.setRGB(new RGB(0,0,255));
                FontData defaultFont = new FontData("Courier",10,SWT.BOLD);
                fd.setFontData(defaultFont);
                FontData newFont = fd.open();
                if(newFont==null)
                    return;
                t.setFont(new Font(d, newFont));
                t.setForeground(new Color(d, fd.getRGB()));
            }
```

Example 17-4. Using the FontDialog (continued)

```
        });
        s.open();

        while(!s.isDisposed()){
            if(!d.readAndDispatch())
                d.sleep();
        }
        d.dispose();
    }
}
```

When you create an instance of FontDialogExample, from Example 17-4, it causes Figure 17-8 to be displayed (you can enter any text you want in the Text widget).

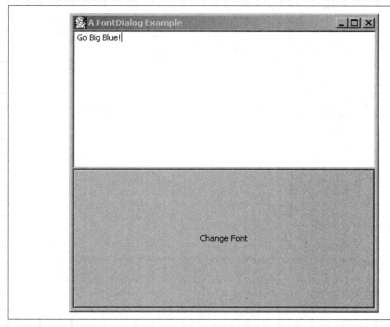

Once again, this is pretty sophisticated behavior with only a small code investment required. The point is this: use the standard dialogs. There's no need to write your own.

Figure 17-8. FontDialogExample

When the user clicks Change Font, the Font dialog is invoked, as shown in Figure 17-9.

If the user makes the selections shown in Figure 17-9 and then clicks the OK button, the result is as shown in Figure 17-10.

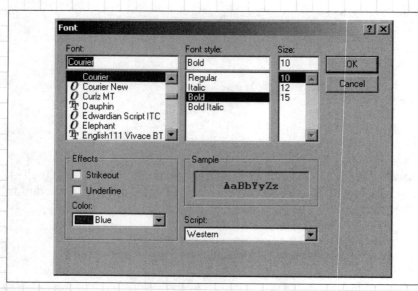

Figure 17-9. Change Font dialog with selections

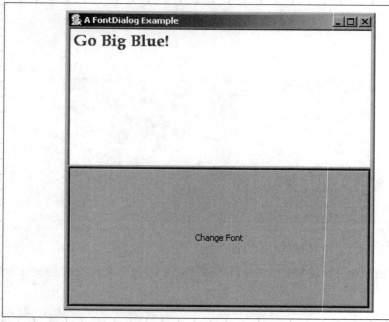

Figure 17-10. The result produced by changing the font

What just happened?

Once again, the code that makes the example work is in the
widgetSelected() method of the SelectionListener attached to Button b:

```
public void widgetSelected(SelectionEvent e) {
        FontDialog fd = new FontDialog(s, SWT.NONE);
        fd.setText("Select Font");
        fd.setRGB(new RGB(0,0,255));
        FontData defaultFont = new FontData("Courier",10,SWT.BOLD);
        fd.setFontData(defaultFont);
        FontData newFont = fd.open();
        if(newFont==null)
            return;
        t.setFont(new Font(d, newFont));
        t.setForeground(new Color(d, fd.getRGB()));
}
```

First, the font dialog is created in the normal manner:

```
FontDialog fd = new FontDialog(s, SWT.NONE);
fd.setText("Select Font");
```

The font dialog is then configured. The first configuration specifies the
color selection that will be displayed when the dialog is opened. I chose
blue for this example:

```
fd.setRGB(new RGB(0,0,255));
```

Next, the default font is specified. This causes the dialog to open with a
preselected font:

```
FontData defaultFont = new FontData("Courier",10,SWT.BOLD);
fd.setFontData(defaultFont);
```

Finally, the dialog is opened. When the dialog is dismissed, the code
checks to see whether a font change has been made; if so, it calls
setFont() and setForeground() to properly configure the Text widget:

```
FontData newFont = fd.open();
if(newFont==null)
    return;
t.setFont(new Font(d, newFont));
t.setForeground(new Color(d, fd.getRGB()));
```

FontDialog offers the simplest way to enable users to select a font for
a Text widget. You should use it in almost any text-centric application.

Using the SWT PrintDialog Class

The final standard dialog is the PrintDialog, which permits the user to
select a print device to which output will be directed. It should be used
in any application that permits the user to send jobs to a printer.

How do I do that?

Creating the Print dialog and obtaining the printer settings is a simple task that is performed in much the same manner as obtaining a font from Font dialog or a color from Color dialog. Example 17-5 demonstrates the technique.

Example 17-5. Using PrintDialog

```
import org.eclipse.swt.widgets.*;
import org.eclipse.swt.SWT;
import org.eclipse.swt.events.*;
import org.eclipse.swt.graphics.*;
import org.eclipse.swt.layout.FillLayout;
import org.eclipse.swt.printing.*;


public class PrintDialogExample {
    Display d;
    Shell s;
    PrintDialogExample()    {
        d = new Display();
        s = new Shell(d);
        s.setSize(400,400);
        s.setImage(new Image(d, "c:\\icons\\JavaCup.ico"));
        s.setText("A PrintDialog Example");
        s.setLayout(new FillLayout(SWT.VERTICAL));
        final Text t = new Text(s, SWT.BORDER | SWT.MULTI);
        final Button b = new Button(s, SWT.PUSH | SWT.BORDER);
        b.setText("Print");
        b.addSelectionListener(new SelectionAdapter() {
            public void widgetSelected(SelectionEvent e) {
                PrintDialog printDialog = new PrintDialog(s, SWT.NONE);
                printDialog.setText("Print");
                PrinterData printerData = printDialog.open();
                if(!(printerData==null))
                {
                    Printer p = new Printer(printerData);
                    p.startJob("PrintJob");
                    p.startPage();
                    Rectangle trim = p.computeTrim(0, 0, 0, 0);
                    Point dpi = p.getDPI();
                    int leftMargin = dpi.x + trim.x;
                    int topMargin = dpi.y / 2 + trim.y;
                    GC gc = new GC(p);
                    Font font = gc.getFont();
                    String printText= t.getText();
                    Point extent = gc.stringExtent(printText);
                    gc.drawString(printText, leftMargin, topMargin +
                            font.getFontData()[0].getHeight());
                    p.endPage();
                    gc.dispose();
                    p.endJob();
```

Example 17-5. Using PrintDialog (continued)

```
                    p.dispose( );
                }


            }
        });
        s.open( );

        while(!s.isDisposed( )){
            if(!d.readAndDispatch( ))
                d.sleep( );
        }
        d.dispose( );
    }
}
```

Creating an instance of PrintDialogExample, from Example 17-5, causes Figure 17-11 to display.

Figure 17-11. PrintDialogExample

Clicking the Print button invokes the Print dialog, shown in Figure 17-12.

Here, the user selects the desired printer and any other configuration options desired, and then clicks OK to send the output to the printer.

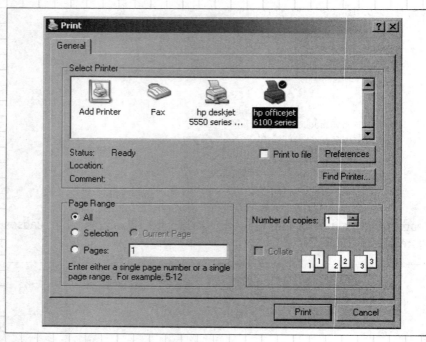

Figure 17-12. Print dialog

What just happened?

The code that makes this example work is in the widgetSelected()
method of the SelectionListener attached to Button b:

```
public void widgetSelected(SelectionEvent e) {
        PrintDialog printDialog = new PrintDialog(s, SWT.NONE);
        printDialog.setText("Print");
        PrinterData printerData = printDialog.open();
        if(!(printerData==null))
        {
            Printer p = new Printer(printerData);
            p.startJob("PrintJob");
            p.startPage();
            Rectangle trim = p.computeTrim(0, 0, 0, 0);
            Point dpi = p.getDPI();
            int leftMargin = dpi.x + trim.x;
            int topMargin = dpi.y / 2 + trim.y;
            GC gc = new GC(p);
            Font font = gc.getFont();
            String printText= t.getText();
            Point extent = gc.stringExtent(printText);
            gc.drawString(printText, leftMargin, topMargin +
                    font.getFontData()[0].getHeight());
            p.endPage();
```

```
            gc.dispose( );
            p.endJob( );
            p.dispose( );
        }
    }
```

After creating an instance of `PrintDialog`, the dialog is opened without the need for any additional configuration:

```
PrinterData printerData = printDialog.open( );
```

TIP

You can use some settings for `PrintDialog`, such as whether to print all pages, or just a range of pages. These settings are specified in the usual manner—by calling a method provided for that purpose.

Most of the code in the `if` block deals with sending the output to the chosen printer, a topic that is beyond the scope of this discussion. The selection made by the user resides in the `PrinterData` object returned from the call to `PrintDialog.open( )`. From that object, an instance of the `Printer` class is created, which permits interaction with the printer.

As you can see from these examples, the SWT standard dialogs make it very easy for you to provide complex functionality to your users. Imagine the hours of coding it would take to present just the File dialog. With the SWT, you have no excuse for not providing color customization or font selection capability when your application calls for it.

Printing in the SWT (actually in all of Java) has a few rough edges. It requires obtaining a graphics context to represent the printer, then "drawing" text on that context.

A Complete SWT Application

To complete the process of learning how to use the SWT, the final step is to complete a fully functioning application. Until now, the examples have been designed to showcase a single technique associated with a single widget. In this chapter, a Text Editor application will be developed and analyzed, as a demonstration of how to pull various techniques into a functional application.

Designing the Application

The first step of any development process is to design the application. For a complex application, the design phase can take at least as long as development time, and might consist of the development of screen layouts or even functional prototypes.

For the purposes of this exercise, making a simple list of the functionality required for the application will suffice. The list should be as comprehensive as possible to serve as a complete guide to exactly what functionality will be included in the application.

The SWT Text Editor will have the following functionality:

- The ability to edit text
- The ability to open files, with the contents being displayed in the text-editing area of the application
- The ability to save the contents of the text-editing area into a file for later use
- The ability to copy selected text from the text-editing area into the clipboard
- The ability to cut text from the text-editing area into the clipboard

- The ability to paste text from the clipboard into the text-editing area
- The ability to display an About dialog with information about the application
- A menu bar that allows access to all functionality
- A toolbar that allows access to the open, save, cut, copy, and paste functionality

The main window for the application should look like Figure 18-1.

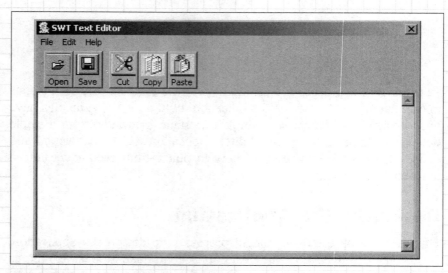

Figure 18-1. The Text Editor Application

When the user selects Help → About from the menu, an informational window is displayed, as in Figure 18-2.

Developing the Application

Once the design is well understood, the development process can begin. In this case, much of the development work has already been done in earlier examples—especially the toolbar example that was built in Chapter 4. From that core, development of the SWTTextEditor class, shown in Example 18-1, can be completed.

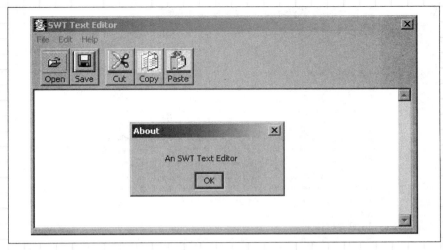

Figure 18-2. The About dialog

Example 18-1. The main SWTTextEditor class

```java
import java.io.*;
import org.eclipse.swt.SWT;
import org.eclipse.swt.events.*;
import org.eclipse.swt.graphics.Image;
import org.eclipse.swt.widgets.*;

public class SWTTextEditor {
        Display d;
        Shell s;
        SWTTextEditor()     {
            d = new Display();
            s = new Shell(d, SWT.CLOSE );
            s.setSize(500,500);
            s.setImage(new Image(d, "c:\\icons\\JavaCup.ico"));
            s.setText("SWT Text Editor");
            final ToolBar bar = new ToolBar(s,SWT.HORIZONTAL);
            final Text t = new Text(s, SWT.MULTI | SWT.V_SCROLL |
                    SWT.H_SCROLL | SWT.WRAP | SWT.BORDER);
            //create images for toolbar buttons
            final Image saveIcon = new Image(d, "c:\\icons\\save.jpg");
            final Image openIcon = new Image(d, "c:\\icons\\open.jpg");
            final Image childIcon = new Image(d, "c:\\icons\\userH.ico");
            final Image cutIcon = new Image(d, "c:\\icons\\cut.jpg");
            final Image copyIcon = new Image(d, "c:\\icons\\copy.jpg");
            final Image pasteIcon = new Image(d, "c:\\icons\\paste.jpg");

            //create ToolBar and ToolItems
            final ToolItem openToolItem = new ToolItem(bar, SWT.PUSH);
            final ToolItem saveToolItem = new ToolItem(bar, SWT.PUSH);
            final ToolItem sep1 = new ToolItem(bar, SWT.SEPARATOR);
            final ToolItem cutToolItem = new ToolItem(bar, SWT.PUSH);
```

Example 18-1. *The main SWTTextEditor class (continued)*

```java
            final ToolItem copyToolItem = new ToolItem(bar, SWT.PUSH);
            final ToolItem pasteToolItem = new ToolItem(bar, SWT.PUSH);

            //create the menu system
            final Menu m = new Menu(s,SWT.BAR);
            final MenuItem file = new MenuItem(m, SWT.CASCADE);
            final Menu filemenu = new Menu(s, SWT.DROP_DOWN);
            final MenuItem openMenuItem = new MenuItem(filemenu, SWT.PUSH);
            final MenuItem saveMenuItem = new MenuItem(filemenu, SWT.PUSH);
            final MenuItem separator = new MenuItem(filemenu, SWT.SEPARATOR);
            final MenuItem exitMenuItem = new MenuItem(filemenu, SWT.PUSH);
            final MenuItem edit = new MenuItem(m, SWT.CASCADE);
            final Menu editmenu = new Menu(s, SWT.DROP_DOWN);
            final MenuItem cutMenuItem = new MenuItem(editmenu, SWT.PUSH);
            final MenuItem copyMenuItem = new MenuItem(editmenu, SWT.PUSH);
            final MenuItem pasteMenuItem = new MenuItem(editmenu, SWT.PUSH);
            final MenuItem help = new MenuItem(m, SWT.CASCADE);
            final Menu helpmenu = new Menu(s, SWT.DROP_DOWN);
            final MenuItem aboutMenuItem = new MenuItem(helpmenu, SWT.PUSH);

        //create reusable named inner classes for SelectionListeners
        class Open extends SelectionAdapter
        {
            public void widgetSelected(SelectionEvent event) {
                FileDialog fileDialog = new FileDialog(s, SWT.OPEN);
                fileDialog.setText("Open");
                fileDialog.setFilterPath("C:/");
                String[] filterExt = {"*.txt", "*.*"};
                fileDialog.setFilterExtensions(filterExt);
                String selected = fileDialog.open();
                if (selected==null)
                    return;
                // code here to open the file and display
                FileReader file = null;
                try {
                    file = new FileReader(selected);
                }
                catch (FileNotFoundException e) {
                    MessageBox messageBox = new MessageBox(s, SWT.ICON_ERROR
                            | SWT.OK );
                    messageBox.setMessage("Could not open file.");
                    messageBox.setText("Error");
                    messageBox.open();
                    return;
                }
                BufferedReader fileInput = new BufferedReader(file);
                String text = null;
                StringBuffer sb = new StringBuffer();
                try {
                    do{
                        if(text!=null)
                            sb.append(text);
```

Example 18-1. The main SWTTextEditor class (continued)

```
                }
        while((text = fileInput.readLine())!=null);
          }
          catch (IOException e1) {
          MessageBox messageBox = new MessageBox(s, SWT.ICON_ERROR
                      | SWT.OK );
              messageBox.setMessage("Could not write to file.");
              messageBox.setText("Error");
              messageBox.open();
              return;
          }
          t.setText(sb.toString());
      }
  }

  class Save extends SelectionAdapter
  {
      public void widgetSelected(SelectionEvent event) {
          FileDialog fileDialog = new FileDialog(s, SWT.SAVE);
          fileDialog.setText("Save");
          fileDialog.setFilterPath("C:/");
          String[] filterExt = {"*.txt", "*.*"};
          fileDialog.setFilterExtensions(filterExt);
          String selected = fileDialog.open();
          if(selected==null)
              return;

          File file = new File(selected);
          try {
              FileWriter fileWriter = new FileWriter( file );
              fileWriter.write( t.getText() );
              fileWriter.close();
          } catch (IOException e) {
              MessageBox messageBox = new MessageBox(s, SWT.ICON_ERROR
                      | SWT.OK );
            messageBox.setMessage("File I/O Error.");
              messageBox.setText("Error");
              messageBox.open();
              return;
          }
      }
  }

  class Cut extends SelectionAdapter
  {
      public void widgetSelected(SelectionEvent event) {
          t.cut();
      }
  }

  class Copy extends SelectionAdapter
  {
```

Example 18-1. The main SWTTextEditor class (continued)

```
        public void widgetSelected(SelectionEvent event) {
            t.copy();
        }
    }

    class Paste extends SelectionAdapter
    {
        public void widgetSelected(SelectionEvent event) {
            t.paste();
        }
    }
    //set the size and location of the user interface widgets
    bar.setSize(500,55);
    bar.setLocation(10,0);
    t.setBounds(0, 56, 490, 395);

    //configure the toolbar
    openToolItem.setImage(openIcon);
    openToolItem.setText("Open");
    openToolItem.setToolTipText("Open File");
    saveToolItem.setImage(saveIcon);
    saveToolItem.setText("Save");
    saveToolItem.setToolTipText("Save File");
    cutToolItem.setImage(cutIcon);
    cutToolItem.setText("Cut");
    cutToolItem.setToolTipText("Cut");
    copyToolItem.setImage(copyIcon);
    copyToolItem.setText("Copy");
    copyToolItem.setToolTipText("Copy");
    pasteToolItem.setImage(pasteIcon);
    pasteToolItem.setText("Paste");
    pasteToolItem.setToolTipText("Paste");

    //add SelectionListeners to the toolbar buttons
    openToolItem.addSelectionListener(new Open());
    saveToolItem.addSelectionListener(new Save());
    cutToolItem.addSelectionListener(new Cut());
    copyToolItem.addSelectionListener(new Copy());
    pasteToolItem.addSelectionListener(new Paste());

    //configure the menu items
    file.setText("&File");
    file.setMenu(filemenu);
    openMenuItem.setText("&Open\tCTRL+O");
    openMenuItem.setAccelerator(SWT.CTRL+'O');
    saveMenuItem.setText("&Save\tCTRL+S");
    saveMenuItem.setAccelerator(SWT.CTRL+'S');
    exitMenuItem.setText("E&xit");
    edit.setText("&Edit");
    edit.setMenu(editmenu);
    cutMenuItem.setText("&Cut");
    copyMenuItem.setText("Co&py");
```

Example 18-1. The main SWTTextEditor class (continued)

```
            pasteMenuItem.setText("&Paste");
            help.setText("&Help");
            help.setMenu(helpmenu);
            aboutMenuItem.setText("&About");

            // add SelectionListeners for the menu items
            openMenuItem.addSelectionListener(new Open());
            saveMenuItem.addSelectionListener(new Save());
            exitMenuItem.addSelectionListener(new SelectionAdapter() {
                public void widgetSelected(SelectionEvent e) {
                    System.exit(0);
                }
            });
            cutMenuItem.addSelectionListener(new Cut());
            copyMenuItem.addSelectionListener(new Copy());
            pasteMenuItem.addSelectionListener(new Paste());
            aboutMenuItem.addSelectionListener(new SelectionAdapter() {
                public void widgetSelected(SelectionEvent e) {
                    AboutDialog ad = new AboutDialog(s);
                    ad.open();
                }
            });
            s.setMenuBar(m);
            s.open();
            while(!s.isDisposed()){
                if(!d.readAndDispatch())
                    d.sleep();
            }
            d.dispose();
    }
    // include a main method to make the class executable
    public static void main(String[] args)
    {
        SWTTextEditor ste = new SWTTextEditor();
    }
}
```

Example 18-2 is then used to create the dialog window that is displayed when the user clicks Help → About.

Example 18-2. Creating the About dialog

```
import org.eclipse.swt.SWT;
import org.eclipse.swt.events.SelectionAdapter;
import org.eclipse.swt.events.SelectionEvent;
import org.eclipse.swt.widgets.Button;
import org.eclipse.swt.widgets.Dialog;
import org.eclipse.swt.widgets.Display;
import org.eclipse.swt.widgets.Label;
import org.eclipse.swt.widgets.Shell;

public class AboutDialog extends Dialog {
```

Developing the Application | 279

Example 18-2. Creating the About dialog (continued)

```
AboutDialog(Shell parent)
{
    super(parent);
}
public void open()
{
    Shell parent = getParent();
    final Shell dialog = new Shell(parent, SWT.DIALOG_TRIM
            | SWT.APPLICATION_MODAL);
    dialog.setSize(200,100);
    dialog.setText("About");
    final Label l = new Label(dialog, SWT.NONE);
    l.setText("An SWT Text Editor");
    l.setBounds(43, 20, 100, 20);
    Button b = new Button(dialog, SWT.PUSH | SWT.BORDER);
    b.setText("OK");
    b.setBounds(80, 45, 40, 25);
    b.addSelectionListener(new SelectionAdapter() {
        public void widgetSelected(SelectionEvent e) {
            dialog.dispose();
        }
    });
    dialog.open();
    Display display = parent.getDisplay();
    while (!dialog.isDisposed())
    { if (!display.readAndDispatch()) display.sleep(); }
    }
}
}
```

Remember to substitute the actual locations of the swt.jar file and the SWT native library on your system. Also, both the SWTTextEditor. class and AboutDialog.class must be in the current directory.

Since SWTTextEditor includes a main() method, it can be executed as a standalone application from the command line. The command required to invoke the Text Editor is:

```
java -classpath .;C:\SWT\swt.jar
     -Djava.library.path=C:\SWT  SWTTextEditor
```

Once you have the Text Editor application running, you can verify that all toolbar buttons and menu items are functional. You can load up a text file, edit the text, and save the file back to disk.

What just happened?

All the techniques used in the Text Editor have been covered in other chapters. You may notice the code layout is slightly different—variable declarations are at the top of the SWTTextEditor constructor instead of being strewn throughout the code. Most Java developers have adopted the approach of grouping all variable declarations together, either at the top of the class for instance variables, or at the top of the method for local variables. Since this example demonstrates a complete, production-quality application, I went with the usual approach.

You also notice that no layout manager is used. Why? The most appropriate layout for this window would have been FillLayout. After all, the entire working area of the window is taken up by a single widget. However, the SWT FillLayout mishandles toolbars—it considers them to be just another widget. If you use FillLayout with a toolbar and a Text widget, the toolbar gets 50% of the window and the Text widget gets the other 50%—not what is appropriate for this application. That leaves the developer to size and position the widgets without the aid of a layout manager.

To keep things in position, the Shell is configured so that it is not resizable. That eliminates the requirement of calculating the new size of the Shell and repositioning the widgets to keep things in proportion. It's not an ideal solution, but it works well for this simple application. Perhaps the SWT developers will address this issue with FillLayout and toolbars in a future release.

Another difference between this application and most of the earlier examples is the use of named inner classes for the SelectionListener attached to the toolbar items and some of the menu items. A named inner class provides the advantage of permitting you to reuse the class multiple times. Since the menu items need to execute the same code as the toolbar items, there were three choices: duplicate the code in anonymous inner classes, put the common code in a method and duplicate the method call in anonymous inner classes, or use a named inner class. Since a named inner class results in fewer lines of code, it's the obvious solution.

MessageBox is used to display information to the user in case of an error reading or writing a file. This is an example of the proper use of MessageBox. Notice that the message does not include a stack trace. I can't emphasize enough that users do not want to see stack traces. Should you think that it's important to preserve a stack trace when an error condition occurs, you should attempt to write the trace to a log file, or print it to the console, not display it to the user.

What about...

the cut, copy, and paste functionality? That's easy to provide—it's built into the Text class:

```
t.cut();
t.copy();
t.paste();
```

These three lines appear in the inner classes that deal with each type of functionality. Nothing else needs to be done to allow your application to interact with the clipboard.

WARNING

The clipboard works completely differently on different platforms. On Windows, the clipboard is shared between different applications running in the operating system. This makes it possible to copy from SWTTextEditor and paste into Notepad.

On some versions of Linux, the clipboard does not work in this manner, but instead allows cutting, copying, and pasting only within a single application.

You must determine and code for the behavior typical of your target platform.

And what about incorporating additional functionality, such as printing? That's left to you to develop as an exercise to see how well you have learned SWT programming techniques. Using the PrintDialog example from Chapter 17, you should have no problem adding that functionality to this application.

The End of the SWT Road

The SWTTextEditor concludes this book's examination of the SWT. I hope you have found the SWT to be as fascinating as I have. If a truly native look and feel is essential to your application, and you don't mind the overhead of shipping an extra runtime library, the SWT is the way to go.

But remember that the SWT is still relatively young. Some elements common in other toolkits are not yet present in the SWT—the ability to write true MDI applications, for example. Although the same comment may be made about other Java-component-based toolkits, such as SWT and SWING, it's even more true of the SWT.

Still, the SWT does enable you to build interfaces using all of the most commonly used widgets—Text, Button, List, and Combo—which is all that's needed for many applications. It is also, in my opinion, much easier to learn and use than the SWING components.

Perhaps after reading this book, you will be in a position to try out the SWT in your next GUI-based application.

Index

Symbols

... (elipses), for omitted or implied
    code, xiv
| operator, combining shell style
    values, 20

A

About dialog (Text Editor
    application), 279
Abstract Windowing Toolkit (AWT), 1
accelerators (keyboard shortcuts), 49
Access database
    populating list from, 112
    populating text fields from, 82
adapter classes, 216
add( )
    Combo class, 124
    Control class, 87
    List class, 109
        two versions of, 110
addSelectionListener( ), 41, 69
anonymous inner classes, 41
    code organization for, 45
    MouseListener implemented
        as, 215
append( ), 83
APPLICATION_MODAL style
    attribute, 26
ARROW style (buttons), 102–104, 243
    specifying direction, 102
attachment points for form
    widgets, 156

attribution for materials from this
    book, xvi
auto-complete, 211
AWT (Abstract Windowing Toolkit), 1

B

background color
    changing for tables, 188–189
    changing for Text widget with
        ColorDialog, 260
    setting to single cell in table
        column, 191
BAR style, 33
BEGINNING setting (GridData), 151
BORDER style
    Composites, 162
    shells, 19
    text fields, 77
    trees, 197
Button class, 95
    getBackground( ), 222
    images, using with, 105
    setBackground( ), 222
    subclassing, 98
buttons, 95–106
    adding to container with FillLayout
        (example), 141
    arrow buttons, creating, 102–104
    ARROW style, 243
    changing color when mouse enters
        and exits, 221

We'd like to hear your suggestions for improving our indexes. Send email to *index@oreilly.com*.

About the Author

Tim Hatton is the president of Millennium Learning Technologies, a company specializing in the custom design of IT courseware and learning technologies. He has taught courses to developers at IBM, Lockheed-Martin, LexisNexis, and other Fortune 500 technology companies. Additionally, he has developed applications for these and other companies using a wide variety of tools, from PowerBuilder to Java. Tim has a BA in political science from Wright State University and a JD from the University of Dayton law school and was a practicing attorney in a prior life.

Colophon

Our look is the result of reader comments, our own experimentation, and feedback from distribution channels. Distinctive covers complement our distinctive approach to technical topics, breathing personality and life into potentially dry subjects.

The *Developer's Notebook* series is modeled on the tradition of laboratory notebooks. Laboratory notebooks are an invaluable tool for researchers and their successors.

The purpose of a laboratory notebook is to facilitate the recording of data and conclusions as the work is being conducted, creating a faithful and immediate history. The notebook begins with a title page that includes the owner's name and the subject of research. The pages of the notebook should be numbered and prefaced with a table of contents. Entries must be clear, easy to read, and accurately dated; they should use simple, direct language to indicate the name of the experiment and the steps taken. Calculations are written out carefully and relevant thoughts and ideas recorded. Each experiment is introduced and summarized as it is added to the notebook. The goal is to produce comprehensive, clearly organized notes that can be used as a reference. Careful documentation creates a valuable record and provides a practical guide for future developers.

Jamie Peppard was the production editor and the proofreader for *SWT: A Developer's Notebook*. Audrey Doyle was the copyeditor. Mary Agner provided production assistance. Sarah Sherman and Claire Cloutier provided quality control. Ellen Troutman wrote the index.

Edie Freedman designed the cover of this book. Clay Fernald produced the cover layout with QuarkXPress 4.1 using the Officina Sans and JuniorHandwriting fonts.

David Futato designed the interior layout, with contributions from Edie Freedman. This book was converted by Julie Hawks to FrameMaker 5.5.6 with a format conversion tool created by Erik Ray, Jason McIntosh, Neil Walls, and Mike Sierra that uses Perl and XML technologies.

The text font is Adobe Boton; the heading font is ITC Officina Sans; the code font is LucasFont's TheSans Mono Condensed, and the hand-writing font is a modified version of JuniorHandwriting made by Tepid Monkey Foundry and modified by O'Reilly. The illustrations that appear in the book were produced by Robert Romano and Jessamyn Read using Macromedia FreeHand 9 and Adobe Photoshop 6. This colophon was written by Colleen Gorman.